PROMPT BOOK

EXPERIMENTS FOR WRITING POETRY AND FICTION

Edited and compiled
with introductions and prompts by
BARBARA HENNING

SPUYTEN DUYVIL
NEW YORK CITY

Acknowledgements

Thanks to all the students over the years who have contributed to my
learning and especially thanks to the writers who contributed their
stories and poems. A special thank you to Tod Thilleman for editing
and publishing *Prompt Book*, to Lewis Warsh for his encouragement,
to Fatima Lundy, Esther Hyneman, and Jessica Caroline Holburn for
help with editing and proofreading. And a big hug for my sister Patti
Henning for hosting me for two summer while writing.

Library of Congress Cataloging-in-Publication Data

Names: Henning, Barbara, author.
Title: Prompt book :
experiments for writing poetry and fiction / Barbara Henning.
Description: New York City : Spuyten Duyvil, [2019]
Identifiers: LCCN 2018053143 | ISBN 9781949966046
Subjects: LCSH: English language—Rhetoric—Study and teaching
(Higher)—United States. | Poetry—Authorship—Study and teaching
(Higher)—United States. | Fiction—Authorship—Study and teaching
(Higher)—United States.
Classification: LCC PE1405.U6 .H42 2019 | DDC 808.02071—dc23
LC record available at https://lccn.loc.gov/2018053143

FLASH FICTION: FROM POEM TO SHORT SHORT   103

Prompts / Examples

CHRONOLOGY OF MIND: FROM JOURNAL TO POEM (OR PROSE)   205

Prompts / Examples by Barbara Henning and Others

APPENDIX

Introduction

When I first started teaching creative writing workshops at Long Island University in Brooklyn, I quickly became aware that most of my students had not read much poetry, more fiction, but even then, not much. They were mostly working class first generation college students. I understood where they were coming from because I also had grown up in a working class family; my parents were not college educated; my mother was the only one to graduate from high school in a family with nine children; and my father earned a GED when I was in elementary school.

It was a different time. We didn't have a television until I was eight or nine years old; the old manual typewriter on my mother's desk was the extent of our technology. I was lucky that my parents had encouraged us to read, and growing up, I read many novels. However, I had a limited knowledge of poetry, reading only a few poets in school, memorizing a poem or two by Robert Frost and Emily Dickinson. Fortunately, I was steeped in the poetic language of novels, spending lots of time with library books.

When I took graduate and undergraduate literature classes at Wayne State University, Charlie Baxter introduced me to two poets who would become my favorites, William Carlos Williams and HD (Hilda Doolittle). And both of these writers also wrote fiction. Under Baxter's direction, I started studying modernist poets and some of the collaborations and arguments they had with each other. Around the time when Charlie became my thesis advisor, I started thinking of myself as a poet. In an independent study, Esther Broner sat side-by-side with me and taught me how to write fiction. I am ever grateful for their teaching and support. Another writer who became a favorite and who I first encountered in school was Virginia Woolf. I loved her poetic stream-of-conscious writing. While attending the university, I was also part of a community of Detroit counter-tradition artists, writers and musicians; we were anarchist, anti-establishment, critical of mainstream culture. In the early 80s, when I moved to New York City, I met many other writers, artists and intellectuals, and I started to research the contemporary roots of the poetics I was already practicing.

At LIU, I wanted to give my creative writing students more than a craft class; I wanted to introduce them to poetic theories and especially the history of off-center poetics. I wanted to be upfront about my ideas about language and poetics so they could make their own choices. In every class, I passed out stacks of handouts, eventually collated into booklets. When I started teaching workshops on the internet, I wrote lectures to accompany the many handouts.

In *Prompt Book*, I have condensed three of my courses, material culled from years of teaching at Long Island University, Naropa University, the Poet's House, the Poetry Center in Tucson, St. Marks Poetry Project, writers.com and elsewhere. The three courses include: (1) "Poetic Prose and the Prose Poem;" this course includes experiments with genre and form, while exploring theory and history of 20th century poetic movements. (2) "Flash Fiction: From Poem to Short-Short;" in this course, students use poetic constraints, forms and techniques as experimental beginnings for writing prose stories. (3) In "Chronology of Mind: From Journal to Poem or Prose," I introduce students to approaches and experiments that over the years have helped me generate poems, stories and novels. The emphasis is on developing multiple ways of gathering material through writing and experimenting with journaling.

One of the first handbooks I put together for an MA poetry workshop was entitled "From the Fragment: A Poetics" (Appendix A). In the early 90s, I spent a great deal of time in New Orleans. Tulane University had a wonderful collection of small press books. I worked in their library constructing most of this extensive collage; it is meant to be a dialogue between poets, philosophers and critics, including their ideas about experimental poetry—the why, when and how.

Another handbook included in the appendix is "An Anthology of Experiments: Prose Poems, Poetic Prose and Prosaic Poems" (Appendix A). This anthology includes a selection from the poems that I started gathering in 2003 when I taught the first class on prose poetry at LIU. I invited a group of poets I admired to each give me a prose poem with an assignment or a process note. The content in this anthology has changed over time.

The prompts, lectures and examples in *Prompt Book* are designed to provide workshop teachers with ideas for teaching, and to provide an individual writer with a guided experience through three full courses. I start each course with the same opening assignment, using the art of haiku writing to write imagist prose poetry and short-short fiction. I begin with this particular assignment to ground writers (no matter what genre) in the importance of learning how to work with particulars. I recommend beginning each section with this same assignment.

To creative writing teachers who choose to use this book, I suggest that you give your students choice. The assignments are not meant to be rigid. If a particular prompt does not work for a student, give her the option of writing another poem or story in response to an earlier prompt or of transforming the prompt to make it work for the student.

To offer a prompt is to encourage someone to take action. The prompts in this book are meant to do just that—inspire something new. They are not meant to curtail or restrict the writing experience; they are more like gestures toward beginning a writing experience. Perhaps a writer will become more inventive by working through parts of this book. Writer's block is an excuse, a misunderstanding; between the mind, the body, the world and the word. In fact, there are infinite possibilities—

LINKS:

At the end of each prompt, I hesitantly include some links to websites. Over time websites change and disappear. They were all accessed on May 10, 2020. Consider these links only as *possible* connections. You may have to search further. You may find other links by scrolling around my website: barbarahenning.com

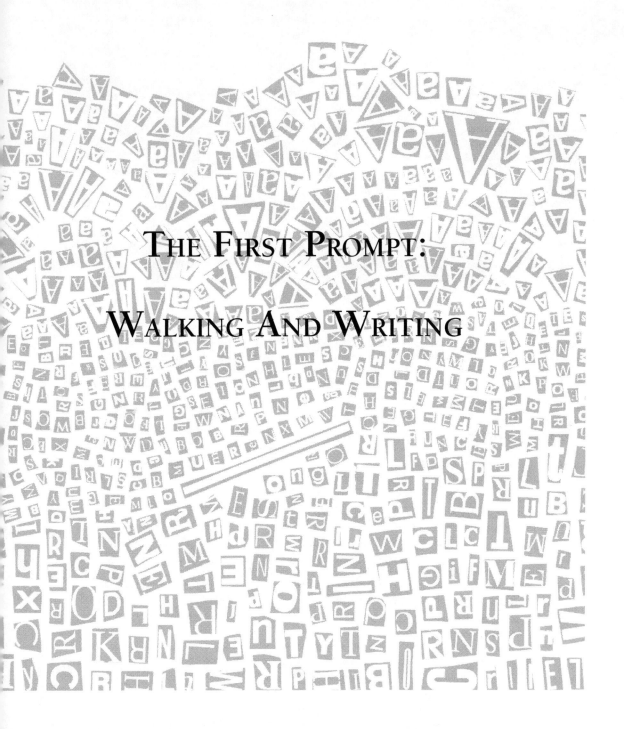

The First Prompt:

Walking And Writing

#1 Prompt: Walking and Writing

The basis for art is change in the universe. . . Moving things change, and because we cannot put a stop to time, it continues unarrested.

Matsuo Bashō, "Learn from the Pine"

At the supreme moment of life and death we just utter a cry or take to action, we never argue, we never give ourselves up to a lengthy talk. Feelings refuse to be conceptually dealt with, and a *haiku* is not the product of intellection. Hence its brevity and significance.

Daisetz T. Suzuki, "Zen and Haiku"

Prompt

Go for a silent walk outside and take notes as you walk; stop intermittently and record everything you see or hear, all the sensory details. Try to focus on haiku-like details. If you are unable to walk outdoors, feel free to transform this assignment. Perhaps you can recall a journey you took in the past. Or take a new journey today. It could be in a car, on a train or on a walk. Or maybe you will walk through the rooms in your house or apartment. Concentrate on just a short part of this trip, ten minutes at most. Then use your notes to write 4 or 5 haiku. Finally write the experience of your walk, as a prose poem, a prose story or a lined poem, and embed the haiku into your writing (as sentences).

Background/Examples

I start each course with the same opening assignment, using the art of haiku writing to write poetry, and/or fiction. The reason I start with this prompt is to ground writers (no matter what genre) in the importance of learning how to be particular. Haiku artists aim to get as close as possible to what they are experiencing.

For many years, I have focused my journal entries on haiku moments. At night, I'd think over the day. Were there any moments when

3

I was stopped by a tiny detail that seemed to resonate simultaneously with peacefulness and action? Some nights there would be no haiku moments to record. The next day I would push myself to stop and see the minute details around me. My journal became a way of life as well as providing material for poems or stories.

The writing of haiku has a rich history of its own, but with this assignment we are focusing only on traditional Bashō-like haiku. **Bashō**, **Issa** and **Buson** spent many years traveling, writing and reading their poetry, staying in monasteries and inns (1644-1827). It was an ancient tradition for Zen poets to wander and train one's mind, writing poetry every day and living their poetry. In his introduction to the anthology, Robert Hass explains that haiku are mysterious:

> The formal reason for this mysteriousness is that they don't usually generalize their images . . . [Roland Barthes] makes a post-modern case for them as deconstructions and subverters of cultural certainties. This case can be made, but the silence of haiku, its wordlessness, also has its roots in Buddhist culture, especially in Zen. (xv)

In the early 20th Century Ezra Pound and HD started a literary movement called "Imagism," and their ideas have been important for poets ever since. Pound was influenced by visual artists of the time as well as by the linguist Ernest Fenollosa's writing on the early Chinese characters and poetry. With an image embedded in the hieroglyph, the word is as close as possible to the thing itself. Here is an example taken from Fenollosa's essay:

人　　　見　　　馬

MAN　　　RIDES　　　HORSE

Pound wanted these same goals for poetry. Direct treatment, no extra words, the word itself carrying a verbal idea of action, without the metronome. Instead of a didactic "telling" poetry that was popular in the 19th century, the imagist poets were trying to get back to something ancient and true: to get as close as possible to "the thing itself." Fiction writers might think of the advice, "Show don't tell." With the imagist poets, the idea was to get even closer than "showing." This sounds a lot like haiku.

Below is a well-known poem by Pound that is similar to a haiku, except for the fact that he uses an overt metaphor, comparing the faces to petals, and also a more subtle metaphor with the word "apparition," describing the faces as ghost-like. Bashō attempts, on the other hand, to stay in contact with the image itself, without calling forth overt metaphors. It's clear that the imagist idea (i.e. Pound, et al) is quite different from Bashō's haiku.

In a Station of the Metro

The apparition of these faces in the crowd;

Petals on a wet, black bough.

How to Write Haiku

Each haiku should **depict a moment in time**, emphasizing time and place; *time* means the season should be apparent in the poem. The Japanese call this seasonal reference, a *kigo*. There should also be some sense of the ever changing nature of life and all things, the relatedness of one to the other, and our inevitable loss. The world turns, the seasons change, everything is moving. See if you can get a sense of this movement and the movement of the season into your haiku.

Haiku are usually three lines. In English haiku writers often count syllables, the first line has five syllables, the second seven and the third five. When haiku are written in Japanese, though, they have a completely different system of sounds that does not translate into our syllables. *For this assignment*: Don't worry about syllable count; instead for each haiku, write one short line, one longer line and another short line.

In each haiku, two images happen simultaneously. For example, from Bashō:

wrapping the rice cakes,	The peasant's child,
with one hand	husking rice, stops
she fingers back her hair.	and gazes at the moon.

In the first poem we see the woman wrapping the rice cakes, and then we look up at her fingers and her hair. In the second, we see the child and then the moon. Also note how the translations are often complete sentences. There is this sense that Bashō is stopped by one image (usually in the first line) and then he develops it as he goes along, bringing in the second image.

Notice how Bashō does not use metaphors, abstract ideas, generalizations and statements about his feelings; he mostly sticks with things in movement. Each poem is located in time and space, but again a haiku is not a still life. There is always movement, tiny and cosmic. There is a sense of a particular time of year, maybe with a word associated with the season (white light, falling leaves, snow trucks).

Haiku do not lecture about truth, goodness and beauty. They *are* truth and beauty. Haiku writers use common simple speech and images, rather than explicit metaphors, symbols or mythology. Usually there are no complicated words or grammar, no rhyming, no moralizing or intellectual comments or abstract ideas or statements about the writer's feelings or sense of herself. The poems are a record or a tracing of the writer's intuitive relationship with the world, but they are not about a "self." They are simple observations.

Here is a haiku by **Richard Wright**, a 20th Century novelist:

A thin mangy dog
Curls up to sleep in the dust
Of a moonlit road.(401)

6

Notice the two images, the dog and the moonlit road, and the simplicity of the images. There are no ideas or overt subjectivity. He is not writing about himself, instead he is concentrating on what he observes. And yet he is there standing beside the dog, or looking out the window.

What's wonderful about Richard Wright's haiku is the way he engages city life; after all, everything about our daily lives—in cities or country—is natural and alive. We can meditate with our haiku vision on anything. Wright writes: "From a tenement, / The blue jazz of a trumpet / Weaving autumn mists." (253). He puts us into the city air with two images, the tenement and the sound of the horn woven together with the mist. Or another example: "What giant spider spun / That gleaming web of fire-escapes / On wet tenements?" (538). Here he steps outside the haiku guidelines (Bashō tradition) and calls forth an imaginary metaphor of a giant spider; in the actual, we see the fire escapes and the wet tenements. His haiku differ from the others included here because they were written in English. He was an American fiction writer, and many of his haiku read like tiny stories.

After you have written your haiku: write another version of your walk in sentences and paragraphs, as a prose poem or a story. Be sure to embed the haiku into the prose. If you consider your life a journey, every event that takes place is part of that journey, every action a part of another action. Even these momentary observations are small actions. Instead of breaking for the lined poem, let the images flow right into the prose as sentences. In this way, you will have a poetic rhythm in your flash fiction or prose poem. The more haiku, the more imagistic the prose poem or story. Another idea: You could also start with three haiku written by someone else and invent a story around them (still embedded). Haiku are momentary observations, tiny actions, tiny stories of their own.

You can use this same technique over and over as a regular journal exercise or as a way to begin a story or a poem. Or perhaps you will be content with only your haiku.

Syntax Experiment

Some writers find it difficult to stay with the image. Perhaps with this exercise you will be able to push yourself out of your normal pattern of seeing and writing. Select a haiku and break it down into its syntax. Take your notes and write your haiku using the same syntax. See example below:

A Student draft of a haiku:

October rose buds
hold on tight to slim branches
bucking west winds

One of Richard Wright's haiku (137):

>   A pregnant black rat
> Poking in a paper bag
>   In a purple dawn.

Article – adjective – adjective – noun
Present participle verb – preposition – article – adjective – noun
preposition – article – adjective – noun.

Possible revision using Wright's Syntax:

October rose petals
clinging to a slim branch
in the West winds

Notice how much simpler the image is with Wright's syntax.

Drafts of student haiku and prose poem:

walking my black bike
blue gum stuck to my white shoe
running down the wind

gasoline puddles
I see me in them filling
my tank with rainbows

he wears his gum balls
one in each ear, look, like that
I whisper nothings

truck hauling beachballs
me lying here in warm sand
I dream it jack knife

Day at the Beach

A truck carrying inflated beach balls just jack-knifed on I-95 near
Roanoke and now beach balls, probably hundreds dot the highway
causing pileups, quite a few flying up into the trees like giant air-filled
jellybeans, causing such a state of joy among the flocks of red-winged
blackbirds and cats now chasing dogs for a change into the median,
dogs that always wanted but never had the courage to enter and those
surviving the chase are relieving themselves like never before and me,
I'm just lying here in the sand listening to the radio, looking at the sun
through my eyelids, waiting for some big new world to come out of
nowhere and bounce off my head.

Charles Springer, October 2016, Writers.com

MATSUO BASHŌ (1644-1694)

On the way to the outhouse—
the white of the moonflower
    by torchlight.

You've heard monkeys crying—
listen to this child
    abandoned in the autumn wind.

The old pond—
a frog jumps in,
    sound of water.

A bucket of azaleas,
in its shadow
    the woman tearing codfish

Autumn moonlight—
a worm digs silently
    into the chestnut.

YOSA BUSON (1716-1783)

Sparrow singing—
its tiny mouth
    open.

The short night—
on the hairy caterpillar
    beads of dew.

In the drained fields
how long and thin
    the legs of the scarecrow.

A flying squirrel
chewing on a bird
in the withered fields.

Before the white chrysanthemum
the scissors hesitate
a moment.

Kobayashi Issa (1763-1827)

The man pulling radishes
pointed my way
with a radish.

Nursing her child
the mother
counts its fleabites.

A huge frog and I,
staring at each other,
neither of us moves.

Last time, I think,
I'll brush the flies
from my father's face.

Pissing in the snow
outside my door—
it makes a very straight hole.

Fukuda Chiyo-Ni (1703-1775)

a single spider's thread
ties the duckweed
　　to the shore

over the flowing water
chasing its shadow—
　　the dragonfly

to tangle
or untangle the willow—
　　it's up to the wind

soaring skylark
what do you think
　　of the limitless sky?

on her day off
the prostitute wakes up alone—
　　the night's chill

Richard Wright (1908-1960)

31

In the falling snow
A laughing boy holds out his palms
Until they are white.

37

Past the window pane
A solitary snowflake
Spins furiously.

72

Droning into the room
The wasp circles angrily,
Then hums slowly out.

223

A highway of black ants
Diagonally bisecting
A sun-hot white wall.

402

In the summer storm
A window shade is flapping
In my neighbor's house

NOTES

Bashō, Matsuo. "Learn from the Pine," Hass, p. 233; poems, pp. 12-37.

Buscon, Yosa. Poems, Hass, pp. 87-121.

Chiyo-Ni, Fukuda. *Chiyo-ni Woman Haiku Master*, Edited and translated by Patricia Donegan and Yoshie Ishibashi, Charles E. Tuttle Co, 1998. pp. 44-177.

Fenollosa, Ernest. "From the Chinese Written Character as a Medium for Poetry," translated by Ezra Pound, *Poetics of the New American Poetry*, Grove Press, 1973. pp. 13-35.

Hass, Robert, Editor and Translator. *The Essential Haiku: Versions of Bashō, Buson and Issa*, Ecco Press, 1994.

Issa, Kobayashi. Poems, Hass, pp. 156-194.

Pound, Ezra. "A Retrospect" and "A Few Don'ts." The Poetry Foundation, https://www.poetryfoundation.org/articles/69409/a-retrospect-and-a-few-donts

—"In a Station in the Metro." *Selected Poems of Ezra Pound*, New Directions, 1957, p. 35.

Suzuki, Daisetz T. "Zen and Haiku." *Zen and Japanese Culture*, Princeton University Press, 2010, pp. 227.

Wright, Richard. Haiku: *The Last Poems of an American Icon*, Arcade Publishing, 1998.

THE PROSE POEM / POETIC PROSE:

POETIC MOVEMENTS & EXPERIMENTS

The Prose Poem / Poetic Prose

Which of us, in his ambitious moments, has not dreamed of the miracle of a poetic prose, musical, without rhythm and without rhyme, supple enough and rugged enough to adapt itself to the lyrical impulses of the soul, the undulations of reverie, the jibes of consciousness?

Baudelaire, *Paris Spleen*, ix

Course Description

When I was in graduate school at Wayne State University, I wrote a series of poems in prose that later became my thesis and then my first book, *Smoking in the Twilight Bar* (United Artists). Because a friend had a typesetting machine in the back of his copy shop, I volunteered to typeset the book for the publisher, Lewis Warsh. I remember rewriting these poems on that typesetting machine. This was before computers were widely available. One week I would typeset them in lines, the next week back into prose. In the end, I liked the way paragraphs and sentences could stream in and out of the narrator's consciousness. Since then, I have written many poems in prose, going back and forth from lines to paragraphs, exploring the difference between line breaks and prose, leaving a poetic rhythm in the prose and prosaic flow to the lined poems.

In the late 80s I became engrossed in studying Mikhail Bahktin, a Russian literary critic and philosopher. I was especially excited about his essay on "The Dialogic Imagination" in which he makes a distinction between poetry and novels, claiming that poetry during his time was monologic while the novel was dialogic, with its many voices. When reading one of his later essays, "On Speech Genres," I started seeing the way the language we speak holds within it a multiplicity of languages, language itself dialogic.

Here's Bahktin:

> Everything that pertains to me enters my consciousness, beginning with my name, from the external world through the mouths of others (my mother, and so forth) . . . Just as the body is formed initially in the mother's womb (body), a person's consciousness awakens wrapped in another's consciousness.

These ideas spoke to me and I started working more diligently against a "uniformity" of presentation. Rather than strict control, I wanted to allow some messiness, some looseness into my writing. This may not be what Bahktin was talking about, but that's where I went with it, into a first person relaxed point of view, stream of consciousness, experimental writing, the prose poem—Baudelaire's pricking of consciousness.

In the early nineties, I read everything I could find about the prose poem, and I designed an early version of this course, teaching it for a graduate writing course at LIU in Brooklyn. Pierre Joris and Jerome Rothenberg had recently published the first volume of their anthologies, *Poems for the Millennium: The University of California Book of Modern and Postmodern Poetry*. The editors provide a clear look back to the different poetic movements that had influenced poets at the time, tracing writers who had worked with language with an intent to change the culture. Their books, as well as Michel Deville's *The American Prose Poem: Poetic Form and the Boundaries of Genre*, were central in the early formation of "The Prose Poem and Poetic Prose" course.

What is a Prose Poem?

If you start searching around in literary dictionaries, you will find a variety of definitions, such as:

> (1) Martin Gray writes, "Short work of POETIC PROSE, resembling a poem because of its ornate language and imagery, because it stands on its own, and lacks narrative: like a LYRIC poem but is not subjected to the patterning of METRE."

(2) An entry in the *Princeton Encyclopedia of Poetry And Poetics:* "A composition able to have any or all features of the lyric except that it is put on the page—though not conceived of—as prose. It differs from poetic prose in that it is short and compact, from free verse in that it has no line breaks, from a short prose passage in that it has, usually, more pronounced rhythm, sonorous effects, imagery, and density of expression. It may contain even inner rhyme and metral runs. Its length, generally, is from half a page (one or two paragraphs) to three or four pages, i.e., that of the average lyrical poem. If it is any longer, the tensions and impact are forfeited, and it becomes—more or less poetic—prose. The term "prose poem" has been applied irresponsibly to anything from the Bible to a novel by Faulkner, but should be used only to designate a highly conscious (sometimes even self-conscious) art form." (John Simon)

(3) In one of the early prose poem anthologies, Michael Benedkt writes, "It is a genre of poetry, self consciously written in prose, and characterized by the intense use of virtually all the devices of poetry.. . . The sole exception . . . we would say, the line break."

(4) A contemporary critic Stephen Fredman—who has written extensively about language poetry calls it "poet's prose." He objects to the above definitions of the prose poem because they rely too heavily on Baudelaire's description of a prose poem. The language poets were often critical of lyrical narrative-oriented poems. Fredman quotes David Antin:

> 'Prose' is the name for a kind of notational style. It's a way of making language look responsible. You've got justified margins, capital letters to begin graphemic strings which, when they are concluded by periods, are called sentences, indented sentences that mark off blocks of sentences that you call paragraphs. This notational apparatus is intended to add probity to that wildly irresponsible, occasionally illuminating and usually playful system called language.

> Novels may be written in 'prose'; but in the beginning no books
> were *written* in prose, they were *printed* in prose, because 'prose'
> conveys an illusion of a common-sensical logical order.

Without writing, we had the sound of our words and poetic language to help us remember; then we had lines perhaps to help us hear the rhythm of our spoken voice. All aids to memory. Sentences and paragraphs are borders for organizing thoughts and pauses between thoughts. I think of a prose poem as *simply* a poem written in sentences and paragraphs, rather than lines. It can be narrative. It can be dramatic. It can be lyrical. It can be scientific. It can be experimental. It can be so many things, but if the language and structure stand out, rather than the information, description, dialogue, plot, then I think of it as a poem. "Poetic prose" might be a little closer to language that explains or elaborates, unless it is fracturing and experimenting with the language of explanation. But of course this can be endlessly debated. If you want to read a long thoughtful exploration on the definition of a prose poem, I suggest reading Michael Deville's book, *The American Prose Poem*.

When writing in response to the prompts in this unit, you may write your poems or poetic prose in sentences and paragraphs; or if your exploration doesn't work as well in prose, write in lines.

The prompts in this collection direct the student to look at their spoken and inner language as ever available material from which to make art. The assignments, background and examples in this section will provide an introduction to the prose poem and to some of the poetic movements in modern and contemporary off-center poetry, such as imagism, surrealism, objectivism, the New York School, Language writing, etc. The prompts are designed to expand a poet's sense of voice and form, offering new constraints and approaches. If you are a prose writer, the assignments may help you work on sentence style and narrative structures.

See Appendix A for a collection of prose poems and prompts by the folllowing poets: Charles Alexander, Martine Bellen, Brenda Coultas, Lynn Crawford, Diane diPrima, Bob Holman, Richard Hell, Alystyre Julian, Bill Kushner, Bernadette Mayer, Harryette Mullen, Maureen Owen, Julie Ezelle Patton, Simon Pettet, Kristin Prevellet. Tom Savage, Cole Swenson, Anne Waldman, Mark Wallace, Lewis Warsh.

Notes

Antin, David. "Some Questions About Modernism." *Occident,* vol. 8, Spring 1974, p. 27. As qtd by Stephen Fredman. *Poet's Prose: The Crises in American Verse*, Cambridge University Press, 1983, pp.126-127.

Bakhtin, Mikhail. "From Notes Made in 1970-71." *Speech Genres and Other Late Essays*, edited by Caryl Emerson and Michael Holquist, Univ of Texas Press, 1986, p.138.

Baudelaire, Charles. *Paris Spleen*, New Directions, 1947. ix.

Benedikt, Michael. *The Prose Poem: An International Anthology*, Dell, 1977, p. 47.

Deville, Michel. *The American Prose Poem: Poetic Form and the Boundaries of Genre*, University of Florida Press, 1998.

Fredman, Stephen. *Poet's Prose: The Crises in American Verse*, Cambridge University Press, 1983.

Gray, Martin. *A Dictionary of Literary Terms*, Longman, 1984, p. 234.

Rothenberg, Jerome and Pierre Joris, editors. *Poems for the Millennium: The University of California Book of Modern and Postmodern Poetry*, vol. 1, University of California Press, 1995.

Simon, John. "Prose Poem." *Princeton Encyclopedia of Poetry And Poetics*, edited by Alex Preminger, Princeton Univ. Press, 1965. Enlarged edititon, 1974.

#2: Day Dreaming / Prose Poems

The moment when vast fissures in the Palace of the World widen into daylight: I would give up the rest of my life—a paltry sum—if only it could endure.   Louis Aragon

---

Prompt

Walk through your city or town when people frequent the streets and shops. Write what you see and what is in your mind. If possible, sit somewhere, focus on something that catches your attention and then let your mind drift. Let your vision become a daydream. Let the marvelous segue into the ordinary everyday experience. Free write including as much material as you can gather. Then later when you are home begin to shape parts of this material into a prose poem. If your daydream becomes overly surreal, rewrite making it more realistic so the dream images give the poem an element of strangeness, but do not push readers into such a state of disbelief that they become uninterested.

Background / Examples

The French symbolist poets **Aloysius Bertrand** and **Charles Baudelaire** made the prose poem popular in the 19th Century. For your reading, I've included two of Baudelaire's city poems from *Paris Spleen*. Following Baudelaire, **Arthur Rimbaud**'s *A Season in Hell* also became important to Surrealists, and then to the Beats and many contemporary poets. Baudelaire resisted writing the pristine refined nature poems of his time. He and Rimbaud celebrated that which was thought to be un-beautiful.

Between WW1 and WW2, the Surrealists rebelled against what they saw as the slavery of a rigid reality-logic. For these poets and artists, writing and speaking the naturally poetic unconscious was a political act. The artwork and the process of creating art were one. Improvisation was privileged. Dreams and wild metaphors became a signature of the movement. Because they were interested in the unconscious/subconscious mind, many of their writings were in prose. Why? Because with prose the mind keeps moving. These writers privileged spontaneity and automatic writing. They were transgressive about speaking their desires and breaking apart norms and inhibitions. The strange was privileged over the ordinary.

According to Patricia Terry, **Pierre Reverdy** "was responsible for the first formulation of what Breton took as his own theory of the image" (xvii). Andre Breton was the surrealist guru, the main leader of the group. In his manifesto, he quotes Reverdy:

> The image is a pure creation of the mind.
> It cannot be born from a comparison, but from a juxtaposition of two more or less distant realities.
> The more the relationship between the two juxtaposed realities is distant and true, the stronger the image will be—the greater is emotional power and poetic reality . . .

CHARLES BAUDELAIRE
EVERY MAN HIS CHIMERA

UNDER a vast gray sky, on a vast and dusty plain without paths, without grass, without a nettle or a thistle, I came upon several men bent double as they walked.

Each one carried on his back an enormous Chimera as heavy as a sack of flour, as a sack of coal, as the accoutrement of a Roman foot-soldier.

But the monstrous beast was no inanimate weight; on the contrary, it hugged and bore down heavily on the man with its elastic and powerful muscles; it clutched at the breast of its mount with enormous claws; and its fabulous head overhung the man's forehead like those horrible helmets with which ancient warriors tried to strike terror into their enemies.

I questioned one of these men and asked him where they were going like that. He replied that he did not know and that none of them knew; but that obviously they must be going somewhere since they were impelled by an irresistible urge to go on.

A curious thing to note: not one of these travelers seemed to resent the ferocious beast hanging around his neck and glued to his back; apparently they considered it a part of themselves. All those worn and serious faces showed not the least sign of despair; under the depressing dome of the sky, with their feet deep in the dust of the earth as desolate as the sky, they went along with the resigned look of men who are condemned to hope forever.

And the procession passed by me and disappeared in the haze of the horizon just where the rounded surface of the planet prevents man's gaze from following.

And for a few moments I persisted in trying to understand this mystery; but soon irresistible Indifference descended upon me, and I was more cruelly oppressed by its weight than those men had been by their crushing Chimeras.

~

WINDOWS

LOOKING from outside into an open window one never sees as much as when one looks through a closed window. There is nothing more profound, more mysterious, more pregnant, more insidious, more dazzling than a window lighted by a single candle. What one can see out in the sunlight is always less interesting than what goes on behind a window pane. In that black or luminous square life lives, life dreams, life suffers.

Across the ocean of roofs I can see a middle-aged woman, her face already lined, who is forever bending over something and who never goes out. Out of her face, her dress and her gestures, out of practically nothing at all, I have made up this woman's story, or rather legend, and sometimes I tell it to myself and weep.

If it had been an old man I could have made up his just as well.

And I go to bed proud to have lived and to have suffered in some one besides myself.

Perhaps you will say "Are you sure that your story is the real one?" But what does it matter what reality is outside myself, so long as it has helped me to live, to feel that I am, and what I am?

~

In "To Every Man His Chimera" by **Charles Baudelaire**, I imagine Baudelaire in the crowd observing people humped over as they walked to work. Maybe he had the thought: "They look like they are carrying monsters on their backs." And from that thought perhaps this strange prose poem came into being. Chimera can also be an unrealizable dream. Perhaps he talked to the people and then watched them go by, deciding if he were to think about them much longer, he would be the one oppressed. So he moved on. In "Windows," perhaps he looked up and saw a window and "the ocean of roofs." Perhaps he saw one woman and then imagined her life, feeling empathy for her., then speculating on what was and wasn't real.

Pierre Reverdy
At Dawn

In my dream the head of a child was in the center.

If the clouds gather on your roof and the rain spares you, will you keep the secret of this double miracle?

But no voice calls you. If you get up, barefoot, you'll get sick. Where would you go, anyway, across these ravines of light.

The quilts kept the silence. Legs folded under, he walks on his wings and goes out. He was an angel and the whiter morning that was rising.

Under The Stars

Maybe I had lost the key, and everyone around me laughs and each shows me an enormous key hanging from his neck.

I am the only one who has no way to get in somewhere. They have all disappeared and the closed doors leave the street sadder. No one. I'll knock on every door.

Insults fly out of the windows and I withdraw.

So, not far outside of town, on the edge of a river and a wood, I found a door. A simple gate with no lock. I got behind it and, beneath the night that has no windows but does have large curtains, between the forest and the river that protected me, I was able to sleep.

The Bruised Air

It is so hot that the air vibrates and every noise becomes deafening. Packs of vicious dogs are barking. Through the open windows the cries of women rival that barbaric fanfare.

The cold has trouble freezing these words. If the birds were silent, if the women were silent, if the dogs were dead.... One moment the gardens are quiet and everything goes to sleep. But soon the terrible noise starts again. This is the call of the sun and each responds to it exuberantly. A few quiet beings who are overwhelmed are unable to protest or avenge themselves. Sovereign noise oppresses them.

In the smoke over the roofs, which are the only things able to protect themselves, I would have had my head turn like an empty bell on the end of a string. Padded speed up to the clouds and let the stream murmur all alone!

The sky came down, the windows were shut again, and the mouths are closed. After the leaves fall, even the birds don't dare to twitter anymore. It's so cold.

Winter, the interval of silence.

~

Reverdy combines surrealism with a spiritual orientation. His writing has influenced many poets. From Patricia Terry:

> Poems, he said, should be "crystals precipitated from the effervescence contact of the mind and reality." The resulting crystals are neither dark nor brilliant, but rather quietly luminous, not just in the texts themselves, but in their lasting effect.... Like these two objects from distant realms that constitute the powerful image, this illumination and this simultaneity may encounter each other, may interpenetrate, as they open in and out."

See other examples of more contemporary dream poems by Diane di Prima (267), Bill Kushner (281) and Richard Hell (271).

Notes

Terry, Patricia. "Introduction." *Roof Slates and Other Poems of Pierre Reverdy*. Edited and translated by Mary Ann Caws and Patricia Terry, Northwestern Univ. Press, 1981, xvii.

Aragon, Louis. *Wave of Dreams*. Translated by Susan de Muth. Thin Man Press, London 2006, 2010. Originally published as *Une Vague de Reves*, Seghers, 1924, 1.

Baudelaire, Charles. "To Every Man His Chimera" and "Windows." *Paris Spleen*. Translated by Louise Varése, New Directions, 1947, pp. 8-9, 76-77.

Reverdy, Pierre. Qtd. by Andre Breton. "Manifesto of Surrealism" 1924. *Manifestos of Surrealism*. Translated by Richard Seaver and Helen R. Lane, University of Michigan Press, 1972, p.20. Originally published in *Nord-Sud*, no. 13, March 1918.

——. "At Dawn," "The Bruised Air" and "Under the Stars." *Prose Poems*. Translated by Ron Padgett. Black Square Editions & The Brooklyn Rail, 2007, pp. 23, 29, 33. Originally published in *Poèmes en prose*, extraits de *Plupart du Temps*, Flammarion, 1967.

#3: Window Improvisation

Prompt

Sit at a window at least once a day for several days (maybe the same time of day) and write whatever comes to mind; let what is outside the window become part of the poem, part of the consciousness of the speaker; remember, see, hear, speculate, think poetically. Let your consciousness fill the page. Then tinker with this material and write a poem. If you like this process, perhaps you will write more poems like this for the coming units.

Background / Examples

This assignment was inspired by **William Carlos Williams'** improvisations from his collection *Imaginations*. Williams was a doctor, practicing in Paterson, New Jersey while writing his poems and prose. In his autobiography, he describes how he worked and he offers some useful advice about how to be a writer.

> Time meant nothing to me. I might be in the middle of some flu epidemic, the phone ringing day and nite, madly, not a moment free. That made no difference . . . Five minutes, ten minutes can always be found. I had my typewriter in my office desk. All I needed to do was pull up the leaf to which it was fastened and I was ready to go. I worked at top speed. If a patient came in at the door while I was in the middle of a sentence, bang would go the machine—I was a physician. When the last patient left, up would come the machine.. . . Finally, after eleven at night, when the last patient had been put to bed, I could always find the time to bang out 10 or 12 pages. In fact, I couldn't rest until I had freed my mind from the obsessions which had been tormenting me all day. Cleansed of that torment, having scribbled I could rest.

Below is one of Williams' improvisations, from *Kora in Hell: Improvisations*. Notice how he includes stories and images from his day as a doctor, and also images from the night of the writing as he spins into his own ecstatic style.

Beautiful white corpse of night actually! So the northwest winds of death are mountain sweet after all! All the troubled stars are put to bed now: three bullets from wife's hand none kindlier: in the crown, in the nape and one lower: three starlike holes among a million pocky pores and the moon of your mouth: Venus, Jupiter, Mars, and all the stars melted forthwith into this one good white light over the inquest table,—the traditional moth beating its wings against it—except there are two here. But sweetest are the caresses of the county physician, a little clumsy perhaps—*mais*—! and Prosecuting Attorney, Peter Valuzzi and the others, waving green arms of maples to the tinkling of the earliest ragpicker's bells. Otherwise—: kindly stupid hands, kindly coarse voices, infinitely soothing, infinitely detached, infinitely beside the question, restfully babbling of how, where, why and night is done and the green edge of yesterday has said all it could.

Hidden inside his thought threads is this story of a death, a murder. And we are carried along by the winds, stars, bullet holes, the body itself as microcosm of the universe, the ragpicker's bells, the trees and all that talk. Michel Deville explains that the "urgent and intimate tone of [Williams'] Improvisations did much to liberate the prose poem from the 'aestheticist' tradition in American writing."

While **Bill Kushner**'s poem, "5/6/87," is not a prose poem, it's lyrical and prosaic. This poem is part of a series of poems, perhaps composed or inspired while looking out a window. For many years, Bill wrote a poem every day. Memory, observation and desire interact with each other. Both Williams' and Kushner's poems were probably rewritten many times, and yet spontaneity is deeply imprinted in the tone and point of view.

BILL KUSHNER
5/6/87

May! & that man with the legs, muscles for forever
I almost yell Come back! for I too believe in hard sports
& there the dark-eyed boy in the doorway, why always alone?
The curious cat black & white nose pressed to window, Wednesday
Morning! cloudy, may clear up, but now's a mess
But nothing's perfect except a thought, & of course love is
But let's not think of that, your face I looked up at, as
The wind, I blew you, I almost remember, I almost forget
You, as you quietly dressed & left, no a whispery Goodnight
& now it's noon, well almost, what's that song? I've heard it
As somewhere in my soft head the D.J. of the moment
A young man turns whistles at a very striking woman on street
"Perfect!" he sings "Perfecto!" he sings again, does almost
A dance, but she never sees it, she never looks back
& he soon calms down, struts the opposite way, perhaps
To go home, write a love poem to her, as I do to him.

~

Other examples that relate to this assignment can be found in the appendix—by Alystyre Julian (279), Kim Lyons (303) and Julie Patton (299). Also see another poem by Bill Kushner (281).

NOTES

Deville, Michel. *The American Prose Poem*, p. 49.

Kushner, Bill. "5/6/87." *That April.* United Artists, 2000, p. 35.

Williams, William Carlos. "Beautiful White Corpse," in "Kora in Hell." *Imaginations,* New Directions, 1938, p. 38.

——. from "Forward." *The Autobiography of William Carlos Williams,* New Directions, 1948, p. xiii.

#4: Epiphany / Anti-Epiphany

Prompt

Remember a moment when you were looking at people or animals (or any event small or large in the natural world), and the observation seemed radiant to you (using a word from Joyce). Tell us the story of this moment in the first person. Include as many images and details in the poem as possible. Let your poem reach a climax, an epiphany when the narrator comes to some understanding or awareness. Maybe your epiphany will end with a sense of openness. Maybe your epiphany will be so subtle that it is almost an anti-epiphany.

Background / Examples

The word "epiphany" originated in early religious revelations. Later with **James Joyce**, the word became connected with moments in poetry or fiction. Many poets and writers live to experience epiphanies and then write about them. In the "Introduction" to *Joyce's Poems and Shorter Writings,* A. Walton Litz writes:

> When he first began to collect his epiphanies Joyce regarded them, in the words of his brother Stanislaus, as "little errors and gestures—mere straws in the wind—by which people betrayed the very things they were most careful to conceal."

In his novel *Stephen Hero*, Joyce's character Stephen defines an epiphany as a moment when an object's radiance is recognized. He explains to his friend Cranly :

> When the relation of the parts is exquisite . . . we recognise that it is *that* thing which it is. Its soul, its whatness, leaps to us from the vestment of its appearance. The soul of the commonest object, the structure of which is so adjusted, seems to us radiant. The object achieves its epiphany.

Almost anything could be an epiphany, depending on how the viewer (writer) depicts the moment. I think of a haiku as a quiet very subtle epiphanic moment.

Joyce collected many epiphanies in prose. As Michel Deville points out in his book, they read like prose poems. Joyce sometimes focuses on one person or a group, and sometimes the epiphany is a memory, or a wide look, or a careful observation, a series of questions, a statement of knowledge, a celebration of beauty, a cry for help, etc. "O, the sunlight in my heart!" "Help!" "Rain begins to fall."

Let's look at one of Joyce's epiphanies, #8:

> Dull clouds have covered the sky. Where three roads meet and before a swampy beach a big dog is recumbent. From time to time he lifts his muzzle in the air and utters a prolonged sorrowful howl. People stop to look at him and pass on; some remain, arrested, it may be, by that lamentation in which they seem to hear the utterance of their own sorrow that had once its voice but is now voiceless, a servant of laborious days. Rain begins to fall.

In this short observation we see clouds, sky, roads, a beach and a dog lying down. We see him howling. We see people on the street and we see the rain beginning to fall. The narrator speculates on how the people feel in relation to the dog's sorrow. The narrator tells us a lot about the people and their laboring lives in that one summarizing speculating thought: "they seem to hear the utterance of their own sorrow that had once its voice but is now voiceless, a servant of laborious days." And then it starts to rain. An anti-epiphany. A sad glimpse at the narrator's world. These kinds of "explanations" work well for Joyce, in between his observations.

Here is another (#6)—

> A small field of stiff weeds and thistles alive with confused forms, half-men, half-goats. Dragging their great tails they move hither and thither, aggressively. Their faces are lightly bearded, pointed and grey as india-rubber. A secret personal sin directs them, holding them now, as in reaction, to constant malevolence. One is clasping about his body a torn flannel jacket; another complains monotonously as his beard catches in the stiff weeds. They move about me, enclosing me, that old sin sharpening their eyes to cruelty, swishing through the fields in slow circles, thrusting upwards their terrific faces. Help!

This prose poem or story begins with an image of men working in a field. Perhaps Joyce squinted and then saw them as if in a daydream as mythic animals of burden. Then he jumps from this image to analyzing them in the third sentence. Then a very detailed image of the one that is wearing a torn jacket. And finally this epiphanic description of being surrounded by them. This piece reminds me of Baudelaire's "To Every Man His Chimera." He is also tracing consciousness with all of its interruptions and detours—a different mind, but a similar flow.

Joyce collected these epiphanies and incorporated many of them into his later writing.

Many contemporary writers do not want to have conclusive endings, closure that shuts the door on the story or poem in the very last line. Some epiphanies can be subtle and quiet like Joyce's, or maybe one can even refuse to end.

Deville, Michel. *The American Prose Poem, pp 19-40*.

"Epiphanies" *The James Joyce Centre,* 3 Nov 2012. http://jamesjoyce.ie/epiphanies/.

"James Joyce's Definition of Epiphany," *The Literary Link,* http://theliterarylink.com/joyce.html. Originally in *Stephen Hero, by James Joyce.* Edited by John J. Slocum and Herbert Cahoon, New Directions Press, 1959.

Joyce, James. "8" (Dull clouds) and "6" (A small field). *Epiphanies: Poems and Shorter Writings,* Faber, 1991, pp.166, 168.

#5: Portraits & Variation

Prompt

Write a prose poem as a character sketch. Focus on a particular person, and use repetition with variations in syntax to help develop the piece. Below are a few examples of experimental approaches by Gertrude Stein and Laura Riding, two modernist poets, as well as a more contemporary story by Jamaica Kincaid. It is not necessary that you write like any of these writers, but maybe you will discover new ideas about how to use repetition and variation in your writing. Sticking with your own style and making slight variations might be the best way to stretch your skills.

How to do this— Freewrite as much as you can, remembering the person. Include some dialogue. Get at the way the person talks and walks. Once you have accumulated enough material, go back and highlight sentences and description that you like. Then as you collage, try repeating some of the words and phrases.

Background and Examples

Before you read **Gertrude Stein** and **Laura Riding**, think about how you receive abstract art and see if you can translate that into your reading experience. When reading Stein, I often wonder, "What is this about?" She seems to be talking about the character, but at the same time about how we can't get at one stable meaning. In much of her writing, she avoids nouns, refusing to "re-present" reality. Rather, she presents the material of writing. Her work is often compared with analytic cubism. Take a look at Marcel Duchamp's "Nude Descending a Staircase," a cubist painting. You can easily find it online. Perhaps the way Stein works with repetition might compare with the fanning out of his image.

Here's what Ulla Dydo writes about Stein's portrait of Picasso, "If I Told Him".

> In the *Autobiography* Stein says that she delighted that summer in the waves on the shore at Antibes, where the portrait was written As was *Geography*. The waves are more than background. Inside the portrait they become Picasso's creative energy; the conquering armies of the leader, whether Napoleon or Picasso; his power over the empire of art, which might yet, like Napoleon's, crumble; and the fickle sexuality, misogyny and flattery characteristic of Picasso. Would he like it if she told him all this . . . Such questions . . . are also never answered, but persistently and rhythmically repeated.

If instead of reading the poem you want to listen to Stein read it, and watch Picasso's paintings becoming more cubist, you might like the YouTube under "Notes." If the YouTube has been removed, you can search for others to hear her read.

GERTRUDE STEIN
IF I TOLD HIM

If I told him would he like it. Would he like it if I told him.

Would he like it would Napoleon would Napoleon would would he like it.

If Napoleon if I told him if I told him if Napoleon. Would he like it if I told him if I told him if Napoleon. Would he like it if Napoleon if Napoleon if I told him. If I told him if Napoleon if Napoleon if I told him. If I told him would he like it would he like it if I told him.

Now.

Not now.

And now.

Now.

Exactly as as kings.

Feeling full for it.

Exactitude as kings.

So to beseech you as full as for it.

Exactly or as kings.

Shutters shut and open so do queens. Shutters shut and shutters and so shutters shut and shutters and so and so shutters and so shutters shut and so shutters shut and shutters and so. And so shutters shut and so and also. And also and so and so and also.

Exact resemblance. To exact resemblance the exact resemblance as exact as a resemblance, exactly as resembling, exactly resembling, exactly in resemblance exactly a resemblance, exactly and resemblance. For this is so. Because.

Now actively repeat at all, now actively repeat at all, now actively repeat at all.

Have hold and hear, actively repeat at all.

I judge judge.

As a resemblance to him.

Who comes first. Napoleon the first.

Who comes too coming coming too, who goes there, as they go they share, who shares all, all is as all as as yet or as yet.

Now to date now to date. Now and now and date and the date.

Who came first Napoleon at first. Who came first Napoleon the first. Who came first, Napoleon first.

Presently.

Exactly do they do.

First exactly.

Exactly do they do.

First exactly.

And first exactly.

Exactly do they do.

And first exactly and exactly.

And do they do.

At first exactly and first exactly and do they do.

The first exactly.

And do they do.

The first exactly.

At first exactly.

First as exactly.

As first as exactly.

Presently

As presently.

As as presently.

He he he he and he and he and and he and he and he and and as and as he and as he and he. He is and as he is, and as he is and he is, he is and as he and he and as he is and he and he and and he and he.

Can curls rob can curls quote, quotable.

As presently.

As exactitude.

As trains

Has trains.

Has trains.

As trains.

As trains.

Presently.

Proportions.

Presently.

As proportions as presently.

Father and farther.

Was the king or room.

Farther and whether.

Was there was there was there what was there was there what was there was there there was there.

Whether and in there.

As even say so.

One.

I land.

Two.

I land.

Three.

The land.

Three
The land.
Three
The land.
Two
I land.
Two
I land.
One
I land.
Two
I land.
As a so.
They cannot.
A note.
They cannot.
A float.
They cannot
They dote.
They cannot.
They as denote.
Miracles play.
Play fairly.
Play fairly well.
A well.
As well.
As or as presently.
Let me recite what history teaches. History teaches.

~

Another writer who worked with repetition in poetry and fiction is Laura Riding (later known as **Laura Riding Jackson**). She was a fan of Gertrude Stein. Riding writes about Stein: "She was only divinely inspired in ordinariness: her creative originality, that is, was original only because it was so grossly, so humanly, all-inclusively ordinary. She used language automatically to record pure ultimate obviousness." For quite a while Riding disappeared from literary history because she wanted to disappear. But since her death, she has reappeared. Some years ago, I made a presentation on Riding at the St. Marks Poetry Project in New York City. The link is below in "Notes."

LAURA RIDING
PRIVATENESS

They have a small bedroom. The bed is small, but they are not fat and they love each other. She sleeps with her knees neatly inside his knees and when they get up they do not get in each other's way. She says, "Put on the shirt with the blue patterns like little spotted plates," and he says, "Put on the white skirt that you wear the purple jacket with." They have no prejudices against colours but like what they have.

Their other room is not larger, but is cleverly arranged, with a table for this and a table for that. He makes the sandwiches at one table while at another she writes a letter to a friend who needs money. She writes promptly to say they have no money and sends their love. It is not true that they have no money; but they are both out of work and must be careful with the little money they have. They are thinking of renting an office and selling advice on all subjects, for they are very intelligent people. The idea seems like a joke, and they talk about it jokingly; but they mean it.

They go to a large park. It costs little to get there and they know the very tree they want to sit under. It is more like a business trip than a holiday. They eat their lunch in a methodical way and afterwards look through the grass around them as a mother looks through her child's hair to see if it is clean.

Then they think about their affairs and change their minds many times.

They walk about on the grass and feel sensible, but when they walk on paved paths they feel they are wasting their time. Finally they decide to commit suicide. They talk about it in natural tones because they may really do it—and they may not. There is an oval pond in the park with solemn brown ducks paddling in it, and they sit down by it, sorry for the ducks but not for themselves.

They go out of the park at a different entrance from the one they came in by. There are strange restaurants all around they would never think of eating in. It makes them feel lonely, so they speed home in a taxi, though they can ill afford this. At home there is the electric light, which makes them look at each other peculiarly. It was worth going out to be able to come home and look at each other in such a way—not a loving way or a tragic way, but as if to say, "It doesn't interest us what our story is—that is for other people."

~

In "Privateness," Riding starts with the pronoun "they" instead of a name. More than one lives in a small bedroom. It's a couple. A small bed is ok because they are small and in love. Spooning. They are content with their lives even though poor, and they are so intertwined with each other that they tell each other what to wear. They are so entwined, so private, but at the same time they avoid being honest with themselves. They consider suicide, but nothing so dramatic, no big drama here, just little glimpses of a couple who won't let us into their lives. This story is about privacy and in being private, also avoiding particularities. Riding offers us an idea, while still protecting their privacy. This story may be about hiding in language.

In **Jamaica Kincaid's** "Girl," the mother is presented with a collage of her advice. This piece is more objective than Stein's or Riding's because Kincaid uses the concrete "sound" of a mother's voice and thereby also minimally developing a character.

Jamaica Kincaid
Girl

Wash the white clothes on Monday and put them on the stone heap; wash the color clothes on Tuesday and put them on the clothesline to dry; don't walk barehead in the hot sun; cook pumpkin fritters in very hot sweet oil; soak your little cloths right after you take them off; when buying cotton to make yourself a nice blouse, be sure that it doesn't have gum on it, because that way it won't hold up well after a wash; soak salt fish overnight before you cook it; is it true that you sing benna in Sunday school?; always eat your food in such a way that it won't turn someone else's stomach; on Sundays try to walk like a lady and not like the slut you are so bent on becoming; don't sing benna in Sunday school; you mustn't speak to wharf-rat boys, not even to give directions; don't eat fruits on the street—flies will follow you; *but I don't sing benna on Sundays at all and never in Sunday school;* this is how to sew on a button; this is how to make a buttonhole for the button you have just sewed on; this is how to hem a dress when you see the hem coming down and so to prevent yourself from looking like the slut I know you are so bent on becoming; this is how you iron your father's khaki shirt so that it doesn't have a crease; this is how you iron your father's khaki pants so that they don't have a crease; this is how you grow okra—far from the house, because okra tree harbors red ants; when you are growing dasheen, make sure it gets plenty of water or else it makes your throat itch when you are eating it; this is how you sweep a corner; this is how you sweep a whole house; this is how you sweep a yard; this is how you smile to someone you don't like very much; this is how you smile to someone you don't like at all; this is how you smile to someone you like completely; this is how you set a table for tea; this is how you set a table for dinner; this is how you set a table for dinner with an important guest; this is how you set a table for lunch; this is how you set a table for breakfast; this is how to behave in the presence of men who don't know you very well, and this way they won't recognize immediately the slut I have warned you against becoming; be sure to wash every day, even if it is with your own spit; don't squat down to play marbles—you are not a boy, you know; don't pick people's flowers—you might catch something; don't throw stones at blackbirds, because it might not be a blackbird at all; this is how to make a bread pudding; this is how to make doukona; this is how to make pepper pot; this is how to make a good medicine for a cold; this is how to make a good medicine to throw away a child before it even becomes a child; this is how to catch a fish; this is how to throw back a fish you don't like, and that way something bad won't fall on you; this is how to bully a man; this is how a man bullies you; this is how to love a man, and if this doesn't work there are other ways, and if they don't work don't feel too bad about giving up; this is how to spit up in the air if you feel like it, and this is how to move quick so that it doesn't fall on you; this is how to make ends meet; always squeeze bread to make sure it's fresh; *but what if the baker won't let me feel the bread?*; you mean to say that after all you are really going to be the kind of woman who the baker won't let near the bread?

~

Other examples of portraits that work with variation and repetition are in the anthology in the appendix, by Bernadette Mayer on page 305 and Lewis Warsh on page 273.

Henning, Barbara. "Mrs. Jackson Is Riding My Thought." *The World*, vol. 53, 1997, 112-121. Also at: http://barbarahenning.com/wp-content/uploads/2016/04/LAURA-JACKSON.pdf.

Kincaid, Jamaica. "Girl." *Sudden Fiction International: 60 Short Short Stories*, edited by Robert Shepard and James Thomas, Norton, 1989, pp. 65-66. Originally published in *At the Bottom of the River*, Farrar, Straus and Giroux, 1984.

Stein, Gertrude. "If I Told Him." Sentiox, https://www.youtube.com/watch?v=1MbWNACKi5A.

——. "If I Told Him." *A Stein Reader*, edited by Ulla E. Dydo. Northwestern University Press, 1993, pp. 464-466.

Riding, Laura. "Privateness." *Progress of Stories*, Dial Press, 1982, 293-294.

Riding, Laura Jackson. "The New Barbarism Essay." *A Survey of Modernist Poetry,* Heiniman, 1927, p. 283.

#6: Cubism & Collaging

Prompt

In this prompt, you will fracture your normal way of seeing things, this time by using collage. Begin by writing a relaxed story/poem about something that happened in one of your ordinary days. Maybe you will retell a story that you once felt compelled to tell someone else, on the phone, on the street, in the laundromat. Include as many particulars as possible. Details. Objects. When you have it formed reasonably well, cut it up and reassemble it using a different organizing principal, rather than chronology. Perhaps you will scramble it or retell it backwards or from different points of view or different voices. If for some reason you don't enjoy collaging, you can always stick with the first draft of your story-poem.

Another possible cubist approach would be to write a "tender button," a Steinian prose poem. Describe someone or something without ever mentioning or alluding to it. Circle around it by using words that sound like the object, rather than describing or defining it..

Background / Examples

Cubist techniques have been important for poets and artists through the 20th and now the 21st century. As we discussed in the last prompt, Picasso was one of the visual artists who used cubist techniques, fracturing an image so that one could see many points of view at once. When you start examining the different poetic movements in the 20th century, you come to realize that they overlap and share a lot of characteristics. For example, the surrealists, as well as the cubists, worked with collage.

But the cubists were not as concerned with the unconscious. Their intent was to include more views than one core meaning, or one central "I". They used language to disrupt logical expectations and to shatter traditional ways of presenting time and space. They used techniques like collage, weird punctuation, unusual patterns of syntax, multiple points of view, etc. They wanted to avoid realistic representations and to inspire the reader to see differently. Playing with language like this requires that the writer see her subject differently.

Sometimes it is difficult to see the strangeness of "cubism" or other modernist techniques because these techniques are now quite common. But in the early part of the 20th Century, this was a new way of writing and making art. Now it is common to question our ability to fully represent someone or something. Then there was hope that with modernization and political changes, we could make a better world. But the World Wars dashed those hopes.

Gertrude Stein's *Tender Buttons* is sometimes described as an example of analytic cubism and she is often described as *the* cubist poet. Below are two of her *Tender Button* poems from "Objects;" notice how she alludes or points to the object without naming it in the body of the poem, talking and walking around it—this is quite different from writing that tries to "re-present" a situation, person or object.

Gertrude Stein
A Dog

A little monkey goes like a donkey that means to say that means to say that more sighs last goes. Leave with it. A little monkey goes like a donkey.

Carafe, That Is A Blind Glass.

A kind in glass and a cousin, a spectacle and nothing strange a single hurt color and an arrangement in a system to pointing. All this and not ordinary, not unordered in not resembling. The difference is spreading.

~

We have already read some of **Pierre Reverdy's** prose poetry and discussed his surrealism. He is also known for his cubism. In his essay "The Cubist Poetry of Pierre Reverdy," Kenneth Rexroth discusses how Reverdy purposefully fractures language and experience, rather than the spontaneous/improvisational slant of most surreal poetry. In the lined poem below, "Late at Night," you can see how Reverdy uses some of the techniques of cubism. The result is far different from Stein's poems; his are almost mystical.

PIERRE REVERDY
LATE AT NIGHT . . .

The color which night decomposes
The table where they sit
In its glass chimney
     The lamp is a heart emptying itself
It is another year
   A new wrinkle
Would you have thought of it
     The window throws a blue square
The door is more familiar
   A separation
    Remorse and crime
Goodbye I am falling
Gently bending arms take me
Out of the corner of my eye I can see them all drinking
    I don't dare move
They sit there
      The table is round
And so is my memory
I remember everybody
Even those who are gone

~

Berger, John. "The Moment of Cubism." *The Sense of Sight*, Vintage, 1985. [If you want to know more about cubism, this is a wonderful essay; Berger explores the ideas and historical background for Cubism.]

Rexroth, Kenneth, "Cubist Poetry of Pierre Reverdy" and "Late at Night." http://www.bopsecrets.org/rexroth/essays/reverdy.htm. Originally published in *Pierre Reverdy, Selected Poems,* translated by Kenneth Rexroth, New Directions, 1969.

Stein, Gertrude. "Dog" and "A Carafe That Is a Blind Glass." *Tender Buttons: Objects, Food, Rooms*, Dover, 1997.

Prompt

Write a poem, in prose or with lines, in which details and language of the here and now, the everyday, the familiar conscious world, become luminous. Concentrate on nouns, things and images from a moment in time when you experienced a startling observation. Be as aware of your language and thoughts, as you are of the things you are observing. Each word in your poem, even thought words, will contribute to the poem and point to the materiality of the language as well as the world observed and lived. This prompt takes the imagist project a step closer to the thing-itself, language.

Background / Examples

A poem is a small (or large) machine made of words. When I say there's nothing sentimental about a poem I mean that there can be no part, as in any other machine . . . that is redundant.

There is no poetry of distinction without formal invention, for it is in the intimate form that works of art achieve their exact meaning, in which they most resemble the machine, to give language its highest dignity, its illumination in the environment to which it is native.
    William Carlos Williams, (*The Wedge*)

A group of poets in the middle of the 20th Century identified themselves as objectivist poets: Louis Zukofsky, George Oppen, Charles Reznikoff, Carl Rakosi, Basil Bunting, Kenneth Rexroth, for a while, and Lorine Niedecker. Here's a description of the movement from Rothenberg and Joris's *Poems for the Millennium:*

Among the "Objectivists" as such—& their cohesion as a group was never clear—the name underscored both an *objective* approach to the world & the idea of the poem as *object*. (For the former, William's formula "no ideas but in things" might serve as a catchphrase; for the latter, his definition of a poem as "a big or little machine made of words." Metaphor came into question or was recast, replaced, by a predilection of immediate experience & an evolving sense of history. For Williams in particular this was accompanied by an American concern to develop a national idiom & a concomitant new measure—in the case of several of the main "Objectivists," a language informed by immigrant particularities (their own included) or by what Williams elsewhere called "the speech of Polish mothers."

There were two trends in this tradition. Both concentrated on the materiality of language. In the first, there is the emphasis on getting close with language to the thing itself. These writers were following Williams Carlos Williams' lead. If you look at "Psalm," a simple lined poem written by **George Oppen**, you will easily get the idea.

GEORGE OPPEN
PSALM

Veritas sequitur ...

In the small beauty of the forest
The wild deer bedding down—
That they are there!

       Their eyes
Effortless, the soft lips
Nuzzle and the alien small teeth
Tear at the grass

       The roots of it
Dangle from their mouths
Scattering earth in the strange woods.
They who are there.

Their paths
Nibbled thru the fields, the leaves that shade them
Hang in the distances
Of sun

The small nouns
Crying faith
In this in which the wild deer
Startle, and stare out.

~

This is an excellent example of an objectivist poem that works with numinous details. As Burt Kimmelman writes in his essay, "Appearances are of the utmost importance. There is a physical tangible landscape, there is a human being's language and there is the appearance of the moment that comprehends them both." Kimmelman adds that the Oppen poem itself is a living language, becoming part of nature. I like the way Oppen moves from what he observes to the concreteness of the language itself. We know these deer through words, and these words, these nouns speak to us.

In "The Red Wheelbarrow," Williams tells the reader what is important: "So much depends / upon" are important words in this poem. Even though they do not point to concrete details, because of the fracturing, each word is highlighted, the words themselves becoming things.

WILLAM CARLOS WILLIAMS
XXII

so much depends
upon

a red wheel
barrow

glazed with rain
water

beside the white
chickens

~

Note: Even though these examples are lined poems, you can experiment trying to discover how to have a similar effect with prose, perhaps using space inside sentences.

Notes

Kimmelman, Burt. "George Oppen's 'Psalm': Manifest Things and a Poet's Words." *Big Bridge*, vol.14, 2009, http://www.bigbridge.org/BB14/OP-KIM.HTM.

Oppen, George. "Psalm." *This is Which*. New Directions, 1962, p. 20.

Rothenberg, Jerome and Pierre Joris, editors. "Prologue to "Objectvists." *Poems for the Millennium: The University of California Book of Modern and Postmodern Poetry*, vol. 1, University of California Press, 1995, p. 526.

Williams, William Carlos. From "Introduction." *The Collected Poems of William Carlos Williams*, vol. II, 1939-1962, pp. 54-55. Originally published in *The Wedge,* The Cummington Press, 1944.

———. "XXII. "*Spring and All. The Collected Poems of William Carlos Williams (1909-1939)*. Edited by A. Walton Litz and Christopher MacGowen, vol. 1, New Directions Press, 1986, p. 224.

Prompt

We all have access to some kinds of documents that represent our communities: letters, newspapers, emails, student essays, etc. See if you can locate a group of documents that might be fruitful for a writing project. Go through them and highlight passages, sentences, phrases and paragraphs that you can rearrange into a collaged poem. The important first step is to find the right passages. Sometimes a random search can be productive, or even a mathematical approach, for example, using the third line in every email.

Background / Examples

The objectivist poets were writing in the middle of the 20th Century. In this second objectivist approach, there is still an emphasis on simplicity and clarity over formal structure and rhyme, but these poets seem more concerned with inventive ways of making social statements with "historic and contemporary particulars," rather than using poetic figures of speech. Often they use language from other documents. Poets can be astute plagiarists, finding language everywhere, just as painters look for color and line in the world around them. The objectivist movement later became very important for many poets who continued to focus on language as material and for those practicing "investigative poetics."

An example of an objectivist poem composed from "found material" is **Charles Reznikoff's** "Testimony," a long text composed and transformed from passages he found in law books. (He was also a lawyer). It is a great picture of America in his time. The style is prosaic, including some long lines (paragraphs) and shorter lines. Reading it, I can't help but think of all the stories locked away in law and medical files. Here is one section from the beginning:

Charles Reznikoff
from Testimony

Amelia was just fourteen and out of the orphan asylum; at her first job—
    in the bindery, and yes sir, yes ma'am, oh, so anxious to please.
She stood at the table, her blonde hair hanging around her shoulders,
    "knocking up" for Mary and Sadie, the stitchers
("knocking up" is counting books and stacking them in piles to be taken
    away).
There were twenty wire-stitching machines on the floor, worked by a
    shaft that ran under the table;
as each stitcher put her work through the machine,
she threw it on the table. The books were piling up fast
and some slid to the floor
(the forelady had said, Keep the work off the floor!);
and Amelia stooped to pick up the books—
three or four had fallen under the table
between the boards nailed against the legs.
She felt her hair caught gently;
put her hand up and felt the shaft going round and round
and her hair caught on it, wound and winding around it
until the scalp was jerked from her head,
and the blood was coming down all over her face and waist.

~

In "Poem Beginning *The,*" **Louis Zukofsky** incorporates fragments from
other texts, including Dante, Mussolini and others. In the original, each
line is numbered with an index at the end. There are over 300 lines.
Here are just a few of the beginning lines. I encourage you to search for
the full text.

Louis Zukofsky
Poem beginning "The"
First Movement: "And out of olde bokes, in good feith"

1 The
2 Voice of Jesus I. Rush singing
3   in the wilderness
4 A boy's best friend is his mother,
5 It's your mother all the time.
6 Residue of Oedipus-faced wrecks
7 Creating out of the dead,—
8 From candle flames of the souls of dead mothers

Note: Even though these examples are lined poems, you can use the same type of prompt to write a prose poem. Or you can use prosaic lines. I once wrote a 28 page novella using found material from books and then spinning off into a narrative. You can find "The Dinner" in *A Swift Passage* (Quale Press) or online. Also, see an excerpt from *My Autobiography* on page 230.

NOTES

Henning, Barbara. "The Dinner," Talisman #38, 39, 40 (Autumn 2010) www.barbarahenning.com/wp-content/upload/2014/11/The-Dinner.pdf.

Reznikoff, Charles. "Testimony: II." *The Complete Poems of Charles Reznikoff*. Black Sparrow, 1976, p. 49.

Zukofsky, Louis. "Poem Beginning 'The.'" *All: The Collected Short Poems 1923-1958*. Norton, 1965, p. 12.

#7 OBJECTIVIST (PART 3)
COMBINING #1 AND #2

Prompt

Choose a subject you want to write about—an event, a day in your life or a particular place. Collect words and phrases from your observations, memories and documents. Make sure the language is not all "about" the topic (expository, summary), but is "of" the topic (coming out of the experience). Include politics, voices of people, casual talk, ruminations, memories, etc. Collage together into a whole.

Background / Examples

Lorine Niedecker's poem "Lake Superior" involves both numinous images and found material. She was the only women member of the objectivist group. Neidecker came from a rural working class background, and for much of her life, worked as a cleaning woman on Black Hawk Island in Wisconsin. She wrote mostly about the life and language of the people around her.

In "Lake Superior," she incorporates her own observations of the lake as well as fragments from other writers. The poem began with a trip driving around Lake Superior. She took notes along the way. Before she went on the trip she researched history and memoirs of explorers. She collaged tiny phrases from others into her poem. Pemberthy writes:

> Niedecker's poem provides us with a textual articulation of the layers of history contained within the Lake Superior region. The voices she collages into her poem may bridge centuries, but as Niedecker told Cid Corman ten days before leaving to drive around the lake, "we are always inhabiting more than one realm of existence—but they all fit in if the art is right."

Here are the beginning sections from her poem:

LORINE NEIDECKER
LAKE SUPERIOR

> In every part of every living thing
> is stuff that once was rock
>
> In blood the minerals
> of the rock
>
> *
>
> Iron the common element of earth
> in rocks and freighters
>
> Sault Sainte Marie—big boats
> coal-black and iron-ore-red
> topped with what white castlework
>
> The waters working together
>   internationally
> Gulls playing both sides
>
> *
>
> Radisson:
> "a laborinth of pleasure"
> this world of the Lake
>
> Long hair, long gun
>
> Fingernails pulled out
> by Mohawks
>
> *

                    (*The long*
                       canoes)
"Birch Bark
   and white Seder
      for the ribs"

                        *

Through all this granite land
the sign of the cross

Beauty: impurity in the rock

                    *

And at the blue ice superior spot

priest-robed Marquette grazed

azoic rock, hornblende granite

basali the common dark

in all the Earth

And his bones of such is coral

raised up out of his grave

were sunned and birch bark-floated

to the straits

                    ∼

Langston Hughes was writing at the same time as the objectivists, but he was considered more of an expressionist. His poem, "Montage of a Dream Deferred," however, seems clearly in the same vein as the objectivists; he is *collecting* the expressive voices of this particular community. There are eighty poems in the Montage, most of them lined.

Below you will find two poems, including the first poem in the collection and another poem where he catalogues the lights and signs in Harlem.

About his process, he writes:

> In terms of current Afro-American popular music and sources from which it has progressed—jazz, ragtime, swing, blues, boogie woogie, and be-bop—this poem on contemporary Harlem, like be-bop, is marked by conflicting changes, sudden nuances, sharp and impudent interjections, broken rhythms, and passages sometimes in the manner of the jam session, sometimes the popular song, punctuated by the rifs, breaks, and disc-tortions of the music of a community in transition.

LANGSTON HUGHES
from MONTAGE OF A DREAM DEFFERED

DREAM BOOGIE

Good morning, daddy!
Ain't you heard
The boogie-woogie rumble
Of a dream deferred?

Listen closely:
You'll hear their feet
Beating out and beating out a—

You think
It's a happy beat?

Listen to it closely:
Ain't you heard
something underneath
like a—

What did I say?

Sure,
I'm happy!
Take it away!

Hey, pop!
Re-bop!
Mop!

Y-e-a-h!

NEON SIGNS
                    WONDER BAR
                         ·
                       ·   ·
                         ·
                    WISHING WELL
                         ·
                       ·   ·
                         ·
                    MONTEREY
                         ·
                       ·   ·
                         ·
                    MINTON'S
            (ancient altar of Thelonious)
                         ·
                       ·   ·
                         ·
                    MANDALAY
                Spots where the booted
                and unbooted play
                         ·
                       ·   ·
                         ·

SMALL'S

.

. .

.

CASBAH

.

. .

.

SHALIMAR

.

. .

.

Mirror-go-round
where a broken glass
in the early bright
smears re-bop
sound

.

. .

.

~

Note: Even though these examples are lined poems, you can use the same prompt to write a prose poem. For an example of a prose poem, see selections from "Twelve Green Rooms" on page 243.

Hughes, Langston. Poems from "Montage of a Dream Deferred." *The Collected Poems of Langston Hughes*, Vintage, 1994. pp. 387-88, 397, 397-398. Originally published as *Montage of a Dream Deferred*, Henry Holt, 1951.

Niedecker, Louise. "Lake Superior." *Collected Works,* University of California Press, 2002, 232-234. Originally published in *North Central,* Fulcrum Press, *1968.* For those who become a fan of Niedecker, a beautiful new book has recently been published by Wave Books: *Lake Superior: Lorine Niedecker's Poem and Journal Along with Other sources, and Documents, and Readings*, 2013. 1-3.

Penberthy, Jenny. *Lorine Niedecker, Woman and Poet*. Modern Poet Series, National Poetry Foundation, July 1, 1996, p. 76. Quoted in Sarah Dimick. "Lorine Niedecker's 'Lake Superior': Articulating Landscape Through Textual Collage." *Friends of Lorine Niedecker,* http://www.lorineniedecker.org/documents/Dimick.pdf.

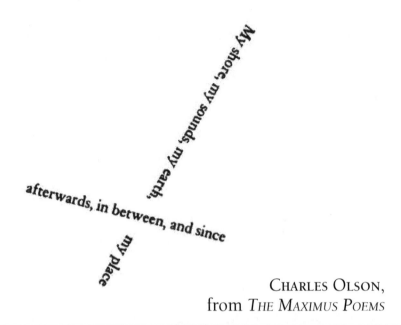

My shore, my sounds, my earth,

afterwards, in between, and since

my place

Charles Olson,
from *The Maximus Poems*

Prompt

The poet Charles Olson writes in his essay, "Projective Verse": "Breath is man's special qualification as animal. Sound is a dimension he has extended. Language is one of his proudest acts." He explains that when one is in the present with all the objects (no subject-object division), a secret can be shared and it has something to do with the breath. These ideas about breath and sound are in unison with mystical breathing and meditation practices, working toward the experience of oneness between poet and world.

Take your notebook outside or sit near a window. Free write for half an hour or more, tracing your mind with your pen or the movement of your fingers on the keys. Look around, let your mind drift and record the drifting. When a word or phrase stands out, leave extra space; when there is hesitancy or emotion, use space within the prose or use other punctuation to indicate the pause. Look closely at people, animals and things in your world and include them in your free-writing. If you find yourself remembering, remember or imagine other objects in the space of the memory (besides object-you). Then when you rewrite, read out loud and attend to the spacing, based on your breathing; this will help you find your form. In Olson's words, the assignment might read as follows: Write a poem with images and perceptions, one following another, energetically expressing your energetic breath/living being.

If you are writing a prose poem, perhaps you will work with space breaks inside the prose. You could use spaces in between each breath   Just as I am putting spaces   here   then you might catch   something of what Olson is saying. Feel free to work   with paragraphs and lines.

Background / Examples

In his poems **Charles Olson** paid tribute to the place where he grew up and lived—Gloucester, Massachusetts. If possible watch the documentary about Olson, *Polis Is This*. It is available as a series of YouTubes. Below under "Notes," you will find links for the documentary as well as for his essay "Projective Verse," and an article I wrote about Olson and his ideas about history.

Olson has influenced a lot of poets, including beat writers, like Allen Ginsberg and Diane di Prima. He was the rector of the experimental Black Mountain College; Many writers and artists taught or attended Black Mountain in the 40s and 50s, writers such as Robert Duncan, Robert Creeley and Denise Levertov. Most of Olson's essays were lectures first. In "Projective Verse" he makes a case for writing poetry with an emphasis on spontaneity (not precluding revision), so the poem becomes an experiment with the consciousness of the writer at the time of composing ("composition by field"). In his essay on organic poetry, Paul Nelson connects this Black Mountain mode of writing with the tradition of Whitman. "It is the epiphanic/transcendent state or heightening of consciousness which the organic poet strives to experience in the process of writing."

Ezra Pound had encouraged poets to write with the musical phrase in mind, rather than a tightly formed and scripted poetry with rhyme and meter. Now Olson quotes Edward Dahlberg "one perception must immediately and directly lead to a further perception." Let the breath of the poet live in the line and in the entire body of the poem. He brings the body and voice (not just the mind) of the poet back into the poem; and if the body of the poet is considered equal to every other object in the world, then with your breath and your ear, you can speak the divine.

He warns poets against relying too much on "description." Why? Because to simply describe is to be outside the work, an observer, separate from what is being written "about." A poem that works is "of the poet" and "of the subject/object" rather than about it. Still, concrete details ground us in time and space (and the reader, too, even in Olsen's writing). But description, he says, takes energy away from the poem. The form of the poem and the details can arrive organically out of the experience of writing. The idea is to get as close as you can to the object until you are writing "of" instead of "about."

The syllable, Olson says, starts in the mouth with the breath. He argues for a poetry that weds the speaking, thinking, and expressing poet. The energy of the poem, the breath of the poet, will be different and so will the length and intensity of the line. He argues for breaking syntax rules, anything to get to energetic heart. Like a Zen haiku poet, he wants to shed the "ego-I", but here the speaker's emotions and attitudes are to be included.

In *The Maximus Poems*, Olson writes history with poetry, tells stories, explores philosophical ideas, examines the economy and the life lived. Following are the last three poems in the collection of many volumes. In this grand epic, he experiments with form, line and page, writing becoming concrete, writing become ecstatic, writing in line and prose. In these few pages, you can see how he uses space on the page.

CHARLES OLSON
from THE MAXIMUS POEMS

I live underneath
the light of day

    I am a stone
on the ground beneath

My life is buried
with all sorts of passages
both on the sides and on the face turned down
to the earth

or built out as long gifted generous northeastern Connecticut stone walls are
through which 18th century roads still pass
as though they themselves were realms

the stones they're made of
are from the bottom such ice-age megaliths

and the uplands the walls are the boundaries of
are defined with such non-niggardly definition

of the amount of distance between a road in & out
of the wood-lots or further passage-ways, further farms
are given

      that one suddenly is walking

in Tartarian-Erojan, Geaan-Ouranian
time and life love space
     time & exact
analogy   time & intellect   time & mind   time & time
spirit

the initiation

of another kind of nation

*

the Blow is Creation
& the Twist   the Nasturtium
is any one of Ourselves
And the Place of it All?
    Mother   Earth   Alone

*

my wife   my car   my color   and   myself

~

Ferrini, Henry."Polis Is This: Charles Olson and the Persistence of Place," http://www.youtube.com/watch?v=evWPIeA_9W4.

Henning, Barbara. "The Content of History Will Be Poetry," no. 5, http://chax.org/eoagh/issuefive/henning.html.

Nelson, Paul. "Introduction to Organic Poetry." Global Voices Radio (March-April 2007), http://www.globalvoicesradio.org/Organic-Poetry-Introductory-Essay-4.8.07.html.

Olson, Charles. "Projective Verse." *Poetics of the New American Poetry*, edited by Donald Allen and Warren Tallman, New Directions, 1974, 147-158. Also published at *Poetry Foundation,* https://www.poetryfoundation.org/articles/69406/projective-verse.

Olson, Charles. *The Maximus Poems*. Edited by George F. Butterick, University of California, 1985, pp 438; 633-635.

#9: The New York School

Prompt

On the back of **Frank O'Hara's** *Lunch Poems*:

> Often this poet, strolling through the noisy splintered glare of
> a Manhattan noon, has paused at a sample Olivetti to type up
> thirty or forty lines of ruminations, or pondering more deep-
> ly has withdrawn to a darkened ware-or firehouse to limn his
> computed misunderstandings of the eternal questions of life,
> co-existence and depth, while never forgetting to eat Lunch his
> favorite meal.

Each locale and each moment is teeming with detail and happenings.
Take a break from work, go outside and record your place by recording
observations and thoughts. While jotting down as many details as possible, allow yourself time to meditate, to let your mind drift. Then write
down your thoughts and what you saw and heard. Shape the material
into a prose poem. When you are writing, remember to assume you are
speaking to another individual, someone you know well. They are leaning over your shoulder, listening.

Background / Examples

New York City is a city full of details, lights, conversations and people;
consciousness is pricked constantly with images and sounds. The idea
with these New York School writers was to highlight ordinary moments
as potentially ecstatic. The poets collaborated with each other and with
other artists; they worked with collage, and were influenced by the
surrealists and dadaists; they experimented with language, and quite
often wrote with an intimate voice. Sometimes the poems seem loose
and chatty, perhaps making the reader think that they were written
without revision (but of course they were revised). Some of the first
generation NY School poets were: LeRoi Jones, Edward Denby, Kenneth
Koch, James Schuyler, Barbara Guest, John Ashbery and O'Hara. Some

of the second generation were: Bernadette Mayer, Anne Waldman, Ted Berrigan, Alice Notley, Lewis Warsh, John Godfrey. The third and fourth and fifth generations continue to evolve.

O'Hara explains in his tongue-in-cheek essay, "Personism" that you could get so ordinary and so anti-literature (in its stilted overly poetic forms) that — "if I wanted to I could use the telephone instead of writing the poem, and so Personism was born.. . . It puts the poem squarely between the poet and the person.. . . I confess that it may be the death of literature as we know it" (353-5).

Once in a class, someone asked why a New York School writer tends not to use extended metaphors or personification in their writing. Well they are trying to write poems that are intimate communications between people. Using a metaphor to structure a poem might make it seem stiff and artificial (unless your everyday language is densely metaphoric).

O'Hara is very well known for a collection of poems, published by City Lights as part of their pocket series, *Lunch Poems*. It's so nice to carry a book around that fits in your pocket or the palm of your hand. Most of these poems are lyrical and lined (not prose poems), but they are prosaic, too, in the same ways we have discussed above. Notice that O'Hara ends some of his lines with "and" and "the," further emphasizing the prosaic nature of his poem. I'm including one of his poems, "The Day Lady Died," written on the day he learned that Billy Holiday had died.

FRANK O'HARA
THE DAY LADY DIED

It is 12:20 in New York a Friday
three days after Bastille day, yes
it is 1959 and I go get a shoeshine
because I will get off the 4:19 in Easthampton
at 7:15 and then go straight to dinner

and I don't know the people who will feed me
I walk up the muggy street beginning to sun
and have a hamburger and a malted and buy
an ugly NEW WORLD WRITING to see what the poets
in Ghana are doing these days
                                    I go on to the bank
and Miss Stillwagon (first name Linda I once heard)
doesn't even look up my balance for once in her life
and in the GOLDEN GRIFFIN I get a little Verlaine
for Patsy with drawings by Bonnard although I do
think of Hesiod, trans. Richmond Lattimore or
Brendan Behan's new play or Le Balcon or Les Nègres
of Genet, but I don't, I stick with Verlaine
after practically going to sleep with quandariness

and for Mike I just stroll into the PARK LANE
Liquor Store and ask for a bottle of Strega and
then I go back where I came from to 6th Avenue
and the tobacconist in the Ziegfeld Theatre and
casually ask for a carton of Gauloises and a carton
of Picayunes, and a NEW YORK POST with her face on it

and I am sweating a lot by now and thinking of
leaning on the john door in the 5 SPOT
while she whispered a song along the keyboard
to Mal Waldron and everyone and I stopped breathing

I'm also including a prose poem by **James Schuyler**, "Wonderful World." This is an good example of a NY School poem in prose: the world of the poem is full of New York details. Maybe the narrator is leaving the Katz household (Alex Katz was an artist many poets collaborated with), then he looks down Prince Street, then off in some memory about Great Danes or maybe he sees them through a window. There is coffee, perhaps he is stopping for coffee, some comments about gangsters living in the neighborhood. It was a hot night. Some memories segue into the prose. And then it ends with Anne Waldman saying "I grew up around here." On a second read, I'm thinking about how the poem could be in conversation with Anne, while also in the mind of the narrator—Don't we sometimes hear ourselves talking with others and the dialogue becomes mixed with our thoughts?

JAMES SCHUYLER
WONDERFUL WORLD
for Anne Waldman
July 23, 1969

"I," I mused, "yes, I," and turned to the fenestrations of the night beyond one of Ada and Alex Katz's windows. Deep in Prince Street lurked thin sullen fumes of Paris green; some great spotty Danes moved from room to room, their tails went whack whack in a kindly way and their mouths were full of ruses (roses). Flames in red glass pots, unlikely flowers, a spot of light that jumped ("Don't fret") back and forth over a strip of moulding, the kind of moulding that spells low class dwelling—I, I mused, take no interest in the distinction between amateur and pro, and despise the latter a little less each year. The spot of light, reflected off a cup of strong blue coffee, wasn't getting anywhere but it wasn't standing still. They say a lot of gangsters' mothers live around here, so the streets are safe. A vast and distant school building made chewing noises in its sleep. Our Lady of someplace stood up in a wood niche with lots and lots of dollar bills pinned around her. The night was hot, everybody went out in the street and sold each other hot sausages and puffy sugared farinaceous products fried in deep fat ("Don't put your fingers in that, dear") while the band played and the lady in the silver fox scarf with the beautiful big crack in her voice sang about the young man and how he ran out in front of the stock exchange and drank a bottle of household ammonia: "Ungrateful Heart." Big rolls of paper were delivered, tall spools of thread spun and spelled Jacquard, Jacquard. Collecting the night in her hand, rolling its filaments in a soft ball, Anne said, "I grew up around here," where, looking uptown on summer evenings, the Empire State Building rears its pearly height.

~

Schuyler, James. "Wonderful World." *Great American Prose Poems: From Poe to the Present.* Edited by David Lehman, Scribner, 2003, p.75. Also published in *Collected Poems*, Farrar, Straus and Giroux, 1993.

O'Hara, Frank. "Personism: A Manifesto." *Poetics of the New American Poetry,* edited by Donald Allen and Warren Tallman, New Directions, 1974, pp. 353-5.

— "The Day Lady Died." *Lunch Hour Poems*, The Pocket Poets Series, no. 19, City Lights Books, 1964, p. 27.

#10: The Contemporary Sonnet

Prompt

Write a sonnet, but in this sonnet, instead of lines, write it as a paragraph with fourteen sentences. You don't have to follow the literary requirements for sonnets (rhyme, meter, form). Your *sentences* may be as long or as short as you'd like.

Perhaps your language will be loose and chatty, like the New York school poems. Maybe people where you come from are not as loose and chatty as NY school writers, but there is a way of being personal. Perhaps you can work that language and life into your poem.

Maybe you will use the sonnet structure with a turn in understanding between the 8th line (or sentence) and the last six.

Or perhaps you can find a well-known sonnet that you are drawn to and transform it using a dictionary of your choice to change the nouns and maybe even the verbs. The Oulipo writers were a group located in Paris who experimented with mathematical transformations of language. A well-known constraint they use is called S + 7 (N + 7 in English). Take each noun and replace it with the 7th noun, counting up or down the dictionary. Feel free to play around with this idea to make the poem your own. The Oulipo writers are often very strict about following rules, but I find it fun to use their ideas in the process of finding the poem.

Background / Examples

The traditional sonnet has a pretty complex history, but generally we can describe it as a poem that sets something up at first and then after about eight lines (sometimes more), there is a pause and a shift in thinking, perhaps a conclusion. Sometimes the sonnet goes on for twelve lines and the turn takes place in the last two. A sonnet is somewhat like an essay, but richer with image, figures of speech and rhythm.

Traditionally, sonnets were also written in meter—iambic pentameter, ten syllables, every other one accented, ending with an accent. There were different rhyme schemes. **Shakespeare**, for example: abab, cdcd, efef, gg. Wordsworth: abbaaccb, dedeff. Here's an example of a Shakespeare sonnet.

WILLIAM SHAKESPEARE
SONNET 130

My mistress' eyes are nothing like the sun;
Coral is far more red than her lips' red;
If snow be white, why then her breasts are dun;
If hairs be wires, black wires grow on her head.
I have seen roses damasked, red and white,
But no such roses see I in her cheeks,
And in some perfumes is there more delight
Than in the breath that from my mistress reeks.
I love to hear her speak, yet well I know
That music hath a far more pleasing sound.
I grant I never saw a goddess go;
My mistress when she walks treads on the ground.
　　　And yet, by heaven, I think my love as rare
　　　As any she belied with false compare.

~

Modern sonnets don't usually lock the readers up with meter and rhyme. The lined poems of New York School poets like O'hara, Mayer and Berrigan often have a loose, chatty, more open feeling.

Ted Berrigan wrote a collection of sonnets and then taught a sonnet workshop at Naropa and at the Poetry Project in the 70s. He made the sonnet a contemporary form by making it very personal. In this unit, I am summarizing, explaining and quoting passages from his workshop.

Ted tells his students how he began writing his sonnet sequence by reading Shakespeare's sonnets. He pinned four of Shakespeare's sonnets that he liked the best on his wall and read them every day so he could absorb the rhythm. He didn't want to write in iambic pentameter or rhyming couplets because that wasn't how he thought or talked. He explains, "I couldn't put my emotions into those rhythms."

"My poems," he writes, "are about what happens to me in my life as I see it or imagine it or fantasize it or do whatever. The 'I' that I'm talking about, the 'me,' is just a person in this world. I don't write my poems about Ted Berrigan the poet, but about 'me' Ted Berrigan" (96). Berrigan wrote the poems quickly. "I didn't have to build conceits, I didn't have to evolve the root metaphor in any way. I simply had to spill out what was inside me and I have a vessel to spill it out into"

That's interesting: he didn't evolve the root metaphor. Like the imagists, objectivists and projectivists, he wasn't interested in setting up an artificial metaphoric structure. The poems are 14 lines long, using lines to emphasize dramatic change and to control the pace of the poem. You can work with sentences and punctuation in a similar way.

> Rather than say "those that have the power to hurt and will do none" I might say, "it is 5:15 a.m. and I'm waiting for the milkman." But still, it was simply notations of what was going on and I never did make a rude metaphor that I would use all the way through the poem or establish any elaborate conceits. Instead I would turn back upon things that I had in the poem. I would come and go out. (91)

In the last six lines, Berrigan moves into thoughts he had about the subject. "I like to make a statement which will cast a certain light on the whole poem and on everything that you've read before.. . . a kind of statement which will identify really clearly what kind of person has been talking to you in this poem"

Sometimes he would use the sonnet form of three quatrains and a final couplet, as Shakespeare does above. Below is "Final Sonnet," a poem included in Berrigan's workshop and as the final sonnet in his collection. Note the way he uses space within the lines (like the projectivists), and also the way the ending of the poem could easily be a beginning.

TED BERRIGAN
"A FINAL SONNET"

How strange to be gone in a minute! A man
Signs a shovel and so he digs   Everything
Turns into writing a name for a day
        Someone
is having a birthday and someone is getting
married and someone is telling a joke   my dream
a white tree   I dream of the code of the west,
But this rough magic I here abjure   and
When I have required some heavenly music   which even
        now
I do   to work mine end upon *their* senses
T hat this aery charm is for   I 'll break
My staff   bury it certain fathoms in the earth
And deeper than did ever plummet sound
I 'll drown my book.
It is 5:15 am.
        Dear Chris, hello

~

The full transcript of his workshop is readily available on the internet. I've included a current link below in "Notes."

Another possible approach might be to write something similar to **Harryette Mullen**'s translation of Shakespeare Sonnet 130 using "synonymous slang and commercial brand names" (perhaps also using an OULIPO constraint, like N + 7). In an interview with Mullen, she explains how she used the "Dictionary of Slang" and the reason why she was drawn to this particular sonnet: "He's in love, or in lust with a flesh-and-blood woman, and he's also making fun of sonnets in the manner of Petrarch, poetic blazons that praise a woman's body parts, comparing her to gold, alabaster, silk, pearls and other precious commodities.

Here's **Harryette Mullen's** prose poem, a transformation of Shakespeare's 130—

HARRYETTE MULLEN
DIM LADY

My huneybunch's peepers are nothing like neon. Today's special at Red Lobster is redder than her kisser. If Liquid Paper is white, her racks are institutional beige. If her mop were Slinkys, dishwater Slinkys would grow on her noggin. I have seen tablecloths in Shakey's Pizza Parlors, red and white, but no such picnic colors do I see in her mug. And in some minty-fresh mouth-washes there is more sweetness than in the garlic breeze my main squeeze wheezes. I love to hear her rap, yet I'm aware that Muzak has a hipper beat. I don't know any Marilyn Monroes. My ball and chain is plain from head to toe. And yet, by gosh, my scrumptious Twinkie has as much sex appeal for me as any lanky model or platinum movie idol who's hyped beyond belief.

~

Perhaps you will be inspired to work on a parody of another well-known poem, or even another translation of Shakespeare's 130. For more information on OULIPO constraints, see Prompt #10 on page 252.

Berrigan, Ted. "Sonnet Workshop." *Ted Berrigan, On the Level of Everyday: Selected Talks on Poetry and the Art of Living.* Edited by Joel Lewis, Talisman Press, 1997, pp. 90-96. Also available on line at: Project Papers,Vol. II, 1989. https://www.poetryproject.org/wp-content/uploads/v2-ted-berrigan.pdf.

Berrigan, Ted. "A Final Sonnet." *The Sonnets*, Penguin, 2000. Originally published by Grove Press, 1964, 72.

Mullen, Harryette. *Looking Up Harryette Mullen: Interviews on Sleeping With the Dictionary and Other Works,* with Barbara Henning, Belladonna Press, 2011. p. 61-62.

——. "Dim Lady." *Sleeping with the Dictionary,* University of California Press, 2002.

Shakespeare, William. "130." *The Sonnets: Poems of Love,* St Martin's Press, 1980.

#11: INVESTIGATIVE POETRY

POET as   Investigator
                      Interpreter of Sky Froth
                      Human Universer
                      Prophet
                      Prophet without death
                      as a consequence.

My statement is this: that poetry, to go forward, in my view, has to begin a voyage into the description of *historical reality*.
Ed Sanders "The Content of History Will be Poetry"

Prompt

Become a re-searcher. Write a poem about your life, your place in the world, the neighborhood where you now live or where you grew up. Gather facts by interviewing people or by working with observation. Or research a particular topic such as the impact of a current or past event on you, your family, your neighbors or the young people working in Mc-Donald's. Or perhaps uncover something with no expectations, no direct question. The idea with this assignment is to bring knowledge from the greater world together with the everyday intimate. You can bring documents into the poem. Perhaps you are steeped in reading and listening to the news. That's a form of research and part of our everyday lives. Let it into the poem. Tell the truth. Gather material, and then rearrange and rewrite.

Background / Example

With investigative poetry, instead of waiting for inspiration, a poet investigates a subject (a place, a problem, a political situation, an untruth) very deeply and then presents the material poetically, putting poetic language and knowledge to the service of unveiling the truth.

In his essay on investigative poetry, **Ed Sanders** looks back to Charles Olson. In "The Special View of History," Olson (also Dean of Black Mountain College) lectures on the place of history in poetics. To Olson, history is a complex organism in which an individual connects to his (her) locale through what she knows, "what he really knows." History is what connects to his/her space and time; it is not a force that acts upon the individual from the outside. Rather it is story, imagination, poetry—History is a verb meaning "to find out for yourself", like Herodotus, "to look for the evidence."(For more on Charles Olson see page 64.)

The poet **Juliana Spahr** writes in an interview:

> I guess what I like about poetry is that it has a certain tradition of exploring intimacy and another tradition of exploring the political, the social, the cultural. And I find myself most amazed by poems where these things happen at the same time. I think the reason why poetry retains an aura of political usability in our culture is because it often mixes intimacy with politics, or even when it is being intimate it has something to say about politics. (2003)

One of Spahr's books that I particularly like and have taught frequently is *thisconnectionofeveryonewithlungs*. I'm including an excerpt (November 30, 2002) from "poemwrittenfromnovember30/2002/tomarch27/2003". Before Spahr begins, she gives some context:

> After September 11, I kept thinking that the United States wouldn't invade Afghanistan. I was so wrong about that.. . . I felt I had to think about what I was connected with, and what I was complicit with, as I lived off the fat of the military-industrial complex on a small island [Hawaii]. I had to think about my intimacy with things I would rather not be intimate with even as (because?) I was very far away from all those things geographically.

Juliana Spahr
from *THISCONNECTIONOFEVERYONEWITHLUNGS*

November 30, 2002

Beloveds, we wake up in the morning to darkness and watch it turn into lightness with hope.

Each morning we wait in our bed listening for the parrots and their chattering.

Beloveds, the trees branch over our roof, over our bed, and so realize that when I speak about the parrots I speak about love and their green colors, love and their squawks, love and the discord they bring to the calmness of morning, which is the discord of waking.

When I speak of the parrots I speak of all that we wake to this morning, the Dow slipping yet still ending in a positive mood yesterday, Mission Control, the stalled railcar in space, George Harrison's extra-large will, Hare Krishnas, the city of Man, the city of Danane and the Movement for Justice and Peace and the Ivorian Popular Movement for the Great West, homelessness and failed coups, few leads in the bombing in Kenya.

Today I still speak of the fourteen that are dead in Kenya from earlier in the week, some by their own choice and some by the choices of others, as I speak of the parrots.

And as I speak of the parrots I speak of the day's weather here, the slight breeze and the blanket I pull over myself this morning in the subtropics and then I speak also of East Africa, those detained for questioning, porous borders, the easy availability of fraudulent passports.

I speak of long coastlines and Alexandre Dumas's body covered in blue cloth with the words "all for one, one for all."

I speak of grandsons of black Haitian slaves and what it means to be French.

I speak of global jihad, radical clerics, giant planets, Jupiter, stars' gas and dust, gravitational accretion, fluid dynamics, protoplane tary evolution, the unstoppable global spread of AIDS.

When I speak of the parrots I speak of the pair of pet conures released sometime in 1986 or 1987 that now number at least thirty

I speak of how they begin their day at sunrise and fly at treetop height southward to rest in the trees near our bed, beloveds, where they rest for about an hour to feed, preen, and socialize before moving on to search for fruits and seeds of wild plum, Christmas berry, papaya, strawberry guava, and other shrubs and trees that were, like them, like us, brought here from somewhere else.

I speak of our morning to come, mundane with the news of it all, with its hour of feeding, preening, and restrained socializing before turning to our separate computers and the wideness of their connections and the probable hourly changes of temperature between 79 and 80 degrees that will happen all day long with winds that begin die day at 12 mph and end it at 8 mph.

When I speak of the green of the parrots I speak of yous and me, beloveds, and our roosts at the bottom of the crater once called Le'ahi, now called Diamond Head, and I speak of those who encourage us to think of them as roosting with us, Mariah Carey, Jermaine Dupri, Jimmy Jam and Terry Lewis, Jay-Z, Cam'ron, Justin Timberlake, Nick Carter, Rod Stewart, and Shania Twain.

And I speak of the flapping of parrots' wings as they come over the tree that reaches over the bed and the helpless flapping of our wings in our mind, our wings flapping as we are on our backs in our bed at night unable to turn over or away from this, the three-legged stool of political piece, military piece, and development piece, that has entered into our bed at night holding us down sleepless as the parrots have entered into this habitat far away from their origin because someone set them free, someone set them free, and they fly from one place to another, loudly, to remind us of our morning and we welcome this even, stuck on our backs in bed, wings flapping, welcome any diversion from the pieces of the three-legged stool.

~

BARBARA HENNING
TOMPKINS SQUARE

Once a swamp, once a military parade ground, once surrounded by shanties, then six-to-seven story tenements, sweatshops,
Eastern European, Puerto Rican, the site of many demonstra-
tions and riots—Charlie Parker lived across the street—heroine culture, chanting love, Hari Krishna, the punks camped on
the southwest side, once a tent city where the homeless staked
a space, then property values climbed, and so a curfew and a
wall of armed police tore the city down   desertion   égress
salida   August 6, 1989 and we were sitting in Lucy's when
the police cavalry charged up Avenue A   agitate   rouse
excite Then the park bench was redesigned with a bar in the
middle. The thinning of trees. Now closed after midnight except
for the tulips, daisies, pigeons, rats and squirrels   the weeds
in the cracks   get away   going along   good-bye for now
Birds of prey migrate into the city for easy feeding. At noon, a
hawk perches in the giant elm with the bird house in the middle,
it's thick branches snaking over the park. Following the curving
iron rails that separate grass from cement, I clasp my hands behind me and hum—*Summertime and your mama's good looking.*
Words and bird sounds on the breeze . . . The guy across the
way is pounding a beat on his hip. All night, all right. A woman
on a bike with big speakers on the back greets her friends at the
circle where the public stage used to be, electric, the center of,
the birds are on, the amps are on, the rain is holding off and we
are wearing clown makeup. Anything can happen here   into a
V again   at any moment   off we go

~

"Tompkins Square" is about the park across the street from where I lived
for many years in the East Village of NYC. Not only did I read the history, but I also lived it.

You might also be interested in reading an essay I wrote in response to Olson's lecture, "The Special View of History." As I was writing the paper, I decided to do exactly what he was calling for, to investigate my place in time and space. I was living in Tucson at the time. See the link in "Notes".

For other examples of investigative poetics, see the prose poems in the appendix by Brenda Coultas on page 268 and Kristin Prevellet on page 311.

Spahr, Juliana. Interview by Joel Bettridge. *How2*, vol. 2, no. 3, 2005, https://www.asu.edu/pipercwcenter/how2journal/archive/online_archive/v2_3_2005/current/workbook/spa/spa.htm.

Spahr, Juliana. from *thisconnectionofeveryonewithlungs*, University of California Press, 2005, pp 13-18.

Henning, Barbara. "The Content of History Will Be Poetry." *Eoagh*, no. 5. 2009, https://chax.org/eoagh/issuefive/henning.html.

Henning, Barbara. "Tompkins Square." *A Swift Passage*, Quale Press, 2013, p. 20.

Olson, Charles. *The Special View of History*, Oyez Press, 1970, pp.19-26.

Sanders, Ed. *Investigative Poetry*, City Lights, 1976, 2019, p. 7. Republished by Spuyten Duyvil (Dispatches Editions), ed. Don Byrd, 2019.

#12: Cut-Ups, Splicing And Plagairism

Writers work with words and voices just as painters work with colors.. . . So let's dispense with this "originality" fetish . . . Look, listen, and transcribe-and forget about being original.
William Burroughs (Cucumbers)

Prompt

Find a paragraph, perhaps a prose poem that you have written and consider finished. Cut it apart into sections, phrases or maybe clip apart every word. Then rearrange. retype, improvise, adding words and re-writing to make this new poem work.

or

Find another text written by someone else, something related tangentially to your prose poem. Extract sentences or phrases and fold them into your prose poem. Rewrite to make this new poem work.

Background / Examples

The dadaists and the beat poets frequently worked with cut-ups and collage. Some writers splice other texts into their writing. Some time ago I was invited to work on a project for a show at MOCAD in Detroit; the show was responding to Italo Calvino's book, *Invisible Cities*. I wrote about each city I had lived in or visited. Then I took a phrase from the middle of each page of Calvino's book and wove these phrases into my prose poems. Cutting and layering. When I look back at the poems, I can't tell where the splicing starts or ends.

from CITIES & MEMORY

Outside the train window, grass, trees, houses. They grow taller and greyer until the city overcomes the vista and whoosh underground straight into Penn Station. Socks and shoes soaking wet. Even *The Confidence Man* is wet and falling apart. Water everywhere, all day long, for two days, dragging a heavy suitcase. Second Avenue Deli closed, a Hooters moving in. Little Esther's rent is higher than my monthly salary. Have trust the cosmopolitan man says. A sign in Cliff's kitchen: Do you really want to work at Sardi's in December? I do not wish your eyes to catch a distorted image. On the corners, smokers congregate and plot some kind of revolution. Under her wide-brimmed hat, Rosemary Mayer waits for me at a table at Greek Delphi. I'm late. I'm running. I'm knocked around, I'm bumped. A network of wires and pipes. Standing outside 158 E. 7th Street, I look through the blinds at my once apartment, now a modeling agency with two guys in front of computer screens, talking on telephones. The leaves from the trees in Tompkins Square drift downward. They crunch under my feet. Up above, the sky and a little bit of blue.

~

Sometimes fracturing and splicing can create new insights for a writer—about one's writing and one's life.

William Burroughs on Plagiarism:

> You see, I had been conditioned to the idea of words as *property*—one's "very own words"—and consequently to a deep repugnance for the black sin of plagiarism. Originality was the great virtue. I recall a boy who was caught out copying an essay from a magazine article, and this horrible case discussed in whispers . . . for the first time the dark word "plagiarism" impinged on my consciousness. Why, in a Jack London story, a writer shoots himself when he finds out that he has, without knowing it, plagiarized another writer's work. He did not have the courage to be a writer. Fortunately, I was made of sterner or at least more adjustable stuff. William Burroughs ("Les Voleurs")

As I understand the law (I'm not a lawyer), artists do not need permission to use images to make collages unless the final product becomes too similar to someone else's work; in that case, you are not inventing your own work. It could also be considered plagiarism if you are selling the text (as advertising, for example) rather than making a new work of art. Picasso does not have a note at the bottom of his painting for the newspaper clipping, *Bottle of Vieux Marc, Glass, Guitar and Newspaper.*

We are born into language. It is passed on to us through others whom we are in dialogue with; that's how we learn to speak, write, read. When we write and speak, we use the language materials we have available to us to make our point or to ask our questions or to speculate. If we just mouth someone else, we're not transforming the material. But if we speak with them, elaborating, adding to and detracting from and so forth, well then, it's new material, a new poem, a new thought.

Throughout literary history, poets and writers have inscribed and responded to each other, often without any citation. Sometimes it is presumed that we will know the reference. Other times, that's not the case. Marjorie Perloff writes about John Ashbery and T.S. Eliot:

> The difference between Ashbery and Eliot: the use of citation. In Eliot's case, we know (or can find out) where the citations come from . . . But in Ashbery's poetry, it is usually impossible to identify the citation, and, even when we do, such identification doesn't necessarily help us to understand the poem.. . . Indeed, in Ashbery, almost everything *sounds* like a citation, sounds like something we've heard before or read somewhere — but where? And that is of course one of the main features of Ashbery's poetic: living at a moment when one's language is so wholly permeated by the discourses that endlessly impinge on it.

When I am bringing someone else's words into my poems, I sometimes mention the author, but it depends on how I use the words. Is the passage common language? If so, no need. If I am usiing longer passages from other written work, I include some notation, some way of pointing back at the author, either inside the poem, as a dedication or part of the title. For example, I named the series of poems I talk about above, "Cities & Memory", and this is the title of many of Calvino's chapters.

Then I also dedicate the poem to him and include a process note in the acknowledgements. Even though it isn't necessary, I feel more comfortable doing this. When the passages are deeply embedded into the work or well known, then no mention is needed.

See other examples by Harryette Mullen on page 276.

Notes

Burroughs, William. "It Belongs to the Cucumbers on the Subject of Randine's Tape Voices." *Talking Poetics from Naropa*, edited by Anne Waldman, July 27, 1865, pp. 63-81, 77, 79.

Burroughs, William. "Les Voleurs." *The Adding Machine*: Selected Essays," Arcade Publishing, 1985, pp. 20-21.

Henning, Barbara. "Cities and Memory." *Cities and Memory*, Chax Press, 2010, p. 144.

Perloff, Marjoire. "Normalizing John Ashbery." *Jacket Magazine*, no. 2, http://jacketmagazine.com/02/perloff02.html.

#13: Refracting Prose Poem

> Tell all the truth but tell it slant—
> Emily Dickinson

Prompt

Take a sentence from your journal, select a word and free associate/write, select a word from the next sentence, free associate/write, until your text takes a series of steps away from the first sentence. Remember again that your reader becomes involved in the poem through detail, image, syntactical direction and compelling ideas that carry them along. Or you may choose to gather lines from your journal and arrange them in the same discontinuous slanting way.

Background / Example

When I was in India, I discovered the Arabic ghazal. Each couplet connects with the next in a somewhat discontinuous way. Moving sideways. I had been writing like this for many years without having read ghazals. Many contemporary writers work against linear-subject continuity.

Following is a ghazal written by **Ghalib (of Agra, India)** in the 19th Century. Notice how each stanza can stand alone. Of course, he is writing in a different age so his poem will reflect his culture, time and place.

GHALIB
XXX

Where I'm going is farther at every step
the desert runs from me
with my own feet

In the lonely night because of the anguish
of the fire in my heart

the shadow slipped from me like smoke
The trail of my madness crosses the desert
red pearls on a page of manuscript

the goblet moves through all its colors because of you
the vision is caught in a single incredulous eye
because of me

And the eye bleeds fire
and the earth and dried leaves of the garden
are lit up because of me

~

In his two prose poems "Lecture" and "Death", **Michael Friedman** refracts from sentence to sentence. What I like about these two poems is the way each sentence leads to the next, but we are not following a logical order. Instead one word sends us in a slanted way toward another thought. We start with a woodpecker tapping, then we are in the range of the "t's". Timber, text. What is the connection? Some kind of discourse. An example and then we are into the personal. In "Death" he writes about a writer who is very present in the poem and then gone like a notation in an encyclopedia. He segues from Rupert's beauty to Rimbaud's beautiful loser. And from there to a lover. Instead of a series of sentences (subject, verb, object) representing a character who is logically living and acting in time, he is following, language, and signifiers always sliding.

MICHAEL FRIEDMAN
LECTURE

The telltale tapping one hears deep in the forest is the woodpecker at work. Timber. Thus, the instability of the text is the necessary underpinning of one's approach to the tree, leaves always in flux or falling, just as, for example, you are not the person you were when you first got here and fell into the abyss of my obsession. I called and you weren't home, so I called someone else instead. She was home. I would propose, then, a discourse that foregrounds and valorizes this instability.

DEATH

Rupert Brooke and his ladyfriend stroll along the Cam. Before long he has gone up in a puff of smoke with "the flower of England's youth"–not a loser, surely, but beautiful, certainly, when I see him beneath the light blue rotunda of Pierson College library at midnight, fall, 1982, on the frontispiece of a first edition of his poems. High cheekbones, blonde hair, a side-part. Rimbaud was a beautiful loser. As we drove up Old Snakey, I realized you were my true love, like the Mysterious Island one has always imagined but never believed in, until waking on its shores. Later I stood alone on the turnpike, programming the possible routes to Beale Street via the Peabody Hotel. As darkness fell the band began to play, couples made their way to the roof.

~

For variations on the assignment see page 192.

NOTES

Friedman, Michael. "Lecture" and "Death." *Great American Prose Poems: From Poe to the Present,* Scribner, 2003, *pp.* 273-274. Originally published in *Species,* The Figures, 2000.

Ghalib (Mirza Asadullah Baig Khan). *Ghazals of Ghalib,* "xxx."
Translated by Aijaz Ahmad and W. S. Merwin, *Poetry Foundation,*
https://www.poetryfoundation.org/
poetrymagazinebrowse?volume=116&issue=5&page=68.

#14: Language Writing

Prompt

> Write a prose poem with one sentence or one fragment for each year you have lived. Perhaps you will concentrate on some particular aspect of each year, making the language come from the experience of remembering and recreating rather than being "about." Perhaps you will disrupt the reader's expectations by collaging different memories and ideas. Use any of the techniques and approaches described below.
>
> ## Background / Examples

In *My Life,* **Lyn Hejinian** wrote a chapter for each year of her life. She composed the same amount of sentences as the number of years she had lived. The text was published in 1980 and covered 45 entries, 45 years, 45 lines. It reads as a reverie of non-sequiturs about the particular year, undoing conventional structuring of time, space and importance.

One of the ideas with language writing is to make the reader participate. In order to get the full meaning, one must question normal syntax, what it means to put a subject and then a verb, what it means to make common sense, what we are really saying with our generalities. Sometimes language writing may seem inaccessible to a reader who isn't accustomed to so much fragmentation, wordplay, and dislocation.

Rather than constructing the narrative of a thinking mind, tracing a mind, as in other prose poems we have read, in Hejinian's prose, the narrator questions the language, the syntax normally used to write a story of one's life. That questioning isn't meant to be read as part of a chronological, thinking mind; it's almost as if the narrator is behind the scenes rearranging and questioning her own telling voice. Hejinian writes, "When I am thinking about my work, I am often thinking about that thinking—its quality, motives, motifs, and instruments. Then, for me, poetry is the site of the consciousness of consciousness" (*Mirage*). The sentences in the entry for her first year of life are fractured, lacking some connections, perhaps because our one-year-old memories are fuzzy and for many of us non-existent. The first sentence barely makes sense syntactially without an independent clause; still there is a father coming home from war and the color yellow. Instead of "The cloudy sky reflects in a little puddle," she writes, "A little puddle is overcast." Even with the dislocation, there are people and things, and midway through, we encounter two grammatically correct sentences with a metaphor: "When daylight moves, we delight in distance. The waves rolled over our stomach, like spring rain over an orchard slope." Rather than working diligently to find meaning, I more or less swim with the prose in a dreamy way, making my own swimmy sense.

In the second entry, for year two, the syntax is closer to standard, but there are leaps between the sentences, as a collage of childhood insight and memory unfolds in the present and past tenses. Occasionally an explanatory sentence: "Unhappily, time seems more normative than place." Just as our language systems form with age and experience—as we start constructing a narrative about our lives—so do the sentences in *My Life* build into a narrative.

The language project was started by a group of poets in the 1970s. They were well versed in contemporary continental philosophy and literary theory. This project of deconstructing conventional reading expectations was also the aim of many other experimental modern and post-modern poets.

Here's a description of language writing, by George Hartley (1989):

> Language writing is often posed as an attempt to draw the reader into the production process by leaving the connections between various elements open, thus allowing the reader to produce the connections between these elements. In this way, presumably, the reader recognizes his or her part in the social process of production. But just as important, the ambiguity of the structure of many of these poems should remind the reader that any connections drawn are arbitrary.

Ron Silliman and others explain: "Our work denies the centrality of the individual artist. . . The self as the central and final term of creative practice is being challenged and exploded in our writing" (Silliman, et al, 1988). Traditional narrative structure, image and logic were seen as participating in the capitalist system, even the syntax of the sentence, with the subject, the ego-I acting on the object. Silliman explains that they were not interested in the "poem as confession of lived personal experience, the (mostly) free verse presentation of sincerity and authenticity that for several decades has been a staple of most of the creative writings in the United States" (1998).

Instead, they wanted to disrupt what a reader might take for granted, a consistent "I", an easy sense, easy reference, a natural look, a lyrical voice, fictional realism, conventional logic, resolution, and unity of presentation. Their writing is full of gaps, jumps and shifts in meaning. They rejected Olson's ideas about breath and speech. Some of their techniques included word play, fragments, parataxis, dislocation, ellipsis, pun, paragram . . . Much of the poetry was written in prose (poet's prose as opposed to prose poems). In "The New Sentence" Silliman describes how the "new sentence" calls attention to the language, technique and structures (88-93).

While certainly undoing an autobiographical "I" and resisting the urge to make many connections for the reader, Lyn Hejinian's *My Life* is still one of the more narrative, imagistic and accessible language texts. Perhaps after reading the first two entries of *My Life,* you will be inspired to order the book.

LYN HEJINIAN
from MY LIFE

A pause, a rose,
something on paper

A moment yellow, just as four years later, when my father returned home from the war, the moment of greeting him, as he stood at the bottom of the stairs, younger, thinner than when he had left, was purple—though moments are no longer so colored. Somewhere, in the background, rooms share a pattern of small roses. Pretty is as pretty does. In certain families, the meaning of necessity is at one with the sentiment of pre-necessity. The better things were gathered in a pen. The windows were narrowed by white gauze curtains which were never loosened. Here I refer to irrelevance, that rigidity which never intrudes. Hence, repetitions, free from all ambition. The shadow of the redwood trees, she said, was oppressive. The plush must be worn away. On her walks she stepped into people's gardens to pinch off cuttings from their geraniums and succulents. An occasional sunset is reflected on the windows. A little puddle is overcast. If only you could touch, or, even, catch those gray great creatures. I was afraid of my uncle with the wart on his nose, or of his jokes at our expense which were beyond me, and I was shy of my aunt's deafness who was his sister-in -law and who had years earlier fallen into the habit of nodding, agreeably. Wool station. See lightning, wait for thunder. Quite mistakenly, as it happened. Long time lines trail behind every idea, object, person, pet, vehicle, and event. The afternoon happens, crowded and therefore endless. Thicker, she agreed. It was a tic, she had the habit, and now she bobbed like my toy plastic bird on the edge of its glass, dipping into and recoiling from the water. But a word is a bottomless pit. It became magically pregnant and one day split open, giving birth to a stone egg, about as big as a foot ball. In May when the lizards emerge from the stones, the stones turn gray, from green. When daylight moves, we delight in distance. The waves rolled over our stomachs, like spring rain over an orchard slope. Rubber bumpers on rubber cars. The resistance on sleeping to being asleep. In every country is a word which attempts the sound of cats, to match an inisolable portrait in the clouds to a din in the air. But the constant noise is not an omen of music to come. "Everything is a question of sleep," says Cocteau, but he forgets the shark, which does not. Anxiety is vigilant. Perhaps initially, even before one can talk, restlessness is already conventional, establishing the incoherent border which will later separate events from experience. Find a drawer that's not filled up. That we sleep plunges our work into the dark. The ball was lost in a bank of myrtle. I was in a room with the particulars of which a later nostalgia might be formed, an indulged childhood. They are sitting in wicker chairs, the legs of which have sunk unevenly into the ground, so that each is sitting slightly tilted and their postures make adjustment for that. The cows warm their own barn. I look at them fast and it gives the illusion that they're moving. An "oral history" on paper. That morning this morning. I say it about the psyche because it is not optional. The overtones are a denser shadow in the room characterized by its habitual readiness, a form of charged waiting, a perpetual attendance, of which I was thinking when I began the paragraph, "So much of childhood is spent in a manner of waiting."

As for we who "love to be astonished"

You spill the sugar when you lift the spoon. My father had filled an old apothecary jar with what he called "sea glass," bits of old bottles rounded and textured by the sea, so abundant on beaches. There is no solitude. It buries itself in veracity. It is as if one splashed in the water lost by one's tears. My mother had climbed into the garbage can in order to stamp down the accumulated trash, but the can was knocked off balance, and when she fell she broke her arm. She could only give a little shrug. The family had little money but plenty of food. At the circus only the elephants were greater than anything I could have imagined. The egg of Columbus, landscape and grammar. She wanted one where the playground was dirt, with grass, shaded by a tree, from which would hang a rubber tire as a swing, and when she found it she sent me. These creatures are compound and nothing they do should surprise us. I don't mind, or I won't mind, where the verb "to care" might multiply. The pilot of the little airplane had forgotten to notify the airport of his approach, so that when the lights of the plane in the night were first spotted, the air raid sirens went off, and the entire city on that coast went dark. He was taking a drink of water and the light was growing dim. My mother stood at the window watching the only lights that were visible, circling over the darkened city in search of the hidden airport. Unhappily, time seems more normative than place. Whether breathing or holding the breath, it was the same thing, driving through the tunnel from one sun to the next under a hot brown hill. She sunned the baby for sixty seconds, leaving him naked except for a blue cotton sunbonnet. At night, to close off the windows from view of the street, my grandmother pulled down the window shades, never loosening the curtains, a gauze starched too stiff to hang properly down. I sat on the windowsill singing sunny lun-ny teena, ding-dang-dong. Out there is an aging magician who needs a tray of ice in order to turn his bristling breath into steam. He broke the radio silence. Why would anyone find astrology interesting when it is possible to learn about astronomy. What one passes in the Plymouth. It is the wind slamming the doors. All that is nearly incommunicable to my friends. Velocity and throat verisimilitude. Were we seeing a pattern or merely an appearance of small white sailboats on the bay, floating at such a distance from the hill that they appeared to be making no prog-ress. And for once to a country that did not speak another language. To follow the progress of ideas, or that particular line of reasoning, so full of surprises and unexpected correlations, was somehow to take a vacation. Still, you had to wonder where they had gone, since you could speak of reappearance. A blue room is always dark. Everything on the boardwalk was shooting toward the sky. It was not specific to any year, but very early. A German goldsmith covered a bit of metal with cloth in the 14th century and gave mankind its first button. It was hard to know this as politics, because it plays like the work of one person, but nothing is isolated in history—certain humans are situations. Are your fingers in the margin. Their random procedures make monuments to fate. There is something still surprising when the green emerges. The blue fox has ducked its head. The front rhyme of harmless with harmony. Where is my honey running. You cannot linger "on the lamb." You cannot determine the nature of progress until you assemble all of the relatives.

~

NOTES

Hartley, George."Textual Politics and the Language Poets (excerpts)." *Penn Sound*, 1989, http://writing.upenn.edu/~afilreis/88/hartley.html.

Hejinian, Lyn. *My Life,* Sun and Moon, 1980, pp. 8-11.

Hejinian, Lyn. *Mirage*, Spring 1989. p. 24.

Silliman, Ron. "Aesthetic Tendency and the Politics of Poetry." *Social Text,* 19/20, Fall 1988. Quoted by Marjorie Perloff. "Language Poetry and the Lyric Subject." http://writing.upenn.edu/epc/authors/perloff/langpo.html.

——. *The New Sentence,* Roof Books, 1977, pp. 88-93.

——. "Who Speaks: Ventriloquism and the Self in the Poetry Reading." *Close Listening*, edited by Charles Bernstein, Oxford Univ. Press, 1998, pp. 360-78. Quoted by Marjorie Perloff. "Language Poetry and the Lyric Subject.". http://writing.upenn.edu/epc/authors/perloff/langpo.html.

FLASH FICTION:

FROM POEM
TO
SHORT-SHORT

Flash Fiction—From Poem To Short-Short

Introduction

[In the short-short] we see human figures in a momentary flash. We see them in fleeting profile.. . . Everything depends on intensity, one sweeping blow of perception.. . . The shorter the piece of writing, the more abstract it may seem to us.. . . [Like the lyric] it strives for a rapid unity of impression, an experience rendered in its wink of immediacy.. . . as if to say, we don't need detail or extension, the whole thing comes to us in a flash. Irving Howe (1982)

[A flash fiction] is intrinsically different from the short story and more like the sonnet or ghazal—two quick moves in opposite directions, dialectical moves, perhaps, and then a leap to a radical resolution that leaves the reader anxious in a particularly satisfying way. The source, the need, for the form seems to me to be the same need that created Norse kennings, Zen koans, Sufi tales, where language and metaphysics grapple for holds like Greek wrestlers, and not the need that created the novel or the short story, even, where language and the social sciences sleep peacefully inside one another like bourgeois spoons. Russell Banks (1986)

Both Irving Howe and Russell Banks compare short-short works of fiction with poetry. What Howe refers to as short short-fiction is between 1500 and 2000 words, quite a bit longer than what contemporary writers are thinking when they hear the term "flash fiction" or "sudden fiction". In this text, I use the term "flash fiction" loosely, for a three line haiku to a 1000 word story.

While I am not a writer of "flash" fiction, per se, as a poet, novelist and teacher, I enjoy working with vignettes, focusing intently on sentence structure, image and framing. Two of the four novels I have written began as journal entries that could easily have become a series of poems; but instead I pulled the narrative thread, following the question: And then what? For me, longer fictions are often a series of overlapping short shorts or prose poems.

Usually with flash fiction there is more emphasis on character, action and dialogue while prose poetry calls our attention to structure, style and sound. Sometimes it is difficult to see the difference. In this sequence of prompts on Flash Fiction, I ask the student to experiment with genre, style, structure, poetic techniques, point of view, sometimes using poetic constraints and forms to help find, evolve, frame or evade the story.

In each course, I ask students to begin by turning back to "Walking and Writing" on page 3. You will write a flash fiction by first writing haiku. If you look carefully at a haiku, you will see a tiny story in three lines. Make it a sentence without line ends and you will have a prose poem or a micro flash fiction. Haiku are incredibly particular, and it is important for a fiction writer to be particular, to bring the reader into the thinking-sensual mind of the narrator with precise detail and description. Once you write your haiku for this section, you will embed them into a short short story.

I recommend that in each prompt you write your draft before you read the sample stories and my comments. That way you will not be overly influenced by someone else's poem or story and instead find your own way into the writing.

Banks, Russell. "Afterwards." *Sudden Fiction: American Short-Short Stories*, edited by Robert Shepard and James Thomas, Peregrine, 1986, p. 244.

Howe, Irving and Ilana Wiener Howe, eds. "Introduction." *Short Shorts: An Anthology of the Shortest Stories*, Godine, 1982. xi-xiii.

Recommended Text:

Burroway, Janet. *Writing Fiction*, 10th ed., Univ. of Chicago Press, 2019. [A helpful book for learning standard approaches to fiction writing.]

#2: The Storyteller

Prompt

Think of a story that someone told you, maybe when you were growing up. Or retell a story that you have told others. Let the voice of the storyteller seem spoken rather than written. Try to retell the story without a lot of explaining, just what's necessary to keep the attention of the listener/reader. If your story is in the first person, focus on the event and the other characters, more than the narrator. Even if the narrator doesn't announce herself inside the story, there will be this sense of a person telling a story rather than an absent narrator. Be sure that you include particular details or images, continuing to use what you learned from the first prompt; in fact, you could write a few haiku (in the voice of the narrator) and embed them into the story..

Background / Examples

In **Sherwood Anderson**'s book *Winesburg, Ohio*, the stories are about characters living in a fictional Midwestern town in the early 20th Century; it was published in 1919. While Anderson doesn't write short-short fiction, you can learn a lot about story writing by reading his work. While William Carlos Williams was writing poems and stories in the language of ordinary Americans, with the ordinary rhythms of American English, Anderson was seeking something similar in his stories:

> There was the language of the streets, of American towns and cities, the language of the factories and warehouses where I had worked, of laborers' rooming houses, the saloons, the farms.
>   It is my own language, limited as it is. I will have to learn to work with it. There was a kind of poetry I was seeking in my prose, word to be laid against word in just a certain way, a kind of word color a march of words and sentences, the color to be squeezed out of simple words, simple sentence construction.. . . [My stories] were simple little tales of happenings, things observed and felt.

A more contemporary fiction writer, **Bobbie Louise Hawkins** was known among the poets, especially in the Kerouac School for Poetics at Naropa University, as a storyteller—on the telephone, on stage and on the page. Stories were always rolling off her tongue. When I interviewed her in 2011, we talked on the telephone for hours at a time; Bobbie told one story after another. The interview is laced with stories about her family, lovers, the news, etc. Parts of it are available on the internet. See the link below in "Notes."

Bobbie Louise Hawkins
Dale Herd's Found Quarter

Dale Herd telephoned me.

"I was just walking down the street and I found a quarter on the sidewalk."

"Good for you."

"Then when I went to pick it up it was epoxied to the cement."

"Hell."

"What I really hated about it was I knew the son-of-a-bitch was somewhere watching me. So I went looking for a good rock and I came back and I knocked the quarter off the sidewalk."

"Spoiled his game."

"Yeah, it would cost him another quarter to keep it up. So then I had this quarter and I wanted to do something with it and I decided to telephone you with it and tell you."

"I'm glad I was home."

Hawkin's story, "Dale Herd's Found Quarter" is short, concise and told with a storyteller's voice. You can find these stories everywhere, on the street, on the kitchen counter or in your texts. Keep a notebook with you at all times. The funny thing about this story is when I met Dale Herd a few years back, I asked him about the story and he told me that it had never happened. Bobbie made it up as a joke.

ANTHONY TOGNAZZINI
SAME GAME

Everyday at the bus stop I see this little kid, about eight years old, hooded sweatshirt and white Nikes, bouncing a blue racquetball against the stippled asphalt.

"Catch," she said yesterday, and threw the ball in my direction.

Its rubber surface felt strange in my fingers, like a piece of fruit I didn't know the name of. It was still pretty early in the morning, and a heavy cloud cover hung low on the buildings. Everything looked like a shadow of itself. I'd seen this kid the day before, and the day before that, and she never seemed to be going anywhere, not school or camp or someone's house. She scared me. Her face was like a slate where you could scribble new expressions.

Finally, she said, "You look sad. Where are you going?"

"To work," I told her. "Everyday I take the bus, same time. See my briefcase? It's an adult thing. When you grow up, you 'll see. it's not sad. You ride the bus, work, come home at night. Like that." I tossed the ball back. "You?" I asked. "Where're you going?"

The built-in reflector on the girl 's sneaker gleamed. She said, "I'm going to be brave in ways you won't recognize." Then she pocketed her racquetball and ran away from me.

~

"Same Game" by Anthony Tognazzini is about 200 words. A first person narrator tells the story of what happened one day when he stopped at a bus stop where a little girl was bouncing a ball. He describes the setting, the ball and the little girl. And the narrator seems to be speaking directly to us: "Every day at the bus stop, I see this little kid . . ." She scares him for some reason because she is expressionless. She looks at him and says, "You look sad. Where are you going?" "To work," he explains and tells her he is not sad. "It's an adult thing." And he asks her where she is going. The whole story hinges on her answer. "I'm going to be brave in ways you won't recognize." Then off she goes. This is a flash fiction. Just a moment or two and it's over. So whenever you encounter little scenes like this, jot them down in your journal. They can become flashes of their own, or flashes that are part of a longer story.

You will find many other examples of storytelling narrators as you progress through the prompts and also in the prose poem anthology in the appendix; one example is Bill Kushner's "Building" on page 281.

NOTES

Anderson, Sherwood. *Winesburg, Ohio: Text and Criticism.* Edited by John H. Ferres, Viking Press, 1966. pp. 13-14.

Hawkins, Bobbie Louise. "Dale Herd's Found Quarter." *My Own Alphabet: Stories Essays and Memoirs,* Coffee House Press, 1989, p. 119.

—"Interview/Discussion with Bobbie Louise Hawkins." *Selected Prose of Bobbie Louise Hawkins*, edited by Barbara Henning, BlazeVox Press, 2012. The Interview is also available on Belladonna Website, 2012, http://www.belladonnaseries.org/wp-content/uploads/2014/04/bobbie_louise_hawkins.pdf

Tognazzini, Anthony "Same Game." *PP/FF: An Anthology*, edited by Peter Connors, Starcherone Books, 2006. 203.

#3: Auto-Flash Fiction

Journal Writing Assignment:

Keep a journal throughout this course. Everyday jot down notes on the stories that happen. Include lots of concrete details and description. This type of a journal has become central to the work of many writers, including thoughts, feelings, reactions and quotations from events and reading. Because you are aiming to use your material to write fiction, it is important that you concentrate especially on what happens, on actions, dialogue and description. These stories do not have to be dramatic; they can be simple and ordinary.

Many writers transform autobiographical material into fiction, some disguising it more than others. Lately, it seems to me that consciousness is so rich that as a writer I can just dip in and pull out a story or a poem. If a day seems uneventful, I still record my seemingly insignificant happenings and thoughts.

Prompt

Take one narrative from your journal and develop it into an auto-flash-fiction (100 to 500 words), a combination of autobiography and flash fiction; perhaps auto can also refer to "automatic," written spontaneously in a voice that seems chatty, available and at ease, i.e. personal. Perhaps there is an event or person you remember from a day when you did not write a journal; you could write an entry using an easy journal voice; then use this material to write an auto-flash-fiction. Even with an easy-going voice, the story will still work better with concrete details and dialogue.

Examples

Lydia Davis
The Caterpillar

I find a small caterpillar in my bed in the morning. There is no good window to throw him from and I don't crush or kill a living thing if I don't have to. I will go to the trouble of carrying this thin, dark, hairless little caterpillar down the stairs and out to the garden.

He is not an inchworm, though he is the size of an inchworm. He does not hump up in the middle but travels steadily along on his many pairs of legs. As I leave the bedroom, he is quite speedily walking around the slopes of my hand.

But halfway down the stairs, he is gone—my hand is blank on every side. The caterpillar must have let go and dropped. I can't see him. The stairwell is dim and the stairs are painted dark brown. I could get a flashlight and search for this tiny thing, in order to save his life. But I will not go that far—he will have to do the best he can. Yet how can he make his way down to the back door and out into the garden?

I go on about my business. I think I've forgotten him, but I haven't. Every time I go upstairs or down, I avoid his side of the stairs. I am sure he is there trying to get down.

At last I give in. I get the flashlight. Now the trouble is that the stairs are so dirty. I don't clean them because no one ever sees them here in the dark. And the caterpillar is, or was, so small. Many things under the beam of the flashlight look rather like him—a very slim splinter of wood or a thick piece of thread. But when I poke them, they don't move.

I look on every step on his side of the stairs, and then on both sides. You get somewhat attached to any living thing once you try to help it. But he is nowhere. There is so much dust and dog hair on the steps. The dust may have stuck to his little body and made it hard for him to move or at least to go in the direction he wanted to go in. It may have dried him out. But why would he even go down instead of up? I haven't looked on the landing above where

113

he disappeared. I will not go that far.

I go back to my work. Then I begin to forget the caterpillar. I forget him for as long as one hour, until I happen to go to the stairs again. This time I see that there is something just the right size, shape, and color on one of the steps. But it is flat and dry. It can't have started out as him. It must be a short pine needle or some other plant part.

The next time I think of him, I see that I have forgotten him for several hours. I think of him only when I go up or down the stairs. After all, he is really there somewhere, trying to find his way to a green leaf, or dying. But already I don't care as much. Soon, I'm sure I will forget him entirely.

Later there is an unpleasant animal smell lingering about the stairwell, but it can't be him. He is too small to have any smell. He has probably died by now. He is simply too small, really, for me to go on thinking about him.

~

In "The Caterpillar," **Lydia Davis** writes about an unusual but ordinary problem. She finds a caterpillar in her bed and walks down the stairs with him. One third of the story is finished. Then she tells of her brief encounters going back to look for him, and finally giving up. The story is 570 words long and the span of the story is a few moments of time. Perhaps like Davis you will write about something that happened while focusing on an object, animal or person. Her piece ends as a meditation on being and smallness.

YASUNARI KAWABATA
MAKEUP

My bathroom window faces the rest room of the Yanaka Funeral Hall. The narrow space between the buildings is the funeral hall's trash dump where they dispose of funeral wreaths and flowers.

The cry of the autumn insects had already grown loud in the

114

graveyard of the funeral hall although it was only the middle of September. I put my hand on my wife's shoulder and led her and her younger sister down the hallway to show them something. It was night. As I opened the door of the bathroom at the end of the hall, the powerful fragrance of chrysanthemums struck us. Surprised, they leaned toward the window over the washbasin. The window was blooming with white chrysanthemums. About twenty wreaths stood in a row, left over from a funeral. As my wife reached out as if to take a flower, she wondered out loud how many years it had been since she had seen so many chrysanthemums at one time.

I turned on the light. The silver wrapping paper of the wreaths sparkled. While I was working that night, time and again I caught the scent of chrysanthemums when I went to the bathroom, and, each time, I felt the weariness of working all night vanish in the fragrance. Finally, in the light of day, the white flowers seemed all the whiter and the silver paper began to glow. As I tended to my business, I noticed a canary perched on the flowers. It was probably a bird released at yesterday's funeral ceremony that had gotten tired and had forgotten to return to the bird shop.

Although this was a beautiful sight, from my bathroom window I also have to look at the funeral flowers on other days as they rot away. Even now at the beginning of March, as I write this, I have been watching a wreath of bellflowers and red roses for four or five days, wondering just how the colors will change as they wither.

I wish the flowers were on living plants.

I also have to look at human beings in the window of the funeral hall rest room. There are a lot of young women. Few men seem to go into the rest room, and the longer the old women stay there the less they look like women. Most of the young women stand there for a moment, then do their makeup. When I see these women in mourning clothes doing their faces in the rest room, putting on dark lipstick, I shudder and flinch as if I've seen the bloody lips of one who has licked a corpse. All of them are calm and collected. Their bodies exhibit a sense of sin, as though they were committing some evil deed while they hide themselves.

I do not want to see such horrible makeup, but the windows face each other all year long, so such disgusting incidents are not at all rare. I always hurriedly look away. I think I may send letters to the women I like, telling them not to go into the rest room at the Yanaka Funeral Hall, even if they should come for a funeral—in order to keep them away from those witches.

Anyway, the other day I saw a girl of about seventeen or eighteen in the window of the rest room, drying her tears with a white handkerchief. Though she wiped her eyes again and again, still the tears overflowed. Her shoulders trembled as she sobbed. Finally, gripped by sorrow, she leaned against the wall. She gave in to her tears without the strength to dry her cheeks.

She was the only one who had come not to hide and put on her makeup. She had surely come to hide herself and cry.

The ill feelings toward women that had grown in me from looking through that window were washed clean by this girl. But then, unexpectedly, the girl took out a small mirror, gave a quick smile, and hurriedly left the rest room. I was so surprised, I felt as though someone had hit me with cold water. I almost called out to her.

It was a puzzling smile.

~

Yasunari Kawabata's *Palm of the Hand Stories* are delicate and perceptive. In his story "Makeup," he includes vivid details, as well as a sense of smell. After reading this story many times, I can't help but wonder why the men in the story don't put on a face. Perhaps they do, but not in the bathroom. What is most interesting to me is the way the story is left unexplained, perhaps unexplainable. We can imagine this story evolving from the author's daily observations. Perhaps from his bathroom window he had a view into a window in a bathroom at a funeral parlor. In my last apartment, I used to look out my window into the bathroom window of a man's apartment. He had a mirror hanging from the window where he would shave. I would watch him while I did my yoga practice. Perhaps he watched me. It's this kind of notation in your journal that could become a seed for a story.

My mother is working the graveyard shift as an elevator operator on 57th Street. She's fine for the first few hours, but around three o'clock in the morning she has all she can do to keep awake. So she goes down to the basement and washes her face in the sink and does some exercises. She does a few chin ups and push ups then goes back upstairs to the lobby. She reads a little, starts to fall asleep, drinks a cup of coffee from her thermos.

At four a.m. Mr. Jones from the Ninth floor enters the lobby from the street. He is an antique collector. He is so drunk that he crawls the whole length of the lobby until he reaches my mother. She is awake. She takes him up to the Ninth floor. When they get there, Mr. Jones wants my mother to come inside with him. He has something to show her, he says. My mother refuses. Mr. Jones then crawls into his apartment.

My mother wears a uniform. She wears bell bottom blue jeans, a fancy coat with brass buttons, high heel shoes. This is a requirement for elevator operators. All elevator operators must wear this same uniform. My father works as a porter at 550 Park Avenue. He too wears a uniform, though it is different from my mother's. His is gray. Both he and my mother try to keep awake.

At about four thirty a.m. the Monsignor arrives at the building where my mother works. He has the results of the tests they have run on my mother. My mother says "What's the verdict!" The Monsignor says "We'll see." The Monsignor says again "We'll see."

Then my mother notices something strange about the Monsignor's face. His face is a large clock, with one hand much larger than the other. My mother stares intently at the Monsignor's face. She wonders if it's quitting time yet.

~

Terence Winch's "Night Shift" is a story about the narrator's mother. It unfolds with a very relaxed voice. "My mother is working the graveyard shift as an elevator on 57th Street." As he tells the story of the night, it gets stranger, a drunk crawling into his apartment and finally she's looking at a man whose face looks like a clock. We get a quick view of her life that becomes dream like in the end at 4:30 am, as life often must for those working in the service industry at night, studying the clock to go home. It's easy for me to imagine this being written from the writer's experience, maybe from listening to his mother talk. When I asked Terence Winch about his process, he wrote:

> That's an interesting question, particularly as it applies to this piece, which mixes autobiography, dream, and imagination. I've written a lot about my mother over the decades, but the mother character in this piece is not her. I was drawing on my own experience as an elevator-operator in Manhattan when I was a student. I worked the graveyard shift from midnight to 8 a.m. one strange summer. My father's last job, however, was as a porter at 550 Park Ave. But, in the end, all of the characters in this story are fictional.

NOTES

Davis, Lydia. "The Caterpillar." *The Collected Stories of Lydia Davis."* Farrar Straus and Giroux, 2009. pp. 531-532. Originally published in *Varieties of Disturbance*, Farrar, Straus and Giroux, 2007, 31-32.

Kawabata, Yasunari. "Makeup." *Palm-of-the-Hand Stories,* North Point Press, 1988. pp.141-143.

Winch, Terence. "Night Shift." *Total Strangers,* The Toothpaste Press, West Branch, Iowa, 1982, pp. 1-2.

Prompt

Write a short-short story with one or two characters in a single place with a definite problem; no more than two incidents, no more than two pages. Make the point of view, the eye of a camera (and the ear if you'd like since in our age we have cameras with ears). Use no obvious metaphors or similes, stick to physical description, only what can be seen by the eye/ear of the camera, stay in the present tense, no memories, only the present, no omniscient narrator, only the eye/ear of the camera. Work with thick visual description.

or

Write a one to three page story where the main character is a group of people doing some ordinary activity in a place that you know well. The narrator will look at them very closely without knowing what they are thinking, zooming in and studying them as if they are a different species, describing their activities as if they were instincts. If you want to zoom in on one person, that's fine, too. Again thick description, but here a camera eye that sees close up and from afar.

Examples

ALAIN ROBBE-GRILLET
A CORRIDOR

A not too dense crowd of people in a hurry, all walking at the same speed, is traveling down a corridor that has no side passages, running between two elbow turns whose obtuse arcs completely hide the final exits, and whose walls are adorned, on the right as well as on the left, by identical advertising posters following each other at equal intervals. The posters display a woman's head, almost as high by itself alone as one of the people of normal height who pass in front of it, walking quickly, without a side glance.

This giant face, with its tightly curled blond hair, its eyes surrounded by very long lashes, its red lips, its white teeth, is shown in a three-quarter pose, smiling as it looks at the passers-by hurrying past one after the other, while beside it, on the left, a bottle of carbonated pop, at a forty-five-degree angle, points its opening at the partially opened mouth. The advertising slogan is written in cursive letters, in two lines: the word "even" placed above the bottle, and the word "purer" below, at the bottom of the sign, on a line that slants upward slightly from the horizontal lower edge of the poster.

The same words are found in the same place on the following poster, with the same tilted bottle whose contents are ready to spill out, and the same impersonal smile. Then, after an empty space covered with white ceramic tile, the same scene again, frozen at the same moment when the lips approach the top of the bottle held forward and the liquid contents about to gush forth, in front of which the same hurrying crowd passes by without turning a head, moving along toward the next poster.

And the mouths multiply, as do the bottles and the eyes as large as hands in the midst of their long, curving lashes. And, on the other wall of the corridor, the same features are exactly repeated (with this difference, that the directions of the glance and the bottle are reversed), following each other at constant intervals on the other side of the dark silhouettes of the travelers, who continue to move by, in a scattered but uninterrupted order, against the sky-blue background of the posters, between the reddish bottles and the pink faces with their parted lips. But, just before the elbow turn at the end of the straight corridor, the crowd is slowed down by a man who has stopped, about a yard away from the left wall. The man has on a gray suit, somewhat worn from wear, and is holding in his right hand, which hangs down alongside his body, a news paper folded twice. He is engaged in staring at the wall, in the vicinity of a nose, bigger than his whole face, which is located level with his own eyes.

In spite of the great size of the drawing and the lack of details in its execution, the observer's head is bent forward, as if to see more clearly. The passers-by have to move aside momentarily from their straight trajectory in order to get around this unexpected obstacle; almost all pass behind the man, but some, noticing too late the scrutiny that they are about to interrupt, or not willing to change their course for such a minor matter, or aware of nothing at all, pass between the man and the poster, cutting straight through the glance.

~

In "A Corridor," **Alain Robbe-Grille** takes his camera eye point of view into the subway system. Some of Robbe-Grillet's films and novels are strange and mysterious. He also wrote some seminal essays on writing fiction. He was associated with a group of French writers, the New Novelists, who aimed to reinvent the novel. Instead of continuing with omniscient godlike narrators, past tense narration, heroes, formulaic dialogue and plot driven texts, they privileged "objects" and what modern science was discussing at the time: knowledge is discontinuous, partial, provisional, even contradictory. In the same way the cinema was inventing new forms, Robbe-Grillet used his camera eye to focus on the immediate present, physical description and movement. He writes, "Art is life. Nothing, in art, is ever won *for good*. Art cannot exist without this permanent condition of being *put in question*." There is an expectation here that the reader will have to do more work as she reads. Instead of trying to go in depth and search for essences, he attempts to stay at the surface, like a roving eye camera, like the new movie-eye of the 20th Century.

In *Tropisms*, **Nathalie Sarraute** aims to capture "movements, which are hidden under the commonplace, harmless appearances of every instant of our lives." She was also associated with the New Novelists, as was Marguerite Duras. Sarraute is observing groups of people in ordinary situations, as if studying groups of insects in their habitat. In her forward, she explains:

What I tried to do was to show certain inner "movements" by which I had long been attracted; in fact, I might even say that, ever since I was a child, these movements, which are hidden under commonplace, harmless appearances of every instant of our lives had struck and held my attention... These movements, of which we are hardly cognizant, slip through us on the frontiers of consciousness in the form of undefinable, extremely rapid sensations. They hide behind our gestures, beneath the words we speak, the feelings we manifest, are aware of experiences and able to define. They seemed, and still seem to me to constitute the secret source of our existence, in what might be called its nascent state. . . . It was also necessary to make them break up and spread out in the consciousness of the reader the way a slow motion film does. . . . I gave them this name [Tropisms] because of their spontaneous, irresistible, instinctive nature, similar to that of the movements made by certain living organisms under the influence of outside stimuli, such as light or heat.

NATHALIE SARRAUTE
from TROPISMS

They seemed to spring up from nowhere, blossoming out in the slightly moist tepidity of the air, they flowed gently along as though they were seeping from the walls, from the boxed trees, the benches, the dirty sidewalks, the public squares.

They stretched out in long, dark clusters between the dead house fronts. Now and then, before the shop windows, they formed more compact, motionless little knots, giving rise to occasional eddies, slight cloggings.

A strange quietude, a sort of desperate satisfaction emanated from them. They looked closely at the piles of linen in the White Sale display, clever imitations of snow-covered mountains, or at a doll with teeth and eyes that, at regular intervals, lighted up, went out, lighted up, went out, lighted up, went out, each time at the same interval, lighted up again and again went out.

They looked for a long time, without moving, they remained there, in offering, before the shop windows, they kept postponing till the next interval the moment of leaving. And the quiet little children, whose hands they held, weary of looking, listless, waited patiently beside them.

~

NOTES

Robbe-Grillet, Alain. *For a New Novel: Essays on Fiction*, Grove Press, 1965.

Robbe-Grillet, Alain. "The Corridor." *Snapshots,* Northwestern Univ. Press, 1962, pp. 55-57

Sarraute, Nathalie. "I." *Tropisms,* George Braziller, 1963, pp. 6-8, 13-14.

#5: LONG SENTENCES

Prompt

Write a one-page story composed of very long sentences. Retell a particular event that took no longer than one hour to occur, better yet a few moments. Long sentences seem to work particularly well with first person narrators. Begin this in your journal and then work on the sentences so they are very long and still grammatically correct. If you need more than two sentences, that's ok. Just try to make the sentences longer than you usually write.

Examples

FIELDING DAWSON
THE VERTICAL FIELDS

In Memory of C.D.K

On Christmas Eve around 1942, when I was a boy, after having the traditional punch and cookies and after having sung 'round the fire (my Aunty Mary at the piano), I, with my sister, my mother and my aunts, and Emma Jackman and her son, got into Emma Jackman's car and drove down Taylor Avenue to church for the midnight service: I looked out the rear window at passing houses, doors adorned with holly wreaths, I looked into windows—catching glimpses of tinseled trees and men and women and children moving through rooms into my mind and memory forever; the car slowed to the corner stop at Jefferson and the action seemed like a greater action, of Christmas in a cold damp Missouri night; patches of snow lay on the ground and in the car the dark figures of my mother and sister and aunts talked around me and the car began to move along in an air of sky—at bottom dark and cold, seeming to transform the car, my face, and hands, pressed close to the glass as I saw my friends with their parents in their cars take the left turn onto Argonne Drive and look for a parking place near the church; Emma Jackman followed, and I watched heavily coated figures make their exits, and move down the winter walk toward the jewel-like glittering church—up the steps into the full light of the doorway—fathers and sons and mothers and daughters I knew and understood them all, I gazed at them with blazing eyes: light poured from open doors; high arched stained glass windows cast downward slanting shafts of color across the cold church-yard, and the organ boomed inside while we parked and got out and walked along the sidewalk, I holding my mother's right arm, my sister held mother's left arm (mother letting us a little support her)—down the sidewalk to join others at the warmly good noisy familiar threshold: spirits swirled up the steps into the church and Billy Berthold handed out the Christmas leaflets, I gripped mine. I looked at the dominant blue illustration of Birth in white and yellow rays moving outward to form a circle around the Christ child's skull as Mary downward gazed; Joseph; kneeling wisemen downward gazed; I gazed down the long center aisle at the rising altar's dazzling cross and we moved down the aisle, slipped in front of Mr. and Mrs. Sloan and my buddy Lorry, Mr. and Mrs. Dart and my buddy Charles, Mr. and Mrs. Reid and my buddy Gene and his brother Ed—we then knelt away the conscious realization of our selves among music in the House of the Lord, I conscious of a voice that, slowly, coarsely, wandered–the I (eye) in see, hear me (I), we were on our feet singing, and the choir swept down the aisle, their familiar faces moving side to side as collective voices raised in anthem I held the hymnbook open and my mother and sister and I sang in celebration of God the crowded and brightly decorated– pine boughs and holly wreaths hung round the walls with candles high on each pew, I glanced at the gleaming cross—my spine arched, and far beyond the church, beyond the front door, beyond the land of the last sentence in James Joyce's *Dubliners* a distant door seemed to open away beyond pungent green of pine gathered around rich red hollyberry clusters, red velvet, white-yellow center of candle flame, white of silk, gold of tassle, and gleaming glittering eternally cubistic gold cross and darkness of wooden beams powerfully sweeping upward—apex for the strange smoky pneuma that so exhilarated me, I who smiled and reeled in a vast cold cold gaze down at myself listening to Charles Kean's Christian existentialist sermon in time before the plate was passed and the choir had singing, gone, and we were outside, I standing by my sister; my mother and aunts were shaking Charles's hand, I shook that solid hand warmly, and I walked down the steps, my mother and sister and aunts again, again, once again it rushed through me taking my breath, my spine arched toward trees and streets walking slowly breathing deep I moved down the sidewalk, eyes crystallizing streets yards houses and all lives within; my perception forked upward through treetops into the vertical fields of space, and a moment later, in the crowded back seat of the car, as Emma Jackman started the engine, I breathed vapor on the rear window, and with my finger, I signed my name.

~

In **Fielding Dawson's** "The Vertical Fields," even though there are only a few actual sentences closed with a period, several semi-colons and colons act as brief stops. What makes me want to read this over again is the odd consciousness of the narrator, the boy who is gazing "with blazing eyes." Let me describe for you, he says, the world of my youth. And the long sentences pull us along to the epiphany at the end: "my breath, my spine arched toward trees and streets walking slowly breathing deep . . ."

Other long sentences below have been excerpted from writing by **Marcel Proust, Robert Bolano,** and **James Joyce**. Notice how each author structures his sentences differently. With Molly Bloom, Joyce ignores standard punctuation rules and just runs it all together. With Bolano and especially with Proust, the sentences mostly follow standard grammar. Proust is, of course, known for his long sentences, long paragraphs, and his novel of several volumes. Each of the sentence styles reveal a different mindset.

MARCEL PROUST
from SWANN'S WAY

But the only one of us for whom Swann's arrival became the object of a painful preoccupation was I. This was because on the evening when strangers, or merely M. Swann, were present, Mama did not come up to my room. I had dinner before everyone else and afterward I came and sat at the table, until eight o'clock when it was understood that I had to go upstairs; the precious and fragile kiss that Mama usually entrusted to me in my bed when I was going to sleep I would have to convey from the dining room to my bedroom and protect during the whole time I undressed, so that its sweetness would not shatter, so that its volatile essence would not disperse and evaporate, and on precisely those evenings when I needed to receive it with more care, I had to take it, I had to snatch it brusquely, publicly without even having the time and the freedom of mind necessary to bring to what I was doing the attention of those individuals controlled by some mania, who do their utmost not to think of anything else while they are shutting a door, so as to be able, when the morbid uncertainty returns to them, to confront it victoriously with the memory of the moment when they did shut the door.

~

In the introduction, Lydia Davis comments on Proust's long sentences.

Proust felt, however, that a long sentence contained a whole, complex thought, a thought that should not be fragmented or broken. The shape of the sentence was the shape of the thought, and every word was necessary to the thought: "I really have to weave these long silks as I spin them," he said. "If I shortened my sentences, it would make little pieces of sentences, not sentences." He wished to "encircle the truth with a single—even if long and sinuous—stroke."

One friend, though surely exaggerating, reported that Proust would arrive late in the evening, wake him up, begin talking, and deliver one long sentence that did not come to an end until the middle of the night. The sentence would be full of asides, parentheses, illuminations, reconsiderations, revisions, addenda, corrections, augmentations, digressions, qualifications, erasures, deletions, and marginal notes. It would, in other words, attempt to be exhaustive, to capture every nuance of a piece of reality, to reflect Proust's entire thought. To be exhaustive is, of course, an infinite task: more events can always be inserted, and more nuance in the narration, more commentary on the event, and more nuance within the commentary. Growing by association of ideas, developing internally by contiguity, the long sentences are built up into pyramids of subordinate clauses.

Roberto Bolaño
from *By Night In Chile*

And a little earlier or a little later, that is to say a few days before being ordained a priest or a couple of days after taking holy vows, I met Farewell, the famous Farewell, I don't remember exactly where, probably at his house, I did go to his house, although maybe I made the pilgrimage to the newspaper's editorial offices or perhaps I saw him for the first time at his club, one melancholy afternoon, like so many April afternoons in Santiago, although in my soul birds were singing and buds were bursting into flower, as the poet says, and there was Farewell, tall, a metre and eighty centimetres, although he seemed two metres tall to me, wearing a grey suit of fine English cloth, hand-made shoes, a silk tie, a white shirt as immaculate as my hopes, gold cufflinks, a tie-pin bearing insignia I did not wish to interpret but whose meaning by no means escaped me, and Farewell invited me to sit down beside him, very close, or perhaps before that he took me into his library or the library of the club, and while we looked over the spines of the books he began to clear his throat, and while he was clearing his throat he may have been watching me out of the corner of his eye, although I can't be sure, since I kept my eyes fixed on the books, and then he said something I didn't understand or something my memory has not retained, and after that we sat down again, he in a Chesterfield, I on a chair, and we talked about the books whose spines we had been looking at and caressing, my young fingers fresh from the seminary, Farewell's thick fingers already rather crooked, not surprisingly given his age and his height, and we spoke about the books and the authors of the books, and Farewell's voice was like the voice of a large bird of prey soaring over rivers and mountains and alleys and ravines, never at a loss for the appropriate expression, the sentence that fitted his thought like a glove, and when with the naiveté of a fledgling, I said that I wanted to be a literary critic, that I wanted to follow in his footsteps, that for me nothing on earth could be more fulfilling than to read, and to present the results of my reading in good prose, when I said that, Farewell smiled and put his hand on my shoulder (a hand that felt as heavy as if it were encased in an iron gauntlet or heavier still) and he met my gaze and said it was not an easy path. In this barbaric country, the critic's path, he said, is not strewn with roses.

~

Throughout **Bolaño's** story, long independent clauses are linked using subordination, interruption, accumulation, transformation, and after a while, another "and" opens up a whole new pattern. In some of my students' long sentences, I point out grammatically, where a student could use a period instead of a comma splice or a run-on "and . . . and . . . and." But the decision depends of course upon the flow of the prose, the narrator's personality, and how you want the reader to interact with your text. Here the entire novel is one paragraph and we spiral along with this priest's run-on mind.

There is no punctuation in Molly Bloom's soliloquy. James Joyce runs on and on following the way her thoughts move.

James Joyce
from *Ulysses*

I love flowers I'd love to have the whole place swimming in roses
God of heaven there's nothing like nature the wild mountains
then the sea and the waves rushing then the beautiful country
with fields of oats and wheat and all kinds of things and all the
fine cattle going about that would do your heart good to see rivers and lakes and flowers all sorts of shapes and smells and colours springing up even out of the ditches primroses and violets
nature it is as for them saying there's no God I wouldn't give a
snap of my two fingers for all their learning why don't they go
and create something I often asked him atheists or whatever they
call themselves go and wash the cobbles off themselves first then
they go howling for the priest and they dying and why why because they're afraid of hell on account of their bad conscience ah
yes I know them well who was the first person in the universe
before there was anybody that made it all who ah that they don't
know neither do I so there you are they might as well try to stop
the sun from rising tomorrow the sun shines for you he said the
day we were lying among the rhododendrons on Howth head in
the grey tweed suit and his straw hat the day I got him to propose
to me yes first I gave him the bit of seedcake out of my mouth
and it was leapyear like now yes 16 years ago my God after that
long kiss I near lost my breath yes he said I was a flower of the
mountain yes so we are flowers all a woman's body yes that was
one true thing he said in his life and the sun shines for you today
yes that was why I liked him because I saw he understood or felt
what a woman is and I knew I could always get round him and
I gave him all the pleasure I could leading him on till he asked
me to say yes and I wouldn't answer first only looked out over
the sea and the sky I was thinking of so many things he didn't
know of Mulvey and Mr Stanhope and Hester and father and old
captain Groves and the sailors playing all birds fly and I say stoop
and washing up dishes they called it on the pier and the sentry
in front of the governors house with the thing round his white

helmet poor devil half roasted and the Spanish girls laughing in their shawls and their tall combs and the auctions in the morning the Greeks and the Jews and the Arabs and the devil knows who else from all the ends of Europe and Duke street and the fowl market all clucking outside Larby Sharans and the poor donkeys slipping half asleep and the vague fellows in the cloaks asleep in the shade on the steps and the big wheels of the carts of the bulls and the old castle thousands of years old yes and those handsome Moors all in white and turbans like kings asking you to sit down in their little bit of a shop and Ronda with the old windows of the posadas glancing eyes a lattice hid for her lover to kiss the iron and the wineshops half open at night and the castanets and the night we missed the boat at Algeciras the watchman going about serene with his lamp and O that awful deepdown torrent O and the sea the sea crimson sometimes like fire and the glorious sunsets and the figtrees in the Alameda gardens yes and all the queer little streets and pink and blue and yellow houses and the rosegardens and the jessamine and geraniums and cactuses and Gibraltar as a girl where I was a Flower of the mountain yes when I put the rose in my hair like the Andalusian girls used or shall I wear a red yes and how he kissed me under the Moorish wall and I thought well as well him as another and then I asked him with my eyes to ask again yes and then he asked me would I yes to say yes my mountain flower and first I put my arms around him yes and drew him down to me so he could feel my breasts all perfume yes and his heart was going like mad and yes I said yes I will Yes.

~

NOTES

Bolano, Roberto. *By Night In Chile,* translated by Chris Andrews, New Directions, 2000. 3.

Davis, Lydia. "IntroductIon." *Swann's Way* by Marcel Proust, translated by Lydia Davis, Viking, 2003. pp. xvii, xviii, ix.

Dawson, Fielding. "The Vertical Fields." *Sudden Fiction: American Short-Short Stories*, edited by Richard Shappard and James Thomas, Gibbs M. Smith, 1986. pp.139-140. Originally published in *Krazy Kat and 76 More*. Black Sparrow, 1982.

Joyce, James. *Ulysses*, Spuyten Duyvil. pp. 766-68.

Proust, Marcel. *Swann's Way,* translated by Lydia Davis, Viking, 2003. 27.

#6: Sestina Story

Prompt

Your assignment is to tell a story using the sestina patterns, but instead of working with lines, you will work with sentences and paragraphs. Use the same patterns as described below, writing the sestina first in a list of sentences, and then make the sentences into a prose story with six paragraphs of six sentences each and one final paragraph with three sentences. Your sentences can be of varying lengths.

A traditional lined sestina is a rather complicated French poetic form invented in the 12th Century. There are six stanzas, with six lines in each stanza. The poem closes with a final three-line stanza. The final words in each line are repeated in each stanza, but in a different order. If you search on line, you will find plenty of instructions on how to write a sestina poem.

Let's say the following letters of the alphabet represent these six words: ABCDEF. The stanzas will follow the following pattern. Stanza one: AB-CDEF; stanza two: FAEBDC; stanza three: CFDABE; stanza four ECB-FAD; stanza five: DEACFB; stanza six: BDFECA. The closing stanza will be ECA or ACE, but it will also contain all of the six words within the three lines.

Background / Examples

In his sestina prose workshops, Harry Matthews recommended that you begin with six end words, no more than one a conspicuous word, at least two of them serving more than one grammatical function (e.g. face and stalk can be either nouns or verbs, routine can be either a noun or an adjective.). In an email to me, Harry wrote, "It would be a good time to point out that whereas in a poem the conspicuousness of the end-words is an arbitrary matter, in prose sestinas they should usually be made as inconspicuous as possible."

Mathews was a member of the French group OULIPO, and he was involved in adding writing constraints to their library. The prose sestina is one of those. In some of Mathews' prose sestinas, he is close to a purist; when he chose a form, he mostly stays with the rules; see "Waiting for Dusk." In others, like "Cigarettes," he allows a more random use of his six words. I've included a prose poem-story I wrote using the sestina form, "Like a Stairway." I started with a narrative I had already written in my journal, then I transformed it using the words I had chosen. I constructed two linked sestinas (following the rules) to initially compose the poem and then I freely revised, completely forgetting the rules. What I found most interesting about using the sestina words was the way the rules pushed me into writing with a different style and a different way of thinking.

Remember your goal is to write a story or a poem in sentences and paragraphs. You are using this poetic form to help inspire your story and to amp up the style.

Harry Mathews
Cigarettes

I sat on the edge of a chair looking out the third-floor window, wondering with a slight concern that could not yet be called worry about my sister, who should have been back from school by then, at least according to my watch. It was a pleasant, hazy spring evening. Shadows were falling on the spot where she would usually appear, often walking with a friend, two distant silhouettes amid the green of our rare surviving elms. Sometimes one or both would be smoking a cigarette—something that in those days had not become a social issue. Indeed the cigarette was omnipresent, as one can tell from movies of the time.

The window in front of me was wide open, it was lovely to drink in the green seasonal smells on this street where few cars passed. I and my sister lived with my mother, widowed for a year now, which put me on the spot as the man of the family, eighteen years to my sister's sixteen, and made me feel obliged to watch out for her well-being and her place in our household; to watch out now for her timely return.

In the deepening shadows I spied the glow of a cigarette down the street on the far sidewalk, coming exactly from the spot where she might appear. It was someone else who emerged, soon passing under my window with slow, somehow sinister steps. For some reason a pang about my sister shot through my breast, I told myself I must go looking for her down the green streets of our peaceful town, a green darkening now so as to be less green than black.

First I made a couple of phone calls, after checking my watch against the kitchen clock, to families whose children were good friends of my sister, but neither parents nor children could tell me anything. I lit a cigarette once I was outside. Looking up, I saw the last light of the sun brightening the window where I had sat with an enchanting orange glow. I walked past the spot where I'd looked for her, and on from there from likely spot to likely spot. I came to the little park, still green in the light of its newly lighted lamps; and there, peering through a kind of window in the shrubbery along its edge, I saw her sitting on a bench, not bothering to watch anything but the young man at her side. Each was fervently puffing on a cigarette while conversing intimately.

The young man, whom I recognized, had an arm around my sister; she leaned against his shoulder. I knew him, but I hadn't known my sister knew him too: Tommy McClough, a nice boy.

I didn't want to put them on the spot. Reflecting on what I might do, I myself lit another cigarette and decided not to butt in. What I did do was whistle "Green grow the lilies, O!", an old song we'd sung many times as kids. I was able to watch her start slightly, say some final words, and stand up. I hurried back to my window.

This time I didn't wait long by the window. My sister came rushing up the street. She was wearing a green dress and her locket watch. I called out to her on the spot. She came in, we hugged, and then each of us sat down and lit a cigarette.

~

Waiting for Dusk

Whoever in the span of his life is confronted by the word "pomegranate"will experience a mixture of feelings: a longing to see at least once the face of a Mediterranean god or nymph or faun; the memory of an old silver mirror decorated with images of varied fruits; a regret at never having known the spell of a summer picnic ending with the taste of acrid seeds spat over the bridge parapet – you look down at your scarlet-stained fingers and up at the weather of the sky as it changes (a black thunderhead, a blue depth), thinking of the same weather crossing centuries and landscapes.

I don't know whether I like the pomegranate as food or dislike it; perhaps neither, thinking of it more as a bridge to other, lost lives. But here now is Simon, with his smiling silly face from which he extracts tough seeds from his teeth with one awkward forefinger, a spell of not unsympathetic bad manners that, if truth be told, is a mirror of our own, perhaps more furtive acts. Then he puts on his mask, made of mirror-like chromed metal, and I think, why, he could face and kill Medusa! Any weather has its charm, even the green tempest surrounding her writhing snakes that spell death to the unwary traveler, snakes like a wreath of leeks in a Dutch still life where a pomegranate cut in two glows idly near the table edge.

I stroll with Simon, averting my eyes from his face, on the path that leads down to the edge of the stream and the pool under the bridge where fanged pike lie deep among bearded stones. The pillars and vaults of the bridge rise sturdily above us and are completed into wavering ellipses in the mirror of the slow-moving water. This is a moment between here and there, between the face of worldly things and their unstable reflections which in the basically sunny weather suggest reveries tending to sleep, and then sadness. Remember the pomegranate sliced on the unvarnished table, I tell myself, that's something sharp and real!

But the spell of the season and the melancholy hour, sweetened and damped with wine, spell another evolution of my afternoon of regrets, far from the Mediterranean and the bridge at Pisa, far from the land of nordic dream where the lemon and the pomegranate drop irregular sweet-and-sour globes on slopes scented and dry that are the dusky mirror of a life so seemingly simple that we think of even the treacherous weather as a seamless warm continuum of sun, moon, and stars. I know that I know better, I try to face my life here, with Simon: he has taken off his mask; it has left on his face a stripe or two like accidental marks of his real pain but that in fact spell nothing but themselves— nothing. He appears relaxed in this comfortable weather, sauntering ahead of me as we cross back over the wood-in-concrete bridge, unaware that in the declining light his silly smiling face is the mirror of my disjunction. The picnic spot is littered with wrecks of pomegranate.

Can my face ever be as actual as a pomegranate? Will the weather ever settle down? What dumb idea will replace the functioning bridge? What spell can make the masks of things real? What mirror will reveal them?

~

Barbara Henning
Like A Stairway

The postman pauses in front of the house—big bushy shrubs, a spindly young maple tree, white curtains half opened, peeling grey paint, a wooden screen door and then a darker solid door with a little window. He stands still, searching through his bag and shuffling a few papers and then he passes by, heading up the street. But we cross the street and slip inside the front door, making a sharp left at the foot of the stairs, passing by a Victorian style chair, covered with a dull gold cloth, bronze tacks, the wooden trim painted dark brown, and then a picture window looking out on a young maple and another grey cinderblock house. To the right, a footstool with chipped gray paint, a big brown stuffed chair and a man with very large ears, sound asleep, his shirt unbuttoned and his armpits covered with perspiration. A checkered tie flops over the arm of the chair and half a pack of Pall Malls rests on the table. A fly buzzes around him. He reaches up and brushes it off his cheek, and then he promptly falls back asleep. Across from him a low green scratchy couch and an end table. Sit down for a moment. The ashtrays are overflowing. In the corner there is a closet with a low rod for the young children and a higher one for the adults. A tv set and a turntable in a cabinet, painted with a mahogany stain. Three ceramic ducks are flying over the archway to the stairs, first the father, then the mother, then the baby.

A sculpted beige carpet leads into a hallway and a bedroom door with yesterday's clothes on a hook and to the right, a dresser cluttered with loose change and an ashtray. On the pale green wall, two painted girls, light skinned and blonde on a turquoise background, tiny yellow flowers laced in their hair. A low dresser with a mirror, a lace doily, hairpins, a white jewelry box and another pack of cigarettes in a brown paper bag. A wicker rocking chair piled with clothes. And a thin woman asleep in the bed, the blankets rumpled, her head falling back into the pillow like a stairway falling down, down, and then the sound of her almost nonexistent breath, her young mouth open, behind her a print of Jesus with the little children. The branches of a lilac bush tap against the window, and the woman reaches up and pulls the covers over her shoulders.

Turn around and cut diagonally across the house into the kitchen, painted a deep yellow. An old oak table and four chairs. Two rows of cupboards with cans of soup and vegetables, and stacks of folded bags. A black wall phone in the corner above the milk box, a glass ashtray with cigarette butts covered with red lipstick, an address book on the counter, a white beagle curled up in a warm spot in the corner, and a child in a diaper dropping clothespins inside the furnace door, the rhythm right in tune with the dog's tale thumping and the washer splashing. Out in back, a young girl, maybe ten years old, takes clothes off the line, white sheets in the wind, the young branches of a pear tree in the beginning stages of hibernation. A newspaper blows across the yard, resting temporarily at the base of the stairs of another gray cinderblock house.

When the dog turns over, the refrigerator starts to hum and the washer goes into spin. The golden rule is pinned above the door. Go back through the kitchen, past the sleeping man into the hallway. Follow the sound of a ball bouncing against a wall. Red plaid pajamas on the floor, a dresser with a fox hunt on top, three ceramic spaniels and a horse. In the bookshelf, fairy tales, hobby books, *Great Expectations* and the *Favorite Poems of Longfellow*. Big yellow sunflowers on the quilt, a toy fire engine in the corner, and the lone yellow ranger riding his horse across the curtains. The little boy bounces his ball at the wall, boing, back again to the bed, boing, hit a book, back again. Shut the door quietly.

In the bathroom, there's a white sink with pink tiles, water is running, a scale behind the door, four toothbrushes in a ceramic holder, and a girl sitting on the toilet, chanting, I'm three, I'm four, I'm free. Her feet are dangling over the edge. Behind her on the wall is a medicine cabinet with a shaving mug, all spice, a whisker brush, on the wall a razor, an extra bar of soap, pepto bismal, and a tube of toothpaste. A big yellow wicker hamper overflowing with clothes, a scale, a bathtub with three pink rags folded into squares and placed into each corner. The little girl pulls up the stool and climbs on top of a telephone book. Water starts to overflow.

Remember you are not the babysitter. You are not the mother. You are just passing through. Go back through the living room past the migrating ducks and up the staircase, past this and that stashed on shelves—a music box, an old doll, and a green library book. Under the rafters, a closet, crawl-throughs, recessed dressers, half built walls, and three beds. A little girl sits on her bed, cross-legged, carefully cutting up Dick and Jane and Sally. Their yellow hair removed, fluttering to the floor, little bits of this and that, a dog, a mother, something is starting to happen. The wind gushes into the room blowing papers all around. A comet, an eclipse, perhaps some star in the evening. A dusty cabinet full of books, an old set of rarely opened Harvard Classics and a worn collection of Mark Twain novels. An old painted dressing table with a cloudy mirror. Behind the walls, throw everything, all the scraps, throw the evidence into the darkness behind the walls. Then stand here, right here and look out the window, a panoramic daytime view of the sky and the yellow maple and oak trees, bare branches, and rows of houses, a block-by-block grid growing into the country.

Sometimes when I was a child and sound asleep, I'd climb up on the ledge, survey the horizon and then I'd jump out the window with my book under my arm—my skirt opening like a parachute, I'd land in the back seat of a black Chevy convertible. I remember looking back at the house the last time, at the lilac bush and the grey walls. My driver was wearing a black leather jacket, his hair was slicked back—he made a fast u turn at the corner, screeching and then he took me far away—never to return—into the city of dark alleys and hidden stars.

~

For another example of a sestina story, see Lynn Crawford's "Fancy" on page 292.

Mathews, Harry. "Cigarettes" and "Waiting for Dusk." Letter to Barbara Henning, Henning Archive, Yale Bieneke Library, New Haven. Manuscript.

Henning, Barbara. "Like a Stairway." *Cities and Memory: Stories and Prose Poems*, Chax Press, 2010. pp. 31-24. *Just Like That,* Spuyten Duyvil, 2018. 193-195. *Jacket Magazine, no.* 35, 2008.

#7 Dream Stories

Prompt

When you wake up from a dream, record what you remember. Write. Write. Write. Bring unusual images together. Then later make whatever changes necessary to make the piece work. Analyze your dream. What can be used to make a more realistic story? Is it the plot structure? The characters? The images? What could change to give it a slightly more ordinary effect? You might have a more successful story if the dream isn't too strange (like many dreams), but still has a dreamy plot and tone. The idea is to use the dream for material to write the story.

Stick with one or two scenes only. Let the dream break through the narrative of daily life. Even though the surrealists were mostly writing wild unbelievable stories, often the wilder the piece the more unbelievable and the better chance of the reader giving up before finishing.

Background / Examples

Between WW1 and WW2, the Surrealists rebelled against the slavery of a rigid reality-logic. For these poets and artists, writing and speaking the unconscious was a political act. They wrote manifestos, created visual art and wrote poetry and fiction. The process of creating the art was considered part of the artwork; they privileged spontaneity. Their stories were laced and structured like dreams with unusual metaphors. The strange was privileged over the ordinary. For more information on surrealism see page 22.

William Burroughs was a beat writer who used surrealist techniques for writing fiction:

> Dreams are a fertile source of material for writing.. . . I began writing dreams down long before I started to write. I have, over a period of years, turned up a number of future references; but more important is the number of characters and sets I have obtained directly from dreams, and at least forty percent of my material

derives from dreams. When I contact a character, I start building up an identikit picture. For example, I meet a character in a
dream; then I may find a photo in a magazine that looks like the
character, or I may meet someone who looks like him in some
respect. Usually my characters are composites of many people—
from dreams, photos, people I know and quite frequently characters in other writings. Over a period of years I have filled a number
of scrapbooks with these identikit pictures.

According to Marcel Jean, the surrealist **Gisèle Prassinos** was "a girl still
in her teens . . . who wrote insolent little tales of a decidedly automatic nature." You can find some background information on Prassinos by Ischell
on line. Ischell writes:

Born in 1920 and discovered at just fourteen by André Breton,
Gisèle Prassinos became the darling of the surrealists. Regarded as
a sort of living incarnation of the surrealist ideal of the child-wom-
an, a pure, uncorrupted talent, she had been writing ecstatic literature from her unconscious with no knowledge of the surrealist
practice of automatism.

GISELE PRASSINOS
HAIR TONIC

A man, a woman, an old man. They are in a hut. The man holds a
newspaper and, with his fingers, takes from his mouth little things
like macaroni. The woman is sitting on the floor. She is naked and
on her body there are pimples with yellow tips ending with a little
filament. She has a canvas bag on her knees and she tries to cut her
toenails with a hairpin.

In a corner a beardless old man watches her. His pink eyes have
no pupils and his eyelids are sewn to his eyebrows as if he were
going for a walk. Little gilded studs are half-buried in his pointed
skull. His ears are projecting and there are long curls of hair behind them. He holds in his black hand a kind of doll made of wire

and wrapped in yellow paper. The other hand is missing. In its place there is a fringe of shoelaces ....

The woman rises. She has put her extraordinary work into a pan and now she wants to cook it. But as she probably has no matches, she beckons to the old man. He comes near her. With a hook he makes a hole in his flesh and extracts a whistle from it. Then he puts it into the pan.

Now they are all three sitting around the pan and they watch it. The old man rises solemnly and says in his ripping voice: "The soup is not worth a scrap." Then the man takes him by the hand and leads him to another room, where he leaves him. He comes back to the woman and says: "O perfumed Chalice, I'll be faithful to you!" Then he goes out, catching on his way a spool of yellow thread, which he takes to the room where he has left the old man. When he comes back, he feels a pin grazing him. Then he takes the spool, puts it into his mouth, and sighs. The old man smiles, then runs toward him. Then they go arm in arm to the neighboring room.

When they arrived, the woman had put a skein of red Algiers silk on her foot.

~

Lydia Davis's "The Moon" was on a Kore Press broadside. In a talk I attended in Tucson, she explained that she would often take an actual happening and rewrite it so it was dreamlike. Or she would take a dream and make it more like daily life. Notice that even though a dream helped her write this little story, the end result doesn't seem surreal.

Lydia Davis
The Moon

I get up out of bed in the night to go to the bathroom. The room I am in is large, and dark but for the white dog on the floor. The hallway is wide and long, and filled with an underwater sort of twilight. When I reach the doorway of the bathroom, I see that it is filled with bright light. There is a full moon far above, overhead. Its beam is coming in through the window and falling directly onto the toilet seat, as if sent by a helpful God.

Then I am back in bed, and I have been lying there awake for a while. The room is lighter than it was. The moon is coming around to this side of the building, I think. But no, it is the beginning of dawn.

~

Richard Brautigan
The Weather In San Francisco

It was a cloudy afternoon with an Italian butcher selling a pound of meat to a very' old woman, but who knows what such an old woman could possibly use a pound meat for?

She was too old for that much meat. Perhaps she used it for a bee hive and she had five hundred golden bees at home waiting for the meat, their bodies stuffed with honey.

"What kind of meat would you like today?" the butcher said. "We have some good hamburger. It's lean.

"I don't know," she said. "Hamburger is something else. "

"Yeah, it's lean. I ground it myself. I put a lot of meat in it."

"Hamburger doesn't sound right," she said.

"Yeah," the butcher said. "It's a good day for hamburger. Look outside. It's cloudy. Some of those clouds have rain in them. I'd get the hamburger," he said.

"No," she said. "I don't want any hamburger, and I don't think it's going to rain. I think the sun is going to come out, and it will be a beautiful day, and I want a pound of liver."

The butcher was stunned. He did not like to sell liver to old ladies.

There was something about it that made him very nervous. He didn't want to talk to her any more.

He reluctantly sliced a pound of liver off a huge red chunk and wrapped it up in white paper and put it into a brown bag. It was a very unpleasant experience for him.

He took her money, gave her the change, and went back to the poultry section to try and get a hold of his nerves.

By using her bones like the sails of a ship, the old woman passed outside into the street. She carried the liver as if it were victory to the bottom of a very steep hill.

She climbed the hill and being very old, it was hard on her. She grew tired and had to stop and rest many times before she reached the top.

At the top of the hill was the old woman's house; a tall San Francisco house with bay windows that reflected a cloudy day.

She opened her purse which was like a small autumn field and near the fallen branches of an old apple tree, she found her keys.

Then she opened the door. It was a dear and trusted friend. She nodded at the door and went into the house and walked down a long hall into a room that was filled with bees.

There were bees everywhere in the room. Bees on the chairs. Bees on the photograph of her dead parents. Bees on the curtains. Bees on an ancient radio that once listened to the 1930s. Bees on her comb and brush.

The bees came to her and gathered about her lovingly while she unwrapped the liver and placed it upon a cloudy silver platter that soon changed into a sunny day.

~

Richard Brautigan's "The Weather in San Francisco" may have started with a dream or maybe Brautigan was dreaming as he was writing. This surreal story starts in an Italian butcher shop. At first, the narrator seems distant, dipping into the butcher's fears and then recording what happens. Once we are outside, we are in the consciousness of the old woman (third person subjective) and her strange relationship to the liver and her body and these amazing bees, her purse becoming a small autumn field and those bees eating the liver, just as the butcher imagined.

146

See other examples of dream-like story-like prose poems by Bob Holman on page 270 and Diane di Prima on page 267.

NOTES

Brautigan, Richard. "The Weather in San Francisco." *Sudden Fiction International: 60 Short Short Stories*, editors Robert Shepard and James Thomas, Norton, 1989, pp. 119-120. Originally published in *Revenge of the Lawn*. Simon Schuster, 1963.

Burroughs, William. "The Technology of Writing." In *The Adding Machine: Selected Essays*. NY: Arcade, 1993, p. 36.

Davis, Lydia. "The Moon," *Can't and Won't,"* Farrar, Straus and Giroux, 2014, p. 94. Originally published on a broadside, Kore Press, 16 October 2007.

Ischell. Review of *Bleak Fairy Tales: Gisèle Prassinos's Surrealist Texts*, *Reading in Translation*, 25 Feb 2014, http://readingintranslation. com/2014/02/25/bleak-fairy-tales-gisele-prassinoss-surrealist-texts-translated-by-ellen-nations/

Prassinos, Gisèle. "Hair Tonic." *The Autobiography of Surrealism*. Edited and translated by Marcel Jean, The Viking Press, 1980, pp. 346-47. Republished in *Poems for the Millennium: The University of California Book of Modern and Postmodern Poetry*, edited by Jerome Rothenberg and Pierre Joris, vol. 1, University of California Press, 1995, pp. 499-500. Originally published in *Minotaure, no. 6*, December 1934.

Examples

JULIO CORTÁZAR
A CONTINUITY OF PARKS

He had begun to read the novel a few days before. He had put it down because of some urgent business conferences, opened it again on his way back to the estate by train, he permitted himself a slowly growing interest in the plot, in the characterizations. That afternoon, after writing a letter giving his power of attorney and discussing a matter of joint ownership with the manager of his estate, he returned to the book in the tranquility of his study which looked out upon the park with its oaks. Sprawled in his favorite armchair, its back toward the door—even the possibility of an intrusion would have irritated him, had he thought of it—he let his left hand caress repeatedly the green velvet upholstery and set to reading the final chapters. He remembered effortlessly the names and his mental image of the characters; the novel spread its glamour over him almost at once. He tasted the almost perverse pleasure of disengaging himself line by line from the things around him, and at the same time feeling his head rest comfortably on the green velvet of the chair with its high back, sensing that the cigarettes rested within reach of his hand, that beyond the great windows the air of afternoon danced under the oak trees in the park. Word by word, caught up in the sordid dilemma of the hero and heroine, letting himself be absorbed to the point where the images settled down and took on color and movement, he was witness to the final encounter in the mountain cabin. The woman arrived first, apprehensive; now the lover came in, his face cut by the backlash of a branch. Admirably, she stanched the blood with her kisses, but he rebuffed her caresses, he had not come to perform again the ceremonies of a secret passion, protected by a world of dry leaves and furtive paths through the forest. The dagger warmed itself against his chest, and underneath liberty pounded, hidden close. A lustful, panting dialogue raced down the pages like a rivulet of snakes, and one felt it had all been decided from eternity. Even to those caresses which writhed about the lover's body, as though wishing to keep him there, to dissuade him from it; they sketched abominably the frame of that other body it was necessary to destroy. Nothing had been forgotten: alibis, unforeseen hazards, possible mistakes. From this hour on, each instant had its use minutely assigned. The cold-blooded, twice-gone-over reexamination of the details was barely broken off so that a hand could caress a cheek. It was beginning to get dark.

Not looking at one another now, rigidly fixed upon the task which awaited them, they separated at the cabin door. She was to follow the trail that led north. On the path leading in the opposite direction, he turned for a moment to watch her running, her hair loosened and flying. He ran in turn, crouching among the trees and hedges until, in the yellowish fog of dusk, he could distinguish the avenue of trees which led up to the house. The dogs were not supposed to bark, they did not bark. The estate manager would not be there at this hour, and he was not there. He went up the three porch steps and entered. The woman's words reached him over the thudding of blood in his ears: first a blue chamber, then a hall, then a carpeted stairway. At the top, two doors. No one in the first room, no one in the second. The door of the salon, and then, the knife in hand, the light from the great windows, the high back of an armchair covered in green velvet, the head of the man in the chair reading a novel.

THE LINES OF THE HAND

From a letter thrown on the table a line comes which runs across the pine plank and descends by one of the legs. Just watch, you see that the line continues across the parquet floor, climbs the wall and enters a reproduction of a Boucher painting, sketches the shoulder of a woman reclining on a divan, and finally gets out of the room via the roof and climbs down the chain of lightning rods to the street. Here it is difficult to follow it because of the transit system, but by close attention you can catch it climbing the wheel of a bus parked at the corner, which carries it as far as the docks. It gets off there down the seam on the shiny nylon stocking of the blondest passenger, enters the hostile territory of the customs sheds, leaps and squirms and zigzags its way to the largest dock, and there (but it's difficult to see, only the rats follow it to clamber aboard) it climbs onto the ship with the engines rumbling, crosses the planks of the first-class deck, clears the major hatch with difficulty, and in a cabin where an unhappy man is drinking cognac and hears the parting whistle, it climbs the trouser seam, across the knitted vest, slips back to the elbow, and with a final push finds shelter in the palm of the right hand, which is just beginning to close around the butt of a revolver.

~

Julio Cortazar's "A Continuity of Parks" is a classic postmodern story. A man sits down to read a novel. We learn a little bit about his life. His business and estate suggest that he is comfortably wealthy, and he has just given up his power of attorney. He relaxes in his armchair. Then we follow the story he's reading until reality intersects with his life. It's a murder story with a trick, the circularity, the story within a story. In the second Cortazar story, "The Lines of the Hand", the narrator draws a line from a letter on a table and then follows it across the room, out the window, through the subway system, in and around particular people, ending in a cabin in a ship where an unhappy man is about to pull the trigger of a revolver. The line draws and implies a connection between the letter, the stops along the way and finally the man's hand.

Cortazar advises fiction writers: "Tell the story as if it were of interest to the small circle of your characters of which you may be one. There is no other way to put life into the story."

~

GEORGES PEREC
TALE

1. It all began almost ten years ago. The evening I had been spending with friends in a Brisbane pub was drawing to a close when a man seated at the bar came over to our table with a mug of beer in his hand:

"Excuse me, gentlemen. Would you allow me to join you for a moment and tell you my story?"

We silently acquiesced. He sat down, took a sip of his beer, and said:

2. " 'My name is Abercrombie Makarenko, I'm forty years old, and a real-estate attorney by profession. It must have been five years ago when a man showed up at my office and requested to speak to me privately. A moment later, seated across form me, he began with these words:

3. " ' "Ezekiel Bridgman-Treyer is my name. About eighteen months ago I found myself in a foreign city. Returning to my hotel room one evening, I discovered a man sitting in my bedroom.

'Forgive the intrusion,' he said, rising to his feet, 'but I have to talk to you.' Curiosity got the better of wariness, and I asked him to explain. This is what I heard:

4.   " ' " 'Have you ever been to Pauvelle-les-Bains? It's a charming spa not far from Chambéry. Last May I went there to take a cure, as I do every year. As I was strolling in the park one Sunday afternoon, a young man dressed in black approached me and insisted on speaking to me. We sat down on a bench, and he told me:

5. " ' " ' "Three weeks ago I travelled to Basle. I shared a compartment with an individual whose face seemed curiously familiar. After several common place remarks, he asked me to listen to hiss tory. I urgently encouraged him to do so. Here is what he revealed:

6. " ' " ' " ' . . . etc.

~

When I first read Georges Perec's "Tale," I laughed. He was an OULIPO writer, who used ideas from mathematics to invent structures for writing. This story is endless. A student in a writers.com class, Ben Magie, had an interesting take on this story:

This story is a literary version of a derivative, which simply takes a function and creates a new mathematical representation of a slope (or change). In physics we can use derivatives to create new information from old functions. For instance if you have time and a change in position you can create a function from that information. If you take the derivative of that function with respect to time you can then find the velocity and if you take another derivative you can find the acceleration. Likewise if you take the integral of the acceleration you can find velocity, and the integral of the velocity leads to position.

So essentially what I'm trying to say is Perec was taking the derivatives of each story and forever leading into new information, just as a physicist would derive all sorts of information from a very simple beginning. This fascinates and confuses me at the same time.

DALE HERD
SPEED LIMIT

In 1958, when I was seventeen, I was seriously injured in a nighttime truck accident, regaining consciousness on my back out in a field, several older men around me, one trying to get whiskey in my mouth.

No, I told him, my body has been crushed and I'm hemorrhaging inside, the alcohol will dilate the blood vessels and speed the hemorrhaging, whiskey is the worst thing. Another man, his arm supporting my head, was telling me an ambulance would arrive soon.

I couldn't tell that I had pain, and I had seen my hips going off to the right in a strange angle with the right leg ballooned and turned wrong inside the pantleg and the right boot crushed flat, but I had been rational enough to talk the man into taking the whiskey bottle away so I knew my thinking was all right and, no longer wanting to look at myself, I turned my head to my left, looking out past the men into the darkness and stopped thinking.

Where I was was in the Moses Lake desert. This is flat desolate country of only some cheatgrass and low clumps of sagebrush with no trees for miles in any direction save for back in the town of Moses Lake. I knew that, and I knew my back must be broken, and again there wasn't any pain, and my last thought had been I hope I am not a paraplegic, and it was easy not to think, and it didn't bother me that out there on the line where the darkness of the land met the lighter darkness of the sky was a stand of trees, large and dark, within an elliptical disc of a strange, brilliant green, the green first flaring up about the boles, moving up in bursts about the tops, then slowing, beginning to flow out around all of the stand, etching each tree in exact location, glowing about them with an intensity I could feel inside me, then not moving, holding, as I knew that was where I was going to go, and would.

And not telling the men what I was seeing, lying there watching that light breaking, then steadying itself about those trees, I thought so this is how it happens, well, it's been a nice life, and only momentarily thought no, it's too soon, knowing immediately that it wasn't, that for me it only went this far, that everything I was supposed to do was already done, and next awoke in an ambulance going at high speed toward Moses Lake and Moses Lake General Hospital.

Years later, in a truckstop garage in Flagstaff, Arizona, I talked with a trucker from Memphis, Tennessee, while an all-night mechanic worked on the heater of a car I was driving east to New York City.

This trucker, a large man in his late fifties, who introduced himself as Earl, had been in a Japanese P.O.W. camp on Luzon during 1942, 43, and 44. During his incarceration he contracted malaria and had it complicated by double pneumonia.

He should have died, he said, but for some miracle he didn't understand. He said due to the severity of the prison rations, as well as his illness, his body had been terribly racked by a lack of water. The crisis of the illness, he said, passed while he was hallucinating.

In his hallucination he knew he was dying and he was desperate for water. He said he found himself crawling in a field that was the slope of a hill. It was nighttime, and what was eerie was that the field was bathed in an unearthly yellowish light that came not from the sky but from the ground, and on the crest of the slope was a series of water spigots. He said he could see himself crawling in that yellow light toward those spigots and the water he absolutely had to have. He said he crawled and crawled and almost reached one of the spigots. He said he was very glad he hadn't because he knew if he had, that the moment he tasted that water he would be dead.

I thought his story was remarkable and told him my story, pointing out the similarity of the eerie lights, and the fact that dying seemed to be a peaceful journey to a new place.

He said perhaps, but he didn't think so. He said from his experience it had been terrifying.

I said in my experience it had not.

He said well, and then told me how to drive across country the fastest way: by getting behind any Semi that has an antenna on top of each of the outside rearview mirrors. Go fast when he goes fast, he said, and slow down when he does; those antennas mean he is two-way radio-equipped and has all the latest information within at least a forty-to sixty mile radius of where all the police and speed traps are.

I thanked him warmly.

We shook hands and he left.

~

In **Dale Herd's** "Speed Limit," The first person narrator tells a story of a terrible truck accident from years ago when he was sure he was going to die. Then he tells another story that another trucker told him about his experience in a P.O.W. camp in WWII. Both of the events are similar, but the revelations about death are different. Then off they go in their own directions. This is a simple honest voice, an easy recollection of a powerful experience with death

For another example of a circular story similar to Cortazars, but more like a prose poem see Kim Lyon's "Tinta" on page 303.

Cortazar, Julio. "A Continuity of Parks." *Flash Fiction,* edited by James Thomas, et al. Trans. by Paul Blackburn. Norton, 1992, pp. 137-139. Originally published in *End of the Game and Other Stories*, Random House, 1967.

——. "The Lines of the Hand." *Cronopios and Famos*. Translated by Paul Blackburn, New Directions, 1969, p. 105.

——. "On the Short Story and Its Environs." Trans. by Thomas Christensen. *The Story and Its Writers*, Compact 7th Edition, edited by Ann Charters, Bedford/St Martins, 2007, pp. 859-860.

Herd, Dale. "Speed Limit." *Empty Pockets: New and Selected Stories,"* Coffee House Press, 2015. Originally published in *Wild Cherries*, Tombouctou, 1980, pp. 77-79.

Perec, Georges. "Tale." *Oulipo Compendium*, translated by Harry Mathews, edited by Harry Mathews & Alastair Brotchie, Atlas Press, London, 1998, p. 133.

#9: Retell A Myth

Prompt

Consider a character or plot from mythology, perhaps a biblical tale. Re-invent this character/story, starring an ordinary imperfect character from the present world. Merge the two together. Or take an ordinary situation and imagine the character as a mythic figure. Include only a couple of scenes; otherwise it will be too much for a flash fiction.

Maybe you will set your story in a supermarket (or someplace else) with a character who is a reincarnation of some mythic figure. Hermes shopping for milk. Or maybe someone else is telling you the story about Hermes shopping for milk in Shoprite. If you were Snow White and you were sitting at your kitchen table drinking tea and all the events of the day had to happen as they do, how would they be different ... Or maybe instead of a myth you would like to work with a pop culture figure, a cartoon or movie star.

Examples

Franz Kafka
Poseidon

Poseidon sat at his desk, doing figures. The administration of all the waters gave him endless work. He could have had assistants, as many as he wanted—and he did have very many—but since he took his job very seriously, he would in the end go over all the figures and calculations himself, and thus his assistants were of little help to him. It cannot be said that he enjoyed his work; he did it only because it had been assigned to him; in fact, he had already filed many petitions for—as he put it—more cheerful work, but every time the offer of something different was made to him it would turn out that nothing suited him quite as well as his present position. And anyhow it was quite difficult to find something different for him. After all, it was impossible to assign him to a particular sea; aside from the fact that even then the work with figures would not become less but only pettier, the great Poseidon could in any case occupy only an executive position. And when a job away from the water was offered to him he would get sick at the very prospect, his divine breathing would become troubled and his brazen chest begin to tremble. Besides, his complaints were not really taken seriously; when one of the mighty is vexatious the appearance of an effort must be made to placate him, even when the case is most hopeless. In actuality a shift of posts was unthinkable for Poseidon—he had been appointed God of the Sea in the beginning, and that he had to remain.

What irritated him most—and it was this that was chiefly responsible for his dissatisfaction with his job—was to hear of the conceptions formed about him: how he was always riding about through the tides with his trident. When all the while he sat here in the depths of the world-ocean, doing figures uninterruptedly, with now and then a trip to Jupiter as the only break in the monotony—a trip, moreover, from which he usually returned in a rage. Thus he had hardly seen the sea—had seen it but fleetingly in the course of hurried ascents to Olympus, and he had never actually travelled around it. He was in the habit of saying that what he was waiting for was the fall of the world; then, probably, a quiet moment would yet be granted in which, just before the end and after having checked the last row of figures, he would be able to make a quick little tour.

Poseidon became bored with his sea. He let fall his trident. Silently he sat on the rocky coast and a gull, dazed by his presence, described wavering circles around his head.

~

In "Poseidon," Kafka's narrator is the Greek God of the sea, but we discover as we read that his work is quite tedious, like an accountant who is bored with his bureaucratic position. The action of the story is Poseidon writing, reflecting and then sitting on a rocky coast. We follow his thoughts about his life.

On the way out to the cliff, the old man kept one hand on the wheel. He smoked with the other hand. The inside of the car smelled of wine and cigarette ashes. He coughed constantly. His voice sounded like a version of the cough.

"I used to smoke Camels unfiltered," he told the boy. The dirt road, rutted, dipped hard, and the car bounced. "But I switched brands. Camels interfered with my eating. I couldn't taste what the Duchess cooked up. Meat, salad, Jell-O: it all tasted the same. So I went to low tar. You don't smoke, do you, boy?"

The boy stared at the road and shook his head.

"Not after what I've taught you, I hope not. You got to keep the body pure for the stuff we're doing."

"You don't keep it pure," the boy said.

"I don't have to. It's *been* pure. And, like I say, nobody is ever pure twice."

The California pines seemed brittle and did not sway as they drove past. The boy thought he could hear the crash of the waves in front of them. "Are we almost there?"

"Kind of impatient, aren't you?" the old man said, suppressing his cough. "Look, boy, I told you a hundred times: you got to train your will to do this. You get impatient, and you — "

"— I know, I know. 'You die.' " The boy was wearing a jacket and a New York Mets cap. "I know all that. You taught me. I'm only asking if we're there yet."

"You got a woman, boy?" The old man looked suspicious. "You got a woman?"

"I'm only fifteen," the boy said nervously.

"That's not too old for it, especially around here."

"I've been kissed," the boy said. "Is that the ocean?"

"That's her," the old man said. "Sometimes I think I know everything about you, and then sometimes I don't think I know anything. I hate to take chances like this. You could be hiding something out on me. The magic's no damn good if you're hiding something out on me."

"It'll be good," the boy said, seeing the long line of blue water through the trees. He pulled the visor down lower, so he wouldn't squint. "It'll be real good."

"Faith, hope, charity, and love," the old man recited. "And the spells. Now I admit I have fallen from the path of righteousness at times. But I never forget the spells. You forget them, you die."

"I would not forget them," the boy said.

"You better not be lying to me. You been thieving, sleeping with whores, you been carrying on in the bad way, well, we'll find out soon enough." He stopped the car at a clearing. He turned the key off in the ignition and reached under his seat for a wine bottle. His hands were shaking. The old man unscrewed the cap and took a long swig. He recapped it and breathed out the sweet aroma in the boy's direction. "Something for my nerves," he said. "I don't do this every day."

"You don't believe in the spells anymore," the boy said.

"I *am* the spells," the old man shouted. "I invented them. I just hate to see a fresh kid like you crash on the rocks on account of you don't believe in them."

"Don't worry," the boy said. "Don't worry about me."

They got out of the car together, and the old man reached around into the back seat for his coil of rope.

"I don't need it," the boy said. "I don't need the rope."

"Kid, we do it my way or we don't do it."

The boy took off his shoes. His bare feet stepped over pine needles and stones. He was wearing faded blue jeans and a sweat-shirt, with a stain from the old man's wine bottle on it. He had taken off his jacket in the car, but he was still wearing the cap. They walked over a stretch of burnt grass and came to the edge of the cliff.

"Look at those sea gulls down there," the old man pointed. "Must be a hundred." His voice was trembling with nervousness.

"I know about the sea gulls." The boy had to raise his voice to be heard above the surf. "I've seen them."

"You're so smart, huh?" the old man coughed. He drew a cigarette out of his shirt and lit it with his Zippo lighter. "All right, I'm tired of telling you what to do, Mr. Know-It-All. Take off the sweatshirt." The boy took it off. "Now make a circle in the dirt."

160

"With what?"

"With your foot."

"There isn't any dirt."

"Do like I tell you."

The boy extended his foot and drew a magic circle around himself. It could not be seen, but he knew it was there.

"Now look out at the horizon and tell it what I told you to tell it."

The boy did as he was told.

"Now take this rope, take this end." The old man handed it to him. "God, I don't know sometimes." The old man bent down for another swig of wine. "Is your mind clear?"

"Yeah," the boy said.

"Are you scared?"

"Naw."

"Do you see anybody?"

"Nope."

"You got any last questions?"

"Do I hold my arms out?"

"They do that in the Soviet Union," the old man said, "but they also do it sitting on pigs. That's the kind of people they are. You don't have to hold your arms out. Are you ready? Jump!"

The boy felt the edge of the cliff with his feet, jumped, and felt the magic and the horizon lifting him up and then out over the water, his body parallel to the ground. He took it into his mind to swoop down toward the cliffs, and then to veer away suddenly, and whatever he thought, he did. At first he held on to the rope, but even the old man could see that it was unnecessary, and reeled it in. In his jeans and cap, the boy lifted himself upward, then dove down toward the sea gulls, then just as easily lifted himself up again, rushing over the old man's head before flying out over the water.

He shouted with happiness.

The old man reached down again for his wine.

"The sun!" the old man shouted. "The ocean! The land! That's how to do it!" And he laughed suddenly, his cough all gone. "The sky!" he said at last.

The boy flew in great soaring circles. He tumbled in the air, dove, flipped, and sailed. His eyes were dazzled with the blue also, and like the old man he smelled the sea salt.

But of course he was a teen-ager. He was grateful to the old man for teaching him the spells. But this—the cliffs, the sea, the blue sky, and the sweet wine—this was the old man's style, not his. He loved the old man for sharing the spells. He would think of him always, for that.

But even as he flew, he was getting ideas. It isn't the style of teenagers to fly in broad daylight, on sunny days, even in California. What the boy wanted was something else: to fly low, near the ground, in the cities, speeding in smooth arcs between the buildings, late at night. Very late: at the time the girls are hanging up their clothes and sighing, sighing out their windows to the stagnant air, as the clocks strike midnight. The idea of the pig interested the boy. He grinned far down at the old man, who waved, who had long ago forgotten the dirty purposes of flight.

Charles Baxter's story is longer than a flash. The characters in "The Cliff" are imperfect and seem realistic rather than mythic, eating Jello and coughing. Then those precise details: "The California pines seemed brittle and did not sway as they drove past." We are following the boy's point of view here, third person subjective. This is what he sees and thinks filtered through a hiding narrator who only knows what the boy knows. Like the boy, we hear the man talking. Right off, I'm worried. This man is a mentor and yet he seems a little sinister and the boy seems somewhat innocent. What's going on, I wonder, caught up in the story. Then I learn about the spells and a kid possibly crashing on the rocks. I still don't know what's going on, but I'm tense. And that tension is important in this story. Everything is revealed through the dialogue. "Do like I tell you," the old man says. Now I'm thinking Icarus—oh, no—he's going to fly and ignore the man's instructions. But Baxter changes the tale again. The father isn't flying, the wings are not made of wax, no wings are necessary. The boy is flying on his own. Now I want to read it again because it's so tight and beautifully written. The boy is ecstatic. It's his mind that allows him to fly. Still like Icarus, he disobeys his father, but we don't know if he will pay the consequences.

In "Poseidon," Kafka tells the story of the character living in mythic time while engaging in a modern activity. In "The Cliff," Baxter uses a few elements from the Icarus myth to structure a more modern story.

Notes

Baxter, Charles. "The Cliff." *Sudden Fiction*, edited by Robert Shepard and James Thomas, Norton, 1989, pp. 43-46. Originally published in *Harmony of the World*, University of Michigan Press, 1984.

Kafka, Franz. "Poseidon." *Parables and Paradoxes*, edited by Nahum N. Glatzer. Translated by Clement Greenberg, et al, Schocken Books, 1935, pp. 85-87.

Background / Examples

In another story, considerably longer than a flash, "Miss Furr and Miss Skeene" **Gertrude Stein's** repetition of words and phrases calls attention to the language, and because of the repetition, meaning is slippery. The story seems to float over the characters, the narrator talking generally about them and their lives, and at the same time pointing to and hiding a secret. Two women meet, live together and then live apart. They are "cultivating something, voices and other things needing cultivation." At the time Stein wrote this story, the word "gay" was an underground word; homosexuality was illegal. Over and over, Stein repeats the word "gay," but some readers at the time didn't realize that she was referring to love between women.

GERTRUDE STEIN
MISS FURR AND MISS SKEENE

Helen Furr had quite a pleasant home. Mrs. Furr was quite a pleasant woman. Mr. Furr was quite a pleasant man. Helen Furr had quite a pleasant voice a voice quite worth cultivating. She did not mind working. She worked to cultivate her voice. She did not find it gay living in the same place where she had always been living. She went to a place where some were cultivating something, voices and other things needing cultivating. She met Georgine Skeene there who was cultivating her voice which some thought was quite a pleasant one. Helen Furr and Georgine Skeene lived together then. Georgine Skeene liked travelling. Helen Furr did not care about travelling, she liked to stay in one place and be gay there. They were together then and travelled to another place and stayed there and were gay there. They stayed there and were gay there, not very gay there, just gay there. They were both gay there, they were regularly working there both of them cultivating their voices there, they were both gay there. Georgine Skeene was gay there and she was regular, regular in being gay, regular in not being gay, regular in being a gay one who was one not being gay longer than was needed to be one being quite a gay one. They were both gay then there and both working there then.

They were in a way both gay there where there were many cultivating something. They were both regular in being gay there. Helen Furr was gay there, she was gayer and gayer there and really she was just gay there, she was gayer and gayer there, that is to say she found ways of being gay there that she was using in being gay there. She was gay there, not gayer and gayer, just gay there, that is to say she was not gayer by using the things she found there that were gay things, she was gay there, always she was gay there.

They were quite regularly gay there, Helen Furr and Georgine Skeene, they were regularly gay there where they were gay. They were very regularly gay.

To be regularly gay was to do every day the gay thing that they did every day. To be regularly gay was to end every day at the same time after they had been regularly gay. They were regularly gay. They were gay every day. They ended every day in the same way, at the same time, and they had been every day regularly gay.

The voice Helen Furr was cultivating was quite a pleasant one. The voice Georgine Skeene was cultivating was, some said, a better one. The voice Helen Furr was cultivating she cultivated and it was quite completely a pleasant enough one then, a cultivated enough one then. The voice Georgine Skeene was cultivating she did not cultivate too much. She cultivated it quite some. She cultivated and she would sometime go on cultivating it and it was not then an unpleasant one, it would not be then an unpleasant one, it would be a quite richly enough cultivated one, it would be quite richly enough to be a pleasant enough one.

They were gay where there were many cultivating something. The two were gay there, were regularly gay there. Georgine Skeene would have liked to do more travelling. They did some travelling, not very much travelling, Georgine Skeene would have liked to do more travelling, Helen Furr did not care about doing travelling, she liked to stay in a place and be gay there.

They stayed in a place and were gay there, both of them stayed there, they stayed together there, they were gay there, they were regularly gay there.

They went quite often, not very often, but they did go back to where Helen Furr had a pleasant enough home and then Georgine Skeene went to a place where her brother had quite some distinction. They both went, every few years, went visiting to where Helen Furr had quite a pleasant home. Certainly Helen Furr would not find it gay to stay, she did not find it gay, she said she would not stay, she said she did not find it gay, she said she would not stay where she did not find it gay, she said she found it gay where she did stay and she did stay there where very many were cultivating something. She did stay there. She always did find it gay there.

She went to see them where she had always been living and where she did not find it gay. She had a pleasant home there, Mrs. Furr was a pleasant enough woman, Mr. Furr was a pleasant enough man, Helen told them and they were not worrying, that she did not find it gay living where she had always been living.

Georgine Skeene and Helen Furr were living where they were both cultivating their voices and they were gay there. They visited where Helen Furr had come from and then they went to where they were living where they were then regularly living.

There were some dark and heavy men there then. There were some who were not so heavy and some who were not so dark. Helen Furr and Georgine Skeene sat regularly with them. They sat regularly with the ones who were dark and heavy. They sat regularly with the ones who were not so dark. They sat regularly with the ones that were not so heavy. They sat with them regularly, sat with some of them. They went with them regularly went with them. They were regular then, they were gay then, they were where they wanted to be then where it was gay to be then, they were regularly gay then. There were men there then who were dark and heavy and they sat with them with Helen Furr and Georgine Skeene and they went with them with Miss Furr and Miss Skeene, and they went with the heavy and dark men Miss Furr and Miss Skeene went with them, and they sat with them, Miss Furr and Miss Skeene sat with them, and there were other men, some were not heavy men and they sat with Miss Furr and Miss Skeene and Miss Furr and Miss Skeene sat with them, and there were other men who were not dark men and they sat with Miss Furr and Miss Skeene and Miss Furr and Miss Skeene sat with them. Miss Furr and Miss Skeene went with them and they went with Miss Furr and Miss Skeene, some who were not heavy men, some who were not dark men. Miss Furr and Miss Skeene sat regularly, they sat with some men. Miss Furr and Miss Skeene went and there were some men with them. There were men and Miss Furr and Miss Skeene went with them, went somewhere with them, went with some of them.

Helen Furr and Georgine Skeene were regularly living where very many were living and cultivating in themselves something. Helen Furr and Georgine Skeene were living very regularly then, being very regular then in being gay then. They did then learn many ways to be gay and they were then being gay being quite regular in being gay, being gay and they were learning little things, little things in ways of being gay, they were very regular then, they were learning very many little things in ways of being gay, they were being gay and using these little things they were learning to have to be gay with regularly gay with then and they were gay the same amount they had been gay. They were quite gay, they were quite regular, they were learning little things, gay little things, they were gay inside them the same amount they had been gay, they were gay the same length of time they had been gay every day.

They were regular in being gay, they learned little things that are things in being gay, they learned many little things that are things in being gay, they were gay every day, they were regular, they were gay, they were gay the same length of time every day, they were gay, they were quite regularly gay.

Georgine Skeene went away to stay two months with her brother. Helen Furr did not go then to stay with her father and her mother. Helen Furr stayed there where they had been regularly living the two of them and she would then certainly not be lonesome, she would go on being gay. She did go on being gay. She was not any more gay but she was gay longer every day than they had been being gay when they were together being gay. She was gay then quite exactly the same way. She learned a few more little ways of being in being gay. She was quite gay and in the same way, the same way she had been gay and she was gay a little longer in the day, more of each day she was gay. She was gay longer every day than when the two of them had been being gay. She was gay quite in the way they had been gay, quite in the same way.

She was not lonesome then, she was not at all feeling any need of having Georgine Skeene. She was not astonished at this thing. She would have been a little astonished by this thing but she knew she was not astonished at anything and so she was not astonished at this thing not astonished at not feeling any need of having Georgine Skeene.

Helen Furr had quite a completely pleasant voice and it was quite well enough cultivated and she could use it and she did use it but then there was not any way of working at cultivating a completely pleasant voice when it has become a quite completely well enough cultivated one, and there was not much use in using it when one was not wanting it to be helping to make one a gay one. Helen Furr was not needing using her voice to be a gay one.

She was gay then and sometimes she used her voice and she was not using it very often. It was quite completely enough cultivated and it was quite completely a pleasant one and she did not use it very often. She was then, she was quite exactly as gay as she had been, she was gay a little longer in the day than she had been.

She was gay exactly the same way. She was never tired of being gay that way. She had learned very many little ways to use in being gay. Very many were telling about using other ways in being gay. She was gay enough, she was always gay exactly the same way, she was always learning little things to use in being gay, she was telling about using other ways in being gay, she was telling about learning other ways in being gay, she was learning other ways in being gay, she would be using other ways in being gay, she would always be gay in the same way, when Georgine Skeene was there not so long each day as when Georgine Skeene was away.

She came to using many ways in being gay, she came to use every way in being gay. She went on living where many were cultivating something and she was gay, she had used every way to be gay.

They did not live together then Helen Furr and Georgine Skeene. Helen Furr lived there the longer where they had been living regularly together. Then neither of them were living there any longer. Helen Furr was living somewhere else then and telling some about being gay and she was gay then and she was living quite regularly then. She was regularly gay then. She was quite regular in being gay then. She remembered all the little ways of being gay. She used all the little ways of being gay. She was quite regularly gay. She told many then the way of being gay, she taught very many then little ways they could use in being gay. She was living very well, she was gay then, she went on living then, she was regular in being gay, she always was living very well and was gay very well and was telling about little ways one could be learning to use in being gay, and later was telling them quite often, telling them again and again.

~

Lydia Davis
Grammar Questions

Now, during the time he is dying, can I say, "This is where he lives"?

If someone asks me, "Where does he live?" should I answer, "Well, right now he is not living, he is dying"?

If someone asks me, "Where does he live?" can I say, "He lives in Vernon Hall"? Or should I say, "He is dying in Vernon Hall"?

When he is dead, I will be able to say, in the past tense, "He lived in Vernon Hall." I will also be able to say, "He died in Vernon Hall."

When he is dead, everything to do with him will be in the past tense. Or rather, the sentence "He is dead" will be in the present tense, and also questions such as "Where are they taking him?" or "Where is he now?"

But then I won't know if the words "he" and "him" are correct, in the present tense. Is he, once he is dead, still "he," and if so, for how long is he still "he"?

People may say "the body" and then call it "it." I will not be able to say "the body" in relation to him because to me he is still not something you would call "the body."

People may say "his body," but that does not seem right either. It is not "his" body because he does not own it, if he is no longer active or capable of owning anything.

I don't know if there is a "he," even though people will say "He is dead." But it does seem correct to say "he is dead." This may be the last time he will still be "he" in the present tense. Or it will not be the last time, because I will also say, "He is lying in his coffin." I will not say, and no one will say, "It is lying in the coffin," or "It is lying in its coffin."

I will continue to say "my father" in relation to him, after he dies, but will I say it only in the past tense, or also in the present tense?

He will be put in a box, not a coffin. Then, when he is in that

170

box, will I say, "That is my father in that box," or "That was my father in that box," or will I say, "That, in the box, was my father"?

I will still say "my father," but maybe I will say it only as long as he looks like my father, or approximately like my father. Then, when he is in the form of ashes, will I point to the ashes and say, "That is my father"? Or will I say, "That was my father"? Or "Those ashes were my father"? Or "Those ashes are what was my father"?

When I later visit the graveyard, will I point and say, "My father is buried there," or will I say, "My father's ashes are buried there"? But the ashes will not belong to my father, he will not own them. They will be "the ashes that were my father."

In the phrase "he is dying," the words "he is" with the present participle suggest that he is actively doing something. But he is not actively dying. The only thing he is still actively doing is breathing. He looks as if he is breathing on purpose, because he is working hard at it, and frowning slightly. He is working at it, but surely he has no choice. Sometimes his frown deepens for just an instant, as though something is hurting him, or as though he is concentrating harder. Even though I can guess that he is frowning because of some pain inside him, or some other change, he still looks as though he is puzzled, or dislikes or disapproves of something. I've seen this expression on his face often in my life, though never before combined with these half-open eyes and this open mouth.

"He is dying" sounds more active than "He will be dead soon." That is probably because of the word "be"—we can "be" something whether we choose to or not. Whether he likes it or not, he "will be" dead soon. He is not eating.

"He is not eating" sounds active, too. But it is not his choice. He is not conscious that he is not eating. He is not conscious at all. But "is not eating" sounds more correct for him than "is dying" because of the negative. "Is not" seems correct for him, at the moment anyway, because he looks as though he is refusing something, because he is frowning.

~

In **Lydia Davis's** "Grammar Questions," the narrator wonders about the connection of language to the body. This is a story about a man who is dying and a narrator who rambles on and on about how to talk about it. She's not hyper-language conscious, but instead distant and language inquisitive. When discussing the relationship between "flash fictions" and other experimental forms, Davis explains in an interview:

> I am simply not interested, at this point in creating narrative scenes between characters. Maybe I'm shying away from a certain artificiality that I perceive to be present in many such scenes as written.. . . We all have an ongoing narrative inside our heads, the narrative that is spoken aloud if a friend asks a question. That narrative feels deeply natural to me. We also hang onto scraps of dialogue. Our memories don't usually serve up whole scenes complete with dialogue. I suppose I'm saying that I like to work from what a character is likely to remember, from a more interior place.

ROBERT WALSER
SHE IS SUCH A NICE WOMAN . . .

She's such a nice woman, who, I wish to point out, had a son and owned a set of lovely teeth. They're still hers to this day, but her son isn't really in her possession any longer. Ran away from her, did he? What an inappropriate tone! Why, of course he didn't, rather the following occurred: he met a halfway pretty young thing who began to baby him, to mother him, so to speak, and he fell victim to this sweet, sneaky little maneuver. Not to say he made a sacrifice or anything. If only he had! Alas, this wasn't the case. He himself became one, falling into the hands, as prey, or rather the little paws with their little claws, of a warrior woman with a not-to-be-underestimated allure. Yesterday I spoke with the betrayed mother. Did her son betray her by letting himself be made a welcome prey? Is it a question of treachery? I think not. I said as much to the good, half-betrayed and -betreacheried mother, offering the opinion that her son had suffered his humble or grand person to be treated in a manner most natural. He was still far too young to start a household of his own, she whispered. Otherwise I like this mother very much.

Now and then I showed her something along the lines of kindness. I once asked her, with an e:xpression she'll never manage to
forget, to drink a bratwurst at my expense, no, eat it, after gently
and neatly slicing it up. She did so and ate a good glass to wash
it down with, no, she drank it. Still, it wasn't so much the glass
she drank as what swam about in it, shimmering redly in all its
leisure, the wine. And she looking so radiant all the while. As she
drank her wine, I lapped up her fine, naive f eatures. That was all
some time ago. But now she insists on complaining that her son, as
it were, abandoned her, letting himself be netted by a net-setter of
a girl. All the same, though, it's quite clever for a young man to let
himself be charmed by a half-nice lass and permanently installed
in the warmth and solidity of a household, if one *can* say so, and
one *can* say so, can't one? A slight oddity of expression, what can
it hurt? I once kissed this woman, the one with the son who,
she believed, had up and left her, run away from his responsibil-
ities, as it were, with surprising speed. I tell you, once I gave this
dear, good woman something like an innocuous little *Mündschi*. A
Mündschi means a kiss. Just a sort of dialect, if you'll permit, and
you will permit, won't you, and now let's keep sliding down this
narrative scree so as to land upon a cosy little green patch. Now
this mother has a husband, and this husband of hers is now out
of work, and this woman now seeks employment for her husband
who has no work, an employment that might perhaps consist in
his taking on something. Sometimes he hangs his support-needy
head, but if she tries hard she'll find, in my opinion, some work
for him, then he won't need to hang his precious head any longer. Is it the son's fault his darling mother, his little mummy, we
want to say, longs for him so? If she longs for him, it only proves
he's dear to her heart and she thinks highly of him, at least she
says so, and says so in such a way one can believe her; who'd be
unwilling to? But now he's gone and made the acquaintance that's
essential for him and his future, there honestly isn't much one
can do about it, and then she truly does realize this, and what a
silly, mundane tale this is I'm telling, apparently I'm not through
with it yet. He was once quite ill, this son when he was one-and-a-

half years old, gravely ill even, and because he escaped with his life she clung to him with all her motherly hands. Well, that's perfectly easy to grasp, and now he left his parents behind to move into the home of his intended, and this, too, can be grasped perfectly easily, but the simplest experiences are, for those who experience them, always perfectly spectacular, momentous, as it were. So now she's rich in longing for her son, and he's rich in his life's new significalities, thanks to the woman he was drawn to, prompting him to throw over father and mother, as the saying goes, and yet this has happened before, as long as the world has existed, and it's existed quite some time now, and all is new and is never new. But, really, I do have to repeat it once more, what a lovely set of choppers she has. She'll just have to resign herself.

~

Robert Walser's story "She's Such a Nice Woman" is an example of a narrator who can't stop talking about people and cannot stop talking period. It's easy to imagine and almost hear the person he is speaking to as he segues from one person to another tripping over his words and giving away his own story, his desire for the woman. "Now let's keep sliding down this narrative screen so as to land upon a cosy little green patch" (142). Walser was a Swiss writer born in the late 19th Century.

Davis, Lydia. "Grammar Questions." *The Collected Stories of Lydia Davis,"* *Farrar Straus and Giroux, 2009.* 527-529. Originally published in *Varieties of Disturbance*, Farrar, Straus and Giroux, 2007, pp. 27-29.

———. Interview by Sarah Manguso, *The Believer*, Fall 2015, https://believermag.com/an-interview-with-lydia-davis/

Stein, Gertrude. "Miss Furr and Miss Skeene." *Geography and Plays*, 1922, Four Seas Company. Dover, 1999, pp.17-21.

Walser, Robert. "She's Such a Nice Woman." *Masquerade and Other Stories*, Trans. Susan Bernofsky, Quartet Books, 1993, pp.141-142.

#11: LIFE STORY / ONE-LINERS

Prompts

Write a life story in 15 paragraphs (or less or more); it can be your life story or someone else's. See if you can dramatize in each paragraph and include details even if they are only two or three sentences. Maybe there will be a problem or some conflict in the life that inspires the search backwards.

or

Collect or write a series of one or two-sentence stories around a single topic or a character in a predicament (be as concrete as possible). Maybe the narrator overhears people telling little stories in a cafe and you write them down. Maybe she remembers stories people have told her about a certain topic. Collage these pieces together, allowing a disjunctive rhythm into the fiction. There is no need to number the list.

Examples

T. CORAGHESSAN BOYLE
THE HIT MAN

Early Years

The hit man's early years are complicated by the black bag that he wears over his head. Teachers correct his pronunciation, the coach criticizes his attitude, the principal dresses him down for branding preschoolers with a lit cigarette. He is a poor student. At lunch he sits alone, feeding bell peppers and salami into the dark slot of his mouth. In the hallways, wiry young athletes snatch at the black hood and slap the back of his head. When he is thirteen he is approached by the captain of the football team, who pins him down and attempts to remove the hood. The Hit Man wastes him. Five years, says the judge.

Back on the Street

The Hit Man is back on the street in two months.

First Date

The girl's name is Cynthia. The Hit Man pulls up in front of her apartment in his father's hearse. (The Hit Man's father, whom he loathes and abominates, is a mortician. At breakfast the Hit Man's father had slapped the cornflakes from his son's bowl. The son threatened to waste his father. He did not, restrained no doubt by considerations of filial loyalty and the deep-seated taboos against patricide that permeate the universal unconscious.)

Cynthia's father has silver sideburns and plays tennis. He responds to the Hit Man's knock, expresses surprise at the Hit Man's appearance. The Hit Man takes Cynthia by the elbow, presses a twenty into her father's palm, and disappears into the night.

Father's Death

At breakfast the Hit Man slaps the cornflakes from his father's bowl. Then wastes him.

Mother's Death

The Hit Man is in his early twenties. He shoots pool, lifts weights and drinks milk from the carton. His mother is in the hospital, dying of cancer or heart disease. The priest wears black. So does the Hit Man.

First Job

Porfirio Bunoz, a Cuban financier, invites the Hit Man to lunch. I hear you're looking for work, says Bunoz.

That's right, says the Hit Man.

Peas

The Hit Man does not like peas. They are too difficult to balance on the fork.

Talk Show

The Hit Man waits in the wings, the white slash of a cigarette scarring the midnight black of his head and upper torso.
The makeup girl has done his mouth and eyes, brushed the nap
of his hood. He has been briefed. The guest who precedes him is
a pediatrician. A planetary glow washes the stage where the host
and the pediatrician, separated by a potted palm, cross their legs
and discuss the little disturbances of infants and toddlers.

After the station break the Hit Man finds himself squeezed
into a director's chair, white lights in his eyes. The talk-show host
is a baby-faced man in his early forties. He smiles like God and
all His Angels. Well, he says. So you're a hit man. Tell me—I've
always wanted to know—what does it feel like to hit someone?

Death of Mateo Maria Bunoz

The body of Mateo Maria Bunoz, the cousin and business as-
sociate of a prominent financier, is discovered down by the docks
on a hot summer morning. Mist rises from the water like steam,
there is the smell of fish. A large black bird perches on the dead
man's forehead.

Marriage

Cynthia and the Hit Man stand at the altar, side by side. She is
wearing a white satin gown and lace veil. The Hit Man has rented
a tuxedo, extra-large, and a silk-lined black-velvet hood.

. . . Till death do you part, says the priest.

Moods

The Hit Man is moody, unpredictable. Once, in a luncheon-
ette, the waitress brought him the meatloaf special but forgot to
eliminate the peas. There was a spot of gravy on the Hit Man's
hood, about where his chin should be. He looked up at the waitress, his eyes like pins behind the triangular slots, and wasted
her.

Another time he went to the track with $25, came back with
$1800. He stopped at a cigar shop. As he stepped out of the shop

a wino tugged at his sleeve and solicited a quarter. The Hit Man reached into his pocket, extracted the $1800 and handed it to the wino. Then wasted him.

First Child

A boy. The Hit Man is delighted. He leans over the edge of the playpen and molds the tiny fingers around the grip of a nickel-plated derringer. The gun is loaded with blanks—the Hit Man wants the boy to get used to the noise. By the time he is four the boy has mastered the rudiments of Tae Kwon Do, can stick a knife in the wall from a distance of ten feet and shoot a moving target with either hand. The Hit Man rests his broad palm on the boy's head. You're going to make the Big Leagues, Tiger, he says.

Work

He flies to Cincinnati. To L.A. To Boston. To London. The stewardesses get to know him.

Half an Acre and a Garage

The Hit Man is raking leaves, amassing great brittle piles of them. He is wearing a black T-shirt, cut off at the shoulders, and a cotton work hood, also black. Cynthia is edging the flowerbed, his son playing in the grass. The Hit Man waves to his neighbors as they drive by. The neighbors wave back.

When he has scoured the lawn to his satisfaction, the Hit Man draws the smaller leaf-hummocks together in a single mound the size of a pickup truck. Then he bends to ignite it with his lighter. Immediately, flames leap back from the leaves, cut channels through the pile, engulf it in a ball of fire. The Hit Man stands back, hands folded beneath the great meaty biceps. At his side is the three-headed dog. He bends to pat each of the heads, smoke and sparks raging against the sky.

Stalking the Streets of the City

He is stalking the streets of the city, collar up, brim down. It is late at night. He stalks past department stores, small businesses, parks, and gas stations. Past apartments, picket fences, picture windows. Dogs growl in the shadows, then slink away. He could hit any of' us.

Retirement

A group of businessman-types—sixtyish, seventyish, portly, diamond rings, cigars, liver spots— throws him a party. Porfirio Bunoz, now in his eighties, makes a speech and presents the Hit Man with a gilded scythe. The Hit Man thanks him, then retires to the lake, where he can be seen in his speedboat, skating out over the blue, hood rippling in the breeze.

Death

He is stricken, shrunken, half his former self. He lies propped against the pillows at Mercy Hospital, a bank of gentians drooping round the bed. Tubes run into the hood at the nostril openings, his eyes are clouded and red, sunk deep behind the triangular slots. The priest wears black. So does the Hit Man.

On the other side of town the Hit Man's son is standing before the mirror of a shop that specializes in Hit Man attire. Trying on his first hood.

~

T. Coraghessan Boyle's three page story "The Hitman" has a structure like a novel. In the first chapter, "Early Years," the third person narrator looks back at events that are central to his career. He sums up each event in a few sentences while also including striking actions, details and description: "lit cigarette," "bell peppers and salami," "black hood," etc. As the narrator continues, some of his statements make him sound a bit like a psychologist: father "whom he loathes and abominates", "deep-seated taboos against patricide that permeate the universal unconscious", etc. He's also humorous. In one paragraph he writes about how the character killed his father and in the next he concentrates on how he dislikes peas. Or the talk show where he is supposedly letting us all know what it's like to be a hit man. The story is about how even a frightening criminal can have an outward appearance of a regular life.

LEWIS WARSH
THE SECRET POLICE

We joined the secret police so we could inform on our relatives & friends

We know the names of the books that our neighbors are reading, & the names of the people who visit

The woman in the apartment below us receives money for sexual favors

I overheard my mother & step-father talking about "guns" & called the police

The policeman directing traffic waves at me as I drive by

My wife's father's father was arrested for selling drugs to a minor

My father's uncle spent a year in jail for molesting young girls

I followed them down an alleyway between two buildings where a meeting was taking place & I wrote a report & sent it to my district officer

I have a key to the building across the street & all the apartments

I bribe the doorman of the building across the street to inform on the occupants, letting me know when someone has gone on vacation so I can ransack their apartment

In the bureau drawer in Madame R's bedroom, there was a passport in someone else's name

I told the police about the gypsies who beg for money on the street corner

With high powered binoculars, I can see Madame R receive her guests

The name of the head of the secret police is a secret, even to me

Every month someone calls me to give me my orders, the names of the people I'm to investigate & inform on

Once, when I was driving home, I saw the woman downstairs climb into the back of a van, with four men

We live in a neighborhood where it's common for women to solicit men for sex

There's a guy who sometimes sleeps in a doorway near the corner, but I won't give him any money

There are the uniformed policemen & women, who carry guns, & then there's the secret police who look like everyone else, but who also carry guns

I carry a revolver under my shirt, at the base of my spine

Once I had to investigate a priest & saw him in the apartment below, with the prostitute, could hear his voice as he offered her money—I have it on tape

I install a camera in Madame R's apartment so I can watch her undress before she goes to bed

Every week I write a report & send it to my supervisor

We have it on tape, the god-worker visiting the sex-worker, round about midnight

There's a meeting tonight, at the end of the alleyway, through a doorway, but they won't let me in

On the top of the bureau, in Madame R's apartment, I find a note about a shipment of guns

I inform my district officer that a shipment of guns is going to arrive on Saturday, February 1

My students tell me I look like Jeff Goldblum, the actor, but it isn't true

It seems like an anti-semetic perception — that I look like Jeff Goldblum — because we're both Jewish

When I asked my students what they were laughing about, Gloria said: "We think you look like Jeff Goldblum"

It occurred to me that some of my students have never seen any people who were Jewish except for me & Jeff Goldblum, but I can't imagine how that could be possible

In the same way that people say all black people look alike or all Chinese people look alike it's possible some people think all Jews look alike as well

People think they're flattering me when they tell me I look like Jeff Goldblum, but I feel hurt instead

There's a movie, starring Jeff Goldblum, about a man in the Middle East who's shipping guns to Israel

There was a rumor that Jeff Goldblum, or someone who looked like him, was importing guns from Rio de Janeiro to Israel

My favorite Russian student told me she thought the Palestinians were all "animals"

In 1995, someone who looked like Jeff Goldblum, massacred 29 Arabs worshiping at the Tomb of the Patriarchs

"It was like a scene in a movie," someone said, "& this guy was the star"

I hire a bodyguard to "take a bullet" just in case anyone tries to assassinate me

The four-star general was last seen leaving the prostitute's apartment after midnight

My bodyguard waited in the hallway while I rifled through the drawers of Madame R's bedroom bureau

Photos of young men dressed up as girls were discovered in the bottom drawer of the general's bureau

There was a rumor that an undercover agent had infiltrated the organization which met once every other Thursday in an apartment at the end of the alley

There was a rumor that many of Bertolt Brecht's most famous plays were written by his girlfriends

It's possible to sign your name to something someone else has written

The paid assassin stood in a doorway outside the general's apartment

Even my best friends act nervous & shy when they're around
me

I make contact with Agent V who tells me that a shipment of
guns is arriving, but doesn't know when

An anonymous call, heavy breathing, no one answers when
I say "hello"

I say "hello" in English & then I say "hello" in all the other
languages I know, but no one answers

It seems like only yesterday that we were lying together on a
blanket near the ocean

I take a ferry, alone, across the English Channel, in the middle of night

I was lying in bed with the curtains drawn, waiting for you
to come

I see my body, pastel colors, on the floor of the ocean

I can hear the sound of the ocean through the open window

We're strangers now, but once we were lovers in a house near
the ocean

We sit on rocks like sirens & wave to men in passing ships

We dress up like women & stretch our legs on the sand

We can see the ocean from above & the clouds passing in
front of the sun

We go down to the ocean, after midnight, & take off our clothes

We fold our gloves on the edge of the horizon & preen on the hot sand

We stare at the sun, into the sun, through the light of the sun & the sun going down over the horizon until the boats on the edge of the horizon resemble brothels on wheels

We lie on a blanket near the ocean watching the sun disappear, islands of clouds dispersing on the horizon

This is the time I like best, late evening, when the sun disappears, & there are no secrets

~

Lewis Warsh's "The Secret Police" is a list of one-liners without ending punctuation. The narrator is a person, who may be a spy for the secret police. The story moves along as he lists what he discovers and the actions he takes. Interspersed are other asides, seemingly unrelated thoughts and observations. He ends with a lover on the beach with no secrets. The piece reads like a collage of his thoughts even though it also seems to have a chronological order. This narrator is a strange, intelligent, dangerous, mysterious guy.

Also see Lewis Warsh's "Suggestions" on page 273.

Boyle, T. Coraghessan. "The Hit Man," *Sudden Fiction: American Short Short Stories*, Peregrin, 1989, pp. 79-80. Originally published in *The North American Review,* June 1980.

Warsh, Lewis. "The Secret Police." *The Origin of the World*, Creative Arts, 2001, pp. 87-92.

#12: List As Story

Prompt

Write a list that becomes a story. Choose a narrator and a point of interest. Let the narrator take a series of glances at this object (person, place, thing). The glance can include (or be limited to) dialogue, description, speculation, etc. Be sure you include details with these glances so the reader gets a sense of what is going on. You'll want to accentuate the problem the narrator is having. For example, if he is obsessed with self-analysis, that will be present in the story. Again put this narrator in a place and let him or her make a list of problems or issues or characteristics or . . . Be sure there are details and anecdotes in the list with not much summary or explanation.

Examples

STEVE KATZ
ON SELF KNOWLEDGE

I have taken all my characteristics—my compulsive eating my inability to make most decisions my fanatical mushroom hunts my cooking with fingers crossed my occasional cruelty my irrational flashes of temper my secret political awareness my nausea when faced with bureaucracy my immobility on humid days my don't take that pill mentality my overwhelming attacks of sheer lechery my tendency to exaggerate some of my exploits the gnawing below my heart when other writers seem to have more success or more luck than I my apparent affability which I have never believed in my indifference to the suffering of other people my cynicism about my mother's situation my body's love for heavy work my suspicion that other writers are geniuses my knowledge that other writers are rich my fingering the change in my pocket my mind's resistance to focus my love for books my inability to remember the books I love my suspicion that anybody is more wise more clearheaded than I my inability to fill out the simplest form my dislike for games of cards chess monopoly go checkers all that shit my preference to sit in a cafe with a drink and gape at the people or watch the swallows if they're flying my indifference to gossip my extreme pleasure at eavesdropping on other people while they gossip my hatred for doctors and hospitals my uncertainty about the writing I do about the writing anyone does my joy at doing certain work that breaks my back my resistance to finish little tasks my compulsive talking about money when I'm broke my compulsion to spend all I've got my buys of vintage wine my Slivovitz my Faville's London Dock Rum my Laphroaig Scotch my Rebel Yell sour mash bourbon brewed exclusively for the deep south my curried oatmeal my tofu in brown bean sauce my deep involvement in the soft discipline of Tai Chi my thrilling thirty six hour fast each week my ears in Cape Breton my mouth in the brook my eyes in the spruce my prick in the gulf the many things I know my inability to dig in and know this well my continually screwing up the facts of any issue my continually screwing as decreasingly many women as I can bear my tendency to feel that anything people do out of kindness cruelty despair loathing talent loneliness joy greed pride ignorance certitude foolishness etc. is interesting my lack of moral conviction my conviction that I am totally moral my tendency to keep myself half hidden my tendency to put on half a show my love for my exlove for my exwife my love for my kids my love for my feeling the woman used me as a stud my beloved vasectomy my love for my love for you my love for myself my inability to love anyone I mean really love my tendency to wake up shouting Bateson is right my love for my friends my feelings of guilt for much of the above my feelings of stupidity for the same my feelings of pride and anger and regret and doom and lust and optimism and grief and anxiety and elation—all of this and anything I have neglected to tell you I have compounded into these pills you see on the table in front of you   you have come into my tent and now you   have   swallowed   the pill   its flavor   is   to open interpretation   its affect will cure the

monotony of these visits   now I am here without myself as you
see me   a sparrow follows   some goose-tongue here
     this plastic cup   my tipi poles   come on with
     occasional blue   effortless the rain
I am the computer of doubt   I will lead you to the chanterelles
     we do fall among raspberries   hang on to this line
of sunlight   I am the twentieth century backing up
       I am the automatic transmission cutting out
      I have fastened my will to your molecules
the hands of these truths are formed by oystershells
closed on the moons of 1959

~

In "On Self Knowledge" **Steve Katz** piles up self-examination, positives, negatives, positives, negatives and then he ends with a situation, a romantic drug-intensified situation that is rendered in poetry. I like the tone and the long unpunctuated (except for a few dashes) run-on sentences. Maybe you'll feel inspired to use this story as a take-off for one of your own ideas.

In **Jamaica Kincaid**'s story "Girl" (see page 43), we follow the point of view of a girl, as she listens to her mother's relentless instructions about how to live. Sandwiched between the mother's tirade, in italics the narrator thinks to herself or possibly speaks to her mother. The mother is pushing her and warning her about womanly issues. Even though there is no specific setting and location mentioned, there are characters and voices from a particular culture, probably Antigua where Kincaid grew up. The cumulative effect of all this advice makes it seem as if it is happening all at once.

If you are going to use this story as a point of departure for your story, I would suggest not writing about a mother and not writing about advice. Otherwise it will always echo this story. Instead take some facet from the story (like overhearing someone or others)—invent a narrator and a situation (far from Kincaid's) and begin there.

Katz, Steve. *Stolen Stories,* Fiction Collective, 1981, pp. 121-122.

Kincaid, Jamaica. "Girl." *Sudden Fiction International: 60 Short Short Stories*, edited by Robert Shepard and James Thomas, Norton, 1989, pp. 65-66. Originally published as *At the Bottom of the River*, Farrar, Straus and Giroux, 1984.

#13: The Refracting Mind

Prompt

Write the first line of a story in the first person. Then allow the narrator's mind to wander. The narrator says something and then her next sentence will follow the connotations of a word in the first sentence, a noun or a verb, or the sound, slipping from one word to another. Let the story unfold by refracting from one sentence to the next, like a wandering mind, someone easily distracted. Of course, each wandering mind will reveal a particular character. Before you begin, It will be important to understand who your narrator-character is, her life, where she is and what's the problem.

Background / Examples

ED DORN
SOME BUSINESS RECENTLY TRANSACTED IN THE WHITE WORLD

It isn't that easy to get a plane. And availability isn't really the place where they put it. The white world is so dangerous, if you are white, the sheer complication of going into it with a ticket, a handkerchief held at your mouth, a cane to ward off the spectators. A lot of the population hangs around airports these days on the pretense they're going someplace and actually end up with tickets so they won't be caught. Airports are located outside towns so that population won't have to be confronted by a destination. In some way they've bought the right not to be involved. But I didn't get on that way and I didn't catch anything, as much because of my own sureness as any of the precautions I took. In New Mexico the colored man still holds the door but fuck that who asked him. I don't want to be bothered by that either.

What I did can only be *thought* permanent, cannot have permanence. We go through that like a verb through sense. If you remember it, that way, as a concrete act the mistake is twofold.

The nature of *it* is twofold. That's surely the heaviest *isolated* problem the white world is going to avoid whether it wants to or not, not color. That assumes itself, it isn't up to *anybody*. Color is an attribute of the character. Commonplace. More on the acquisition of something a century later when it can be looked at. There are certain aspects present which should be left as all over. Finished in the definitions they've acquired spread uniformly across time. Concrete time flows out the hole of a mixer truck around a cornerstone with some unknown local Christian's name trying to get fixed on it. It's going to have the retentive power of an ice-cube. A time capsule which when broken open will reveal the man inside turned into the name his chums called him from the simple frustration of being unable to think of something else. New York. Or you can forget the debt and call it Boston. I can't quite deal with the man who remembers to speak my name alongside a load of other matter about me he's trying hard to forget. A white man, any man who makes himself white discovers spirit he covers himself with the ashes of the blowing sign of the universe, local materials. The population has managed to embarrass itself enough to forget that too. On the turf inside the Racetrack there are still a few jockeys of refusal. The spare numerical presentations we are. We are of the end of the leeching which produced us. A spoonful left at the bottom, very refined, pure stuff, the final dry powder, the dust that lives. The crack it will go into, the crack in the real. the quality is obvious to everyone though of course like quality it can be faked as some revival called a revolution. It isn't automatic by living that you get your own song. But if you want it off your back, if you want to, turn the scab off, the social off.

In the first day of the horse of December crossing Barcelona in those taxis she had something literal to do, when she could speak in a picked up tongue, learn how it's done with a new monkey wrench, sharp teeth, wieldable. The light traveled from behind her eyes like spirit flashes and focused on the thing to be shone. My function was to be there, pay the cabbie, say much as gracias, keep my fingers out of slammed doors and smile like I knew what was up, the useful, respectable function machines have when they feel good. That was it. But the highest kind of help is simply hand-work. That was occasionally possible. Opening the closed. it may not be as exciting as jumping around but that depends on what's inside. Some figures must be given a sum to find. Their growth is based somewhat on a variation of finding the thimble in the universe. He, on the other hand, was not of routine birth, came in differently as a piece of luck, from a conception sprung. So he has his life, others just notice what they think he is. Now is now, like it was then. If there is something called man, which is used to mean *mean* unless it's in a picture book. If there is something of the animal still in man it might be interesting to see what that is before killing it with a request to remember what Happened.

The Garden Of Birth

His mother smoked hashish. She was herself a garden and its outward expression was in the rich loam of the brown sense of her blue eyes ringed within a slightly black edging. Truly, it could be said that drug was her companion from the botanica. More than Grass. And she spoke of it as to an old acquaintance, and Grass she thought No that's close to a football game, in the end, you have to use your head, therefore it must be thick. Sometimes I miss Miss? I miss my sister. I miss my identical. When I turn around I miss her on the other side of me. Then I enter a state in which I find her. She is my There. I am her Here.

Sometimes when she turns to get into a more comfortable po-sition he feels a new crowding in his bag and moves accordingly, an adjustment she could feel. Her sister could feel it. This is the way he formed the first notion of his mother's sister. He can begin to feel how the new people walk through the old world amazed, an amazone.

And in this period of his life, if you understand, along with the work that follows conception, turning into his nativity, he saw trees. She was sitting on the screen porch. A hot slowly undulating afternoon. A maroon tree and a yellow green tree moved the con-tacts together at the point where the tree would be. Later, in him, all trees would be.

And when she played the flute her heartbeat would enter in the score and guide the playing with sometimes the accompaniment, his heart under hers. Learning to beat the source of relation. The still sway of treetops in the sidereal wind, a motion far slower than centuries.

So he had two trees in her eyes and his mother was his sister. And his mother as well as his mother's sister, could feel him outside her while he was in her, opening his hands in the precategorical fluid of his home.

~

Ed Dorn is predominantly known as a poet, but he also wrote a novel and several short stories. As you read these two stories, I am sure you will notice a wandering poetic voice. "Some Business Recently Transacted in the White World" is presented as an interior monologue that invites the reader to decipher the mind presented. The story starts with a problem the narrator has with getting on a plane. Then he segues into the "white world" and how easy it is for whites to get a ticket. He feels as if he is being watched. Maybe he is one of those he describes as hanging out in the airport, but really not really going anywhere.

He seems to have done something that he's not telling us. Instead he segues from one thought to another. Maybe he lived in New York and Boston. He's critical of the way people forget and hide what is important. "It isn't automatic by living that you get your own song. But if you want it off your back, if you want to, turn the scab off, the social off." We could talk about the way the social world inhibits individuality and intelligence.

After all the seguing and circling, I start expecting a story. A man loses his sense of self in coupling. He ends with: "If there is something called man, which is used to mean *mean* unless it's in a picture book, if there is something of the animal still in man it might be interesting to see what that is before killing it with a request to remember what Happened." I start wondering what the desire to tell a story about the past has to do with his manhood. At the same time, there is this sense of a spiritual search in and out of the logical/illogical turns of the mind.

I am mesmerized by the way this narrator tries to avoid telling us the story and yet we try to tell it, try to make sense of it by analyzing his twists and turns, perhaps ending up inflicting a narrative on this rambling monologue.

When reading "In the Garden of Birth" I feel as if I am entering into a hashish dream with the narrator as he tries to imagine his mother's twin sister. In his vision trees and people are related to each other. This dreamy story is filtered through a wandering mind, maybe the mind of a seer. It seem as if we are experiencing someone birthing into an awareness of the sexing of our lives.

See "Refracting Prose Poem" on page 92.

NOTES

Dorn, Ed. "Some Business Recently Transacted in the White World" and "The Garden of Birth." *Some Business Recently Transacted in the White World*, Frontier Press, 1971, pp. 77-83.

#14: RETELLING / REFRAMING

Prompt

Think of an encounter that you witnessed, perhaps one with a conflict or when something strange occurred. Then imagine another "moment" later in the day when something happens to one of the characters, maybe something anti-climactic. Tell this story first in a very relaxed fashion, as if you are telling a good friend or family member about it. Remember it should take place in only a few moments.

Then retell the story at least twice, but make each one far different from the first. Transform the story. You can change the narrator or change the emotion and character of the person observing. Or you can use a poetic form. Or a different rhetorical stance or pattern (argument, description, congratulations, etc.). Or a figure of speech (metaphor, simile, hyperbole, personification, etc.). Or any literary approach, playing with language, such as alliteration or assonance or you can invent some different way to tell the story. Just be sure there is similarity in the plot, but be playful with the transformations.

Or take a tiny fiction that you have already written and tell it again in three or more ways (as above). Sometimes trying out some of these far-out exercises can push a writer into a different style or at least an awareness of all the writerly possibilities.

Background / Examples

The above assignment was inspired by **Raymond Queneau's** *Exercises in Style*. Queneau begins with the "notation" form and then transforms his simple little account of two anecdotes in 99 different ways. Some of these are crazy and fun. He was one of the original OULIPO writers. Below I have included a selection of his transformations.

In the "Preface," to Queneau's book, Barbara Wright quotes Queneau in conversation with Georges Ribemont-Dessaignes:

In *les Exercises de Style*, I started from a real incident, and in the first place I told it 12 times in different ways. Then a year later I did another 12 and finally there were 99. People have tried to see it as an attempt to demolish literature—that was not at all my intention. In any case my intention was merely to produce some exercises; the finished product may possibly act as a kind of rust-remover to literature, help to rid it of some of its scabs.

RAYMOND QUENEAU
from *EXERCISES IN STYLE*

Notation

In the S bus, in the rush hour. A chap of about 26, felt hat with a cord instead of a ribbon, neck too long, as if someone's been having a tug-of-war with it. People getting off. The chap in question gets annoyed with one of the men standing next to him. He accuses him of jostling him every time anyone goes past. A sniveling tone which is meant to be aggressive. When he sees a vacant seat he throws himself on to it.

Two hours later, I meet him in the Cour de Rome, in front of the gare Saint-Lazare. He's with a friend who's saying: "You ought to get an extra button put on your overcoat." He shows him where (at the lapels) and why.

Metaphorically

In the centre of the day, tossed among the shoal of travelling sardines in a coleopter with a big white carapace, a chicken with a long, featherless neck suddenly harangued one, a peace-abiding one, of their number, and its parlance, moist with protest, was unfolded upon the airs. Then, attracted by a void, the fledgling precipitated itself thereunto.

In a bleak, urban desert, I saw it again that self-same day, drinking the cup of humiliation offered by a lowly button.

Dream

I had the impression that everything was misty and nacreous around me, with multifarious and indistinct apparitions, amongst whom however was one figure that stood out fairly clearly which was that of a young man whose too-long neck in itself seemed to proclaim the character at once cowardly and quarrelsome of the individual. The ribbon of his hat had been replaced by apiece of plaited string. Later he was having an argument with a person whom I couldn't see and then, as if suddenly afraid, he threw himself into the shadow of a corridor.

Animism

A soft, brown hat with a dent in his middle, his brim turned down, a plaited cord round his crown, one hat among many others, jumping only when the bumps in the road were transmitted to him by the wheels of the automobile vehicle which was transporting him (the hat). At each stop the comings and goings of the passengers caused him to make certain lateral movements which at times were fairly pronounced, and this ended by angering him (the hat). He expressed his ire by the intermediary of a human voice which was attached to him by a mass of flesh structurally disposed round a sort of bony sphere perforated by a few holes, which was situated below him (the hat). Then he (the hat) suddenly went and sat down.

One or two hours later I saw him (the hat) again, moving about at roughly 1m. 66cm. above the ground and up and down in front of the gare Saint-Lazare. A friend was advising him to an extra button put on his overcoat…an extra button…on his overcoat…to tell him that…him…(the hat).

Blurb

In this new novel, executed with his accustomed brio, the famous novelist X, to whom we are already indebted for so many masterpieces, has decided to confine himself to very clear-cut characters who act in an atmosphere which everybody, both adults and children, can understand. The plot revolves, then, round the meeting in a bus of the hero of this story and of a rather enigmatic character who picks a quarrel with the first person he meets. In the final episode we see this mysterious individual listening with the greatest attention to the advice of a friend, a past master of Sartorial Art. The whole makes a charming impression which the novelist X has etched with rare felicity.

Logical analysis

Bus.

Platform.

Bus Platform. That's the place.

Midday.

About.

About midday. That's the time.

Passengers.

Quarrel.

A passengers' quarrel. That's the action.

Young man.

Hat. Long thin neck.

A young man with a hat and a plaited cord round it. That's the chief character.

Person.

A person.

A person. That's the second character.

Me.

Me.

Me. That's the third character, narrator.

Words.

Words.

Words. That's what was said.

Seat vacant.

Seat taken.

A seat that was vacant and then taken. That's the result.

The gare Saint-Lazare.

An hour later.

A friend.

A button.

Another phrase heard. That's the conclusion.

Logical conclusion.

~

CLARICE LISPECTOR
THE FIFTH STORY

This story could be called "The Statues." Another possible title would be "The Killing." Or even "How to Kill Cockroaches." So I shall tell at least three stories, all of them true, because none of the three will contradict the others. Although they constitute one story, they could become a thousand and one, were I to be granted a thousand and one nights.

The first story, "How To Kill Cockroaches," begins like this: I was complaining about the cockroaches. A woman heard me complain. She gave me a recipe for killing them. I was to mix together equal quantities of sugar, flour and gypsum. The flour and sugar would attract the cockroaches, the gypsum would dry up their insides. I followed her advice. The cockroaches died.

The next story is really the first, and it is called "The Killing." It begins like this: I was complaining about the cockroaches. A woman heard me complain. The recipe follows. And then the killing takes place. The truth is that I had only complained in abstract terms about the cockroaches, for they were not even mine: they belonged to the ground floor and climbed up the pipes in the building into our apartment. It was only when I prepared the mixture that they also became mine. On our behalf, therefore, I began to measure and weigh ingredients with greater concentration. A vague loathing had taken possession of me, a sense of outrage. By day, the cockroaches were invisible and no one would believe in the evil secret which eroded such a tranquil household. But if the cockroaches, like evil secrets, slept by day, there I was preparing their nightly poison. Meticulous, eager, I prepared the elixir of prolonged death. An angry fear and my own evil secret guided me. Now I coldly wanted one thing only: to kill every cockroach in existence. Cockroaches climb up the pipes while weary people sleep. And now the recipe was ready, looking so white. As if I were dealing with cockroaches as cunning as myself, I carefully spread the powder until it looked like part of the surface dust. From my bed, in the silence of the apartment, I imagined them climbing up one by one into the kitchen where darkness slept, a solitary towel alert on the clothesline. I awoke hours later, startled at having overslept. It was beginning to grow light. I walked across the

201

kitchen. There they lay on the floor of the scullery, huge and brittle. During the night I had killed them. On our behalf, it was beginning to grow light. On a nearby hill, a cockerel crowed.

The third story which now begins is called "The Statues." It begins by saying that I had been complaining about the cockroaches. Then the same woman appears on the scene. And so it goes on to the point where I awake as it is beginning to grow light, and I awake still feeling sleepy and I walk across the kitchen. Even more sleepy is the scullery floor with its tiled perspective. And in the shadows of dawn, there is a purplish hue which distances everything; at my feet, I perceive patches of light and shade, scores of rigid statues scattered everywhere. The cockroaches that have hardened from core to shell. Some are lying upside down. Others arrested in the midst of some movement that will never be completed. In the mouths of some of the cockroaches, there are traces of white powder. I am the first to observe the dawn breaking over Pompei. I know what this night has been, I know about the orgy in the dark. In some, the gypsum has hardened as slowly as in some organic process, and the cockroaches, with ever more tortuous movements, have greedily intensified the night's pleasures, trying to escape from their insides. Until they turn to stone, in innocent terror and with such, but *such* an expression of pained reproach. Others— suddenly assailed by their own core, without even having perceived that their inner form was turning to stone!— these are suddenly crystallized, just like a word arrested on someone's lips: I love . . . The cockroaches, invoking the name of love in vain, sang on a summer's night. While the cockroach over there, the one with the brown antennae smeared with white, must have realized too late that it had become mummified precisely because it did not know how to use things with the gratuitous grace of the *in vain*: "It is just that I looked too closely inside myself! it is just that I looked too closely inside . . . "From my frigid height as a human being, I watch the destruction of a world. Dawn breaks. Here and there, the parched antennae of dead cockroaches quiver in the breeze. The cockerel from the previous story crows.

The fourth story opens a new era in the household. The story begins as usual: I was complaining about the cockroaches. It

202

goes on up to the point when I see the statues in plaster of Paris. Inevitably dead. I look towards the pipes where this same night an infestation will reappear, swarming slowly upwards in Indian file. Should I renew the lethal sugar every night? like someone who no longer sleeps without the avidity of some rite. And should I take myself somnambulant out to the terrace early each morning? in my craving to encounter the statues which my perspiring night has erected. I trembled with depraved pleasure at the vision of my double existence as a witch. I also trembled at the sight of that hardening gypsum, the depravity of existence which would shatter my internal form.

The grim moment of choosing between two paths, which I thought would separate, convinced that any choice would mean sacrificing either myself or my soul. I chose. And today I secretly carry a plaque of virtue in my heart: "This house has been disinfected."

The fifth story is called "Leibnitz and The Transcendence of Love in Polynesia." It begins like this: I was complaining about the cockroaches

~

Clarice Lispector is a Brazilian writer. In "The Fifth Story," the narrator begins by telling a simple story of how she killed some cockroaches, but she tells the story five times and each retelliing carries the story along further. The first is simple; the second elucidates on some other motives and actions; the third looks into the life of and disaster for the cockroaches; in the fourth she acts anyhow, murdering the cockroaches; and in the fifth she begins again now with a more philosophical angle. So the story is about murder, trivia, the life of insects, guilt and some of the possible ways a story can unfold.

See also Georges Perec's "Tale" on page 151.

Lispector, Clarice. "The Fifth Story." Translated by Giovanni Pontiero. *Sudden Fiction International: 60 Short Short Stories*, edited by Robert Shepard and James Thomas, Norton, 1989, pp. 264-267. Originally published as *The Foreign Legion*, Carcaner Press, 1964, 1986.

Queneau, Raymond.   "Notation," "Metaphorically," "Dream," "Animism," "Blurb," "Logical Analysis." *Exercises in Styles*, translated by Barbara Wright, New Directions,1981, pp. 19-20; 24; 27; 48; 56; 60-61. Originally published as *Exercises de Style*, Edition Gallimard, 1947.

CHRONOLOGY OF MIND:

FROM JOURNAL
TO POEM (OR PROSE)

CHRONOLOGY OF MIND
FROM JOURNAL TO POEM (OR PROSE)

Introduction

The prompts in this workshop come from experiments that have helped me over the years to generate poems and novels. Some of the experiments were passed on to me by others, but most of them were my own inventions.

Writing in response to this series of experiments may help to circumvent your habitual writing patterns and help you write a story or a poem outside of the comfortable voice and framework to which you are accustomed. The emphasis in this sequence of prompts is first on gathering material through journal writing and research, and then questioning, interrupting, dislocating, rearranging and pushing the language material into different corners and crevices where sometimes a new idea or image or thought might appear.

The focus here is on working with autobiographical material (the self extending into the world) while at the same time disrupting or redirecting an easy logic and/or chronology. Examples in this workshop come mostly, but not entirely, from my own writing.

Journal Writing

To prepare to work on these assignments, begin today to be prolific with your journal writing. You may feel more comfortable working on a computer, but I am going to suggest that you also try writing on paper with a pen. Choose a journal in which you enjoy writing. I like working on smaller size pages, about 4 x 6, smooth paper, sometimes Japanese folding books. Then I purchase pens that glide along, easily following thought. Later I type material into a computer file, but I find that the initial choice of writing material influences the depth of thought.

Perhaps you will write on every other page and then later come back and write on the blank pages while rereading your earlier entry. If you are writing on a computer, you might try working with two columns. Write frequently, several times a day if possible, but at least once. Write about what you see and hear and what is important to you. Include sensory impressions, as well as thoughts. The more material you have for the later experiments, the easier it will be. Write freely. When you are reading or studying something, copy passages that you find meaningful or delightful or horrifying and put them in your journal.

Sometimes I find it useful to limit my journal writing to a page at a time. Then if I have a lot to say, I write very tiny. You might want to try writing at the same time every day, one small page a day. You could even choose to write at a certain time in the middle of the night. Gather as much material as possible.

Begin this sequence of prompts with "Walking and Writing" (page 3). After you finish your haiku and the embedded poem, be sure that as you go along, you continue to record as many haiku moments as possible in your journal. This will help you with the experiments that come later in the workshop.

#2: Oulipo And 14 X 14 X 14

MAY 15, 2011

9. Woke up looking at the still trees & the grey misty sky
10. Wrote an email, a thanky, and then stretch out my mat & my bod
11. Busy mind coming back to losses, creating new losse
12. Also a leaves at the Korean bodega. Hurray!
1. Grey sky. My downstairs Neighbor rolling & rising falling piano s ca
2. Why go outdoors when such beauty rolls from one studio to anoth
3. "Summering" is a word the very well-off use
4. When Jacqueline plays the piano, and dawn sits here
5. looking out the window at the formed leaves & broods
6. then I never want to leave this cave
7. Charmed except when I realize that my significant other
8. has forgotten I'm significant — Entropy Megantropy
9. A yogic mind takes years to develop.
10. Some old people suffer & others hang in there with the
   world word hacka

Prompt

In 2010, Martine Bellen and I were collaborating on a Belladonna project. When we were finished with our editing work, Martine mentioned that she was in between writing projects and was unsure about what to do next. I picked up a 4 x 6 card from my desk and counted the lines: 14! Let's write a poem a day, one line an hour for 14 days. And we did just that, carried around a stack of index cards and wrote 14 lines, for 14 hours, for 14 days. Your assignment is to write 7 lines a day for only 7 days or one line every other hour (or for seven hours straight). Then write seven drafts with 7 lines each. Feel free to revise. Or invent some variation on the assignment that works for you. For this week these cards will be your journal and your first draft. As you are writing your first draft of your lines, focus as much as possible on observation and sounds; if it is a summarizing thought, be sure the language or the thought itself calls attention to itself (but not as a cliché).

Background / Examples

When we came up with this constraint, Martine and I had been working for six months or so on my interviews of Harryette Mullen for *Looking Up Harryette Mullen* (Belladonna, 2011); Martine was the Belladonna editor for my project. While working on Mullen's book, we were steeped in thinking and talking about Oulipo experiments. Writing 14 x 14 x 14 was an apt finale for our collaborative experience. My 14 x 14 x 14 poem combines an OULIPO constraint with a New York School chatty record of a day. While I was writing these poems, sometimes I'd be in a situation where I couldn't write a line in an hour; sometimes I'd write 2 or 3 lines at a time. As you can see, even with the same prompt, Martine and I have very different styles.

Following are the first poems in our project. Our sequences were published by *Peep Show Poetry*. See "Notes" for the current link. Both of our poems have since been revised.

BARBARA HENNING
MAY 9, 2011

The locust trees are under constant revision.
Passersby are wearing hats. These things seem
innocuous, but when he says my body feels like home,
a chair falls on my head, an omen three years short
of medicare and my heart racing like a teenager.
A drummer on Astor Place catches the beat. Crouched
in a doorway on Avenue A, my hand over my left ear,
listening to Cleveland in my right. Trucks, motorcycles
and busses blowing smoke. At home a check for poetry
and the sound of birds and muffled voices in the park.
My neighbor's dog barks for an hour while I fold towels
into small rectangles, branches swaying high over Tompkins
Square. Politicians want to privatize education, kill
medicare, log the forests, 15,000 species cut off, cut out.
Verizon and AT&T donate to the tea party. Sign here.
Quiet. Distant traffic rushing in and out like the sea.

~

Martine Bellen

1.

I declare a holiday for radical architecture—
Maidens locked behind iron doors, rusted since grandees
Seduced your great, great aunt near the aspidistra in the garden below.
Ancestors chopping off milady's viper rage
While waxy Daily Alice chases herself into public space,
3 for 5 and her pleasure paid for with plastic
(You're killing me with your chop-stick watusi).
Beyond the wild woods comes the Wide World,
Lace hands and laurel hair to still the metamorphosis.
Babies pushed by pregnant houses
And cubby holes within ear and nostril sockets.
Don't tell me the work's too dear,
That structure can't be concocted of fur and claws,
And talons and feathers, and I-beams and Moon-rays.

~

I'm also including a few pages from **Harry Mathew's** *20 Lines a Day*. When because of grief he was experiencing a writer's block, Mathews decided to write at least 20 lines a day. In the first poem, "When the wind blows hard", he follows an outside weather event as it enters the room and affects his thinking. Throughout he addresses himself as a "you." The narrative of the wind and the point of view weave this piece together. "Last night I spent" is another descriptive narrative about a happening in NYC, outside Caffe Lucca. I might call some of these poems miniatures, written at the border between a short-short essay and a prose poem.

OULIPO is short for *Ouvroir de Littérature Potentielle*, Workshop of Potential Literature. If you want to know more about Oulipo, you can find a lot of material on the internet. Also, see a link below for my interview with Harry on May 27, 2011; we discuss Oulipo and Harryette Mullen's book. Also, see Harry Mathews' handout on page 258.

Harry Mathews
from *20 Lines A Day*

[5}

When the wind blows hard, you can lock it out, you can let it in but give it no place to go, or you can let it through. The first two ways are suitable for a cold wind; for a hot one, the last is best, unless you like being stifled or being pummeled with heat. There are still disadvantages: when you let the wind through, especially through your bedroom, especially at night, you have to give up in exchange for coolness all hopes of rest. The wind tumbles in, puffing up the curtains, lifting them high enough to reveal a sky whose stars no longer suggest ecstatic calm. The wind blows, the night stares in at you relentlessly, and the day will never come. Lying awake, after you have learned to give up hoping for rest, you begin hoping for day, and then for peace, and then for strength, if not now at least in a foreseeable future: because now you are lying on your bed in utter weakness. Over you moves the tumbling, clattering wind, and although you know that it's only air and holds no real danger for you, you are nonetheless filled with an emotion worse than terror—a knotted, knowledgeable anxiety that comes to feel like the pit and kernel of your life. It is a dismaying conviction that you have neither substance nor consistency nor even the capacity to resign yourself to this sad condition. This awareness is what makes you so weak that you cannot move (except to turn from your left onto your right side and slip your right arm under the pillow); or perhaps your being unable to move simply becomes the proof of what you are aware of. You go on lying there, too wakeful to sleep, too sleepy to take advantage of being awake (or so you not quite honestly tell yourself), you only let the wind continue its noisy work.

St. Bart's, 3/ 17/83

[63]

Last night I spent a few minutes on Father Demo Square, on the sidewalk in front of the buildings that include the Caffe Lucca. It was six o'clock, quite dark now that we're back on standard time, but warm—warm for the hour, warm for the season. On the island in the middle of the square, a number of people were sitting summerwise on the benches. This might be the last evening on which they could sit out. The outermost benches of the triangular island face inward—I noticed this because I wanted to sit looking across Bleecker Street at the Caffe Lucca, and couldn't. The square's designer evidently thought benchsittcrs would prefer watching each other to watching traffic, a mistake, I think, not because cars and trucks are nicer than people but onlookers enjoy varied more than static scenes.

The Caffe Lucca lay open to the evening. Throughout my vigil, a black man stood talking to a white man seated at one of its terrace tables. To the south, the window of Avignone's drugstore displayed a large volume opened to a double page of pasted-in prescription labels (signed by Moroni, Peroni, and yet another -oni), and a mobile sculpture advertising Swiss army knives—an oblong vertical block fitted with opening and closing outsized scissors- and knife-blades. North of the cafe, two bearded barbers in their thirties were razor-cutting the hair of two girls in their early teens. Lace of great cleanliness adorned the door pane and the neighboring window of a tenement building. On the benches in the square both blacks and whites were sitting. Around the corner, in another triangular parklet on Sixth Avenue, all the sitters were black.

New York, 11/4/83

~

NOTES

Bellen, Martine and Barbara Henning. "14 x 14 x 14." *Peep / Show Poetry,* no. 4, July 2011, http://peepshowpoetry.blogspot.com/2011/07/font-face-font-family-arialp.html.

Henning, Barbara. "14 x 14 x 14." *A Swift Passage*, Quale Press, 2013.

Mathews, Harry. Interview by Barbara Henning. *Eoagh*, 27 May 2011, https://eoagh.com/an-interview-with-harry-mathews/.

——. *20 Lines a Day*. Dalkey,1989. pp. 5, 63.

#3: Lines, Letters And Ladders

Prompt

Select a communication from another person, a letter or an email or a text. Take a rather ordinary sentence from the writing. Break it down into its alphabet and write another sentence. Then write the poem in between these two sentences, using details from your journal and daily life. You might want to make each line a step from the beginning to the end like a ladder; that is, segueing from one sentence to the next by some connotation or association in one sentence that leads to another thought or sentence that is slightly related. Or you might prefer to just write a story in between these two sentences.

Background / Examples

I remember one day not being sure what my next project would be. I had a stack of letters from my son on my desk. He was in an exchange program in college in Costa Rica at the time. I made a list of sentences and phrases from his letters. For example: "So please excuse my grammatical errors."

Then I broke the sentence down into the letters. For example the first one became:

    vowels: aaaa eeee i oo   u y
    consonants: cc g l mmm rrrr ssss t p l x

Then I used these letters to make another sentence. This is an anagram-like process, rearranging the letters of a word or phrase to make the new words or phrases.

The final draft of the first poem, "Inheritance," ends with "So please excuse my grammatical errors," but I'm not sure where the anagrammatic sentence went. It might have been clipped in the revision process. It now begins with "I am going to go now". Maybe I worked on the letters for a while and then they became inspiration for another sentence.

After I wrote the two sentences and made them either at the beginning or end, I wrote a prose poem in between, using sentences from my day's events and thoughts recorded in my journal. I tried to invent the movement from one sentence to the next, following the way a mind drifts, segueing away from one word or idea and the connotations or elaborations that might follow. I wanted to make a ladder from the first sentence to the last, but not always with logical narrative constructions.

Of course you can revise this process as you'd like. When I write, I usually write a series, so I wrote 8 poems with this experiment. They were published under the title "Eight Prose Poems," part of a collection published in *Detective Sentences* (Spuyten Duyvil 2001). Here's the first one and another from later in the series.

INHERITANCE

I am going to go now and put some air in the tires of my bicycle. It's been sitting in the living room for six months and both tires are flat. The flat "a" tells us where you were born and where you grew up. Some place in the middle. The crack in your voice tells us what you have not been doing for the past few years. Without exercising the possible range of movement, an inevitable stiffness arrives. The cowboy rode his horse across the plains. I straighten up the mess in the kitchen. If an animal is mistreated and dies violently and you eat the fruit of those acts, you come to identify with the position of a victim. Take the peels from the orange and place them into a plastic bag with the rest of the remains. Place the pillow back on the bed. The blue numbers on my alarm clock are sequential and repetitious. Often the cause of acute sinusitis. First it belonged to Mike's aunt, then Mike, then Allen and now it sits on this desk. So please excuse my grammatical errors.

PLEASE DO NOT ALLOW

another knot to form in the dog's leash. She doesn't have much room left to wander. In forty-five minutes, I'll emerge from the door and head over to the poetry project. Cruising down I94, it takes only ten seconds to pass by the neighborhood where my grandparents raised my parents and then grew old. Ankles crossed under the computer. An e-mail from here to Detroit. Space conquered. They zero in on a bridge in Serbia with a cross-bow and a computer and we watch it blow up on television. We don't take out their television though because that's a human rights issue. But then the next week it isn't. There were already 84 other Mooks, so he took the number 85. One day the Detroit arts community was present. We were stunned. Yesterday there was a little storm in San Jose and access was lost. A student asks me, what's real—your life here or the life in your dreams.

~

NOTES

Henning, Barbara. "8 Prose Poems." *Detective Sentences*, Spuyten Duyvil Press, 2001.13-22.

#4: Words & the Times

Prompt

You have been writing in your journal since the beginning of this workshop, and collecting many haiku moments. Go back now and select one
entry that has images or a poetic spin that you like or a narrative thread
that might work. Work on the piece, shaping it into a poem, revising as
needed, adding whatever you'd like. Then at some point, select three or
four words inside your text, go to the *New York Time Archive* (or another
newspaper, preferably your local paper) and search for that word—maybe limit the search by the day or the week in which you were writing
the poem.

Collect some interesting phrases or sentences. If a word does not lead
to material that you find interesting, you might have to select another
word. Then collage some of this new material into the poem. In this way,
you will be combining the personal and the public.

Background / Examples

In 1976, City Lights published a pamphlet including Ed Sanders' essay
"Investigative Poetry: The Content of History Will be Poetry." Sanders
calls on poets to use "*every* bardic skill and meter and method . . . to
describe *every* aspect (no more secret governments!) of the historical
present." In this "Words and the Times" exercise we are combining present day personal concerns with politics and events worldwide, using

collage and OULIPIAN techniques. Some poets avoid the political as if it isn't woven into every part of our lives; we are especially aware of this inter-weaving now with the internet. See discussion of investigative poetry on page 81.

On the first day of 2012, I decided to write one small page every night, no more no less, and I did this for a complete year. I wasn't sure what I was going to do with the material—write a novel, write poems, or another experiment. And what a year it was, the ups and downs of a new relationship, climaxing in the fall with Hurricane Sandy and then at the end of the year with my own personal hurricane, an illness and operation. In the winter of 2013, I went to Tucson to stay with friends. For a couple of months I worked on excerpting poems, rewriting and editing them. I sifted through the writing looking for interesting narratives or poetic spins, sometimes only a sentence here and there. When I finished I had about 150 rough draft poems. There was still the possibility that these poems would become a novel. (I often work with lines even when I finally decide to go back to prose; it slows down my writing process, with more attention to style and rhythm.)

From the time I started the process, it took me a year and a half to finish with about 100 poems. In each poem I selected 4 to 5 words, went to the *New York Times Archives* and searched for these words in the month in which the material originated. If the poem was written in January, I'd search through the archive for January 2012. Then I would make a catalogue of phrases and sentences that I thought might work with the poem. Sometimes I would be long lost in just reading about the events. Sometimes I would have pages of material and only collage a few words. The research was tedious and I swore many times I would never start such a big project again. Nonetheless, I liked working with the repetition and I liked the way the public world of news interacted with the personal. The title of the collection is *A Day Like Today*.

Here are three poems from *A Day Like Today*, written in 2012 and 2013; I think you can tell by looking at the poems which material I brought in from *The Times*.

On The Bottom Rung

Logan slips on the bottom rung
of the slide. He stands up and starts
to cry. Looking at me, he frowns
and says, Gramma, I'm always
falling down. Some say hitting
bottom is a prelude to a rebound.
Fleas were ten times bigger
then and their mouths were
sharp enough to feed on dinosaurs.
Our mouths, teeth and tongues are
orchestrated to enunciate the inner
and the outer. Crouched down,
Patti Smith is naked and clutching
the top rung of a radiator while
staring directly into Mapplethorpe's
camera. The strange and sulky
beauty of always. A reflection
of gas flames from the fireplace,
flickering on the window
as the planet moves closer and closer
to the end of its life span—
this ravishingly beautiful earth.

A Bedouin Man

A Bedouin man isn't certain
whether joining a revolt was
life's proudest moment or its
ruination. The object in your
pocket is a tracking device
that just happens to make calls.
Just perch the clock near the bed
and put your phone on the stand
and it will record your sleep

patterns. Hello. Good night.
The days are going so quickly.
Perhaps we perceive quickness
more in our busy lives than
people did in previous centuries.
Yesterday, Americans used
their sizable advantage to run
others ragged. We lay the child
down into his bed and find
each other under the sheet.
Now with four arms, four legs
and two heads, we circulate qi.
Then the arm starts turning
sideways in a gentle curve, tracing
an S shape, the thumb heading
up as the palm turns parallel,
our bodies and souls parallel.
Oh, the grief of separation.
Don't think, dear, stay here.

WHEN I OPEN MY EYES

A knuckleboom loader plucks up
the mighty oak as if it were a twig.
Dust in my sinuses, throat, lungs.
I lie on the floor, propped up
on pillows covered with a quilt.
At a lookout where Kerouac
once sat, a small seated silhouette
watches for a spark. My acupuncturist
takes burning moxa-mugwart,
lifts up the blanket and holds it
over particular points on my legs,
arms and stomach. Over 100
burned bodies are lined up
on the floor of Tazreen Fashions

in Bangladesh. Bus-size boilers
from Texas prop up our steam
systems and bring heat into cold
dark public housing. I bike home
from Union Square in the icy rain—
covered in plastic, my glasses steaming,
rain rolling down my cheeks, cars
and pedestrians cutting here and there.
In the long run, so they say, the ice
and the middle class will slowly disappear.

Later in 2016-17 when almost everyone I knew was consumed with the political disaster-to-be, the election of Donald Trump, I used the same process, but I took it one step further, translating the poems into a form similar to a telegram. I call them, Digigrams, messages from me to the world, through the digital screen. I was influenced by the Baroness, Elsa Von Freytag-Lorenhaven's poems. Here is one of my digigrams.

STRING BALL

> for Nevine Michaan and Charles Blow

*—the body's organized—on a square—*so says Yogi Nevine—I walk around Tompkins Square—all four corners—surely this is the center—of the universe—*the goal in life—should be joy—*in Larung Gar—the Chinese—are tearing apart—Tibetan monastic—dwellings—*plan your life—like a chess game—move analytically—with intent—it's very practical—the way to attain joy—*even for civilians—trapped in Aleppo—with artillery shelling overhead—*defeat in life—is bitterness—*buck up—writes Charles Blow—it's over—the bully's—in the white house—for the time being—alt-right is not—a computer command—they're a batch of fanatical racists—*if you're happy—you'll help everyone—if you're miserable—you*

222

won't help anyone—in Shuafat—a refugee camp—in Jerusalem—
Baha helps the orphans—work, find direction, survive—then a
drive-by—ten bullets—one of the children—will surely—take his
place—you can follow—fake news sites—from one to another—
unravel the molecular structure—of ribosomes—a tangled mess of
rubber bands—and coiled wires—a new pattern—of income equal-
ity—life expectancy in the US—declines slightly—*be careful*—*it's*
like a string ball—*if we keep going around*—*in the same direction*—
we will surely unravel—
(1 Dec 2016)

NOTES

Henning, Barbara. *A Day Like Today*, Negative Capability Press, 2015. pp.
25, 70, 107.

——. "String Ball." Digigrams, United Artists books, 2020, p. 33.

Sanders, Ed. *Investigative Poetry*, City Lights, 1976. p. 7. Republished by
Spuyten Duyvil (Dispatches Editions), ed. Don Byrd, 2019.

#5: THINKING THE OPPOSITE / IN BETWEEN

Prompt

Write a lot in your journal. Collect. Collect. Freewrite. Then select poetically interesting sentences or phrases. For each phrase, sentence or
paragraph, write an opposite and then a middle. You will have to determine what an opposition is. Put these together as a poem with a series of
stanzas. See if you can keep the reader interested by including stories and
images, as well as ideas.

Background / Examples

I started practicing yoga seriously in 1995. In one of my early classes,
my teacher Sharon Gannon talked about one of *The Yoga Sutras* (2:33).
When having negative thoughts, think the opposite. This has been a very
helpful sutra for me. If I'm fixated on some thought or worry, I repeat
the bothersome thought in my mind, then construct an opposite, then
try to let the thought go. Of course it reoccurs, but then I do the same
thing, and eventually (with a lot of practice) I'm sometimes moved out of
a stuck place.

When I first encountered this sutra, I started wondering if it was really
possible to think the opposite. And could I use this in a writing experiment? Could I take each word in the sentence and reconstruct it with an
opposition?

And what is an opposition anyhow? Dog: cat. Not really the opposite, but fun to play with. I guess the opposite would really be "no dog". Even absence and presence are not opposites, just variations in our linguistic stream. Then I started thinking that if you have two opposites, in the Buddhist sense, you might want to end up in the middle instead of swinging back and forth.

I decided to play with the idea of opposites and middles. I took my journal and broke it apart selecting sentences and paragraphs. It's important, of course, to select the right material and to edit it. In the process, I realized that all the messages on my answering machine were in between two people, so I put the messages into the long series of poems. I titled it *In Between* and it was published later by a press in England, Spectacular Diseases. The books are not available anymore, printed in a limited edition. Following is a selection from this series.

BARBARA HENNING

from IN BETWEEN

warped timber
& the shadow of desire

*

My body is the only home I can count on & it is enough.
Your eye is the empty spot I'm lost in & this is insufficient.
The act of turning exists & we wonder if this is necessarily adequate.

*

Perhaps captured by your willingness to sit in place.
Reluctantly, suspended by a perpetual plan for future mobility.
Yes, freed by your negative reactions.

*

After the pharmacist sends the boy to the doctor, he agrees to remove his
eyebrow ring. Prior to the witch's refusal to offer a remedy, the mother puts
a stake in her womb. In the interim, tangled indecipherable designs are tat-
tooed on our breasts by big Teddy in Brooklyn.

*

The wicked rumor at the university might have started from a kernel of truth.
The run of the mill lecture on the street corner was finished off with a lie.
It is my opinion that the owner of this cafe is making a small fortune on
    refills.

*

Men, he says, need to be admired.
Women, she thinks, don't really invite humiliation.
We, the middle one disclaims, prefer to be left alone.

*

The dramatic bohemian yells at a noisy family eating at the table beside her
and they throw food back. An academic whispers a compliment to a polite
man across the room who smiles at someone else. The broker calmly discusses daily events with another broker who listens intently.

*

No one flinches. I am an observer. Everyone complains. You are not pay-
ing attention. A few bear it. They are half listeners, half talkers, half asleep.

*

Emerson & courage.
Edgar Allen Poe & terror.
Hester Prynne & the scar of balance.

*

this is lewis um if you see michael tonight um maybe you can tell him
to call me um i left my   cap in a taxi cat cab and he knows the name of
the taxi driver and i need to know the name so if you're connecting i'm
at home   it's about nine something nine thirty   tell him to call and if
i'm not here tell him to tell me the name of the driver   i know it sounds
insane but it is the hat i bought in tibet so i really like it so i want to get
it back okay kay bye bye.

*

A typical relationship between a man and a woman. I never learned how
to play. A rather unusual monologue. I practiced diligently from morning
to night. This moribund dialogue. A smattering of haphazard thought in
the afternoon.

*

barbara michael calling, i don't know what time you're coming in or what
the story is but i would suspect   as you know i'll be at school and i'll be
back here about five to five thirty   i have a car for the day to do some
errands and stuff and wanted to pick up food anyway and it's a good day

to blow off things you know with a car   any way i can always run in and pick you up and take you back whatever you know and um later this evening   anyhow so let's be in touch   i tried to reach you a couple of times yesterday and as you know the answering machine wasn't working and i didn't hear from you on the machine when i went out so i just figured you were busy doing things   whatever   so i'll talk to you soon.

*

The wind blows the coupons off the kitchen table. Everything stands still, breathless, the bills in their envelopes, unopened. Economically balanced, a pocket of air accumulates.

NOTES

Barbara Henning. *In Between*. Spectacular Diseases, Peterborough, England, 2000, pp. 7-11.

#6: Found In The Library

Prompt

Select 14 books in your library, perhaps 14 in alphabetic order. Scan the beginning pages of the first book until you come to a phrase or line that you would like to use to begin your poem. Then in the next book, go a little further inside the book and scan looking for a phrase that begins with the same sound as the last word of the first line. Use alliteration. If you ended a line with "not," maybe you would start the next line with "now." Then keep working through the books until you have fourteen lines. A found sonnet. A collaged sonnet. You may decide to play a bit with your lines (rearranging a little), tinkering a little with verbs or connectors to make the grammar work. Make the lines connect with each other. Go ahead tinker! Maybe you will write two or three poems using this technique.

Background / Examples

Some years ago, my friend—and often time collaborator—Miranda Maher and I were out to dinner talking about her new project. She was planning an installation, asking a limited number of friends to write a line about each of their books; then she planned to clip the corner off each of the books. Miranda's installation never evolved into a finished project, but I become consumed with the idea. I couldn't write a sentence or a phrase; I tried, but the result was too explanatory, too much about the book rather than evolving out of the language. So instead I selected 999 books and invented a process of taking a line or phrase out of each book. In the first book, I scanned a few pages and I began looking for a line. After that I went to the next book with the last word in the first line in mind, and I began looking for a word that started with the same sound. As I went through the books, at first I took passages from the beginning, slowly moving into the middle of the next book, and then the end sections of the final books. I constructed the poem by taking a word, a phrase, or passage or two from each of these books, using alliteration as the knot between the lines, and then finally allowing myself the freedom to end and begin each line where I wanted, often letting the alliteration fall away, but leaving the natural rhythm that either preceded or followed the sound. Most of the time, I made minimal changes. Sometimes I rearranged the lines. The surprise was that many of the poems took shape without much revision; one line seemed to find its partner effortlessly in the next book, from Agee, Artaud and Apollinaire to Zukofsky and all the way into the kitchen to my cookbooks.

This was an objectivist project, a poem unfolding from found pieces of text, similar to Zukofsky's "Poem, Beginning 'The'" constructed from 330 lines taken from other texts. Or Reznikoff's "Testimony," a long text composed and transformed from passages he found in law books. For more information on the objectivists, see pages 50-62. Eventually I titled the book *My Autobiography,* and Miranda Maher made the cover, using some of the clipped corners. United Artists published it with an index in the back. Below is the fourth and the final sonnet, #72, as well as the index for the poems.

from *My Autobiography*

4

one is tempted to add as a postscript
color slides of the warm climates

perhaps its hard brown crust
kamikakazes mixed

moon poppies backdrop
billions. Of course it also explains why

the baboons have all been dead for ages
a sentence says you know

the middle ground of care in particulars
requires a firm wham of the fingers

family finances, everything but desire
it always struck me as a bit ludicrous

later I learned that he was only twenty
take off your head; un-loose your duck

72

through it all, Yudhistra
went out in the hot sun

the infinite pilgrimage
obstacles we have gone through

with paper, separate and inside
figures ducking carelessly

on the threads of midnight
an indispensable sea

it's an old experience
a tall birth appearing

sideways increasing error
darling, the salt rum

can barely project the title
in this house experimental

~

4

Margery Evans	Baudelaire and Intertextuality
Charles Baxter	Imaginary Paintings
Charles Baxter	The South Dakota Guidebook
Paul Beatty	Big Bank Takes Little Bank
Martine Bellen	10 Greek Poems
Michael Benedikt	Night Cries
Kenneth Bernard	The Baboon in the Nightclub
Charles Bernstein	Content's Dream
Charles Bernstein	A Poetics
Anne Waldman	Nice to See You: Homage to Ted Berrigan
Ed Foster	Code of the West: Memoir of Ted Berrigan
Aaron Fischer	Ted Berrigan: An Annotated Checklist
Ron Padgett	Ted: Personal Memoir of Ted Berrigan
Ted Berrigan	A Certain Slant of Sunlight

72

R. K. Narayan	The Mahabharata
Donald Keene	Anthology of Japanese Literature
Rabindranath Tagore	Songs of Kabir
Haruki Murakami	Sputnik Sweetheart
Muhammad Umar Memon	The Tale of the Old Fisherman
Roland Barthes; Ted Berrigan; S. Foster Damon	A Lover's Discourse; A Certain Slant of Sunlight; A Blake Dictionary
Allen Ginsberg; Mitch Highfill	Howl; Liquid Affairs
Nicole Brossard	Picture Theory
Harry Mathews	Immeasurable Distances
Charles Olson; Toni Morrison	Reading at Berkeley; Jazz
Tyrone Williams; G. Leech; Louis Zukofsky	Callaloo, 22.1; A Linguistic Guide; Complete Short Poetry
Dennis Teichman	Edge to Edge
Douglas Messerli	Language Poetries
James Agee; Alan Young	Let Us Praise These Famous Men; Dada and After

As you can see, in the last poem, the alliteration remained only in the drafts. Later I worked on a similar project but instead wrote a lengthy story (using about 200 lines from books), entitled "The Dinner," inventing a narrative between the lines. It was published by Talisman and then included in the book, *A Swift Passage* (Quale Press).

Notes

Henning, Barbara. "4" and "72." *My Autobiography,* United Artists, 2007.

Henning, Barbara. "The Dinner." *A Swift Passage,* Quale Press, 2013, pp. 103-130. Originally published in *Talisman, #38. 39, 40: Summer 2010.*

Reznikoff, Charles. "Testimony." *The Complete Poems of Charles Reznikoff,* Black Sparrow, 1976.

Zukofsky, Louis. "Poem Beginning 'The.'" *All: The Collected Short Poems (1923-1958),* Norton, 1965.

#7: Repetition and the Pantoum

M C Escher 1943 Reptiles

Prompt

Go through your journals excerpting lines that you like, as many as possible. Sort between your haiku-like imagistic descriptive lines and your more abstract/general lines. Then write a pantoum, making four line stanzas, the second and fourth lines of each stanza becoming the first and third of the next. You may then circle around so that the 2nd line and the 4th line of the last stanza become the 1st and the 3rd lines of the first stanza.

Feel free to invent new lines (not necessarily in your journal). Your poem can be any length, long or short. Or if the pantoum doesn't work for you, you might invent your own way of working with repetition. Perhaps read Allen Ginsberg and Walt Whitman for other ideas for working with repetition.

Background / Examples

A pantoum is a very old form, originally from Malaysia. When it was still a folk form, the couplets would be rhymed, probably as an aid to memory. Later the rhyming disappeared. Often writers make tiny adjustments in the repetition of lines so that the grammar and logic of the poem works.

I was first inspired to try the form after reading **John Ashbery's** pantoum, "Hotel Lautréamont." Somewhere I read that besides the pattern of repetition in the lines of the pantoum, there was often a play between the concrete and the more general. Maybe Ashbery talked about this in an interview somewhere. If you would like to hear him reading and discussing this poem, go the Poetry Foundation website. A link is in the notes. The back of his book offers some context for reading his poem:

> John Ashbery's title *Hotel Lautréamont* alludes to the psedonymous Comte de Lautréamont, a nineteenth century poet remembered for his epic prose poem *The Songs of Maldoror.* Little is known about him, save his real name (Isidore Ducasse) and that he spent his brief adult life in various hotels in Paris, checking out of his transient existence in 1870 at the age of twenty-four.

I remember taking my journal that I had just finished, excerpting lines that I liked and then dividing them into two lists, one of those tending toward concrete/particular and the other more general/abstract. Then I used the pantoum form and started weaving the lines. In the first stanza, line 1 and 3 had concrete (or particular) images while lines 2 and 4 would be more general (or perhaps abstract); then that pattern would reverse in the following stanzas." I wrote two pantoums,"Central Booking" and "In a Lavender Room." They were later published in a chapbook, *Me & My Dog.*

JOHN ASHBERY
HOTEL LAUTRÉAMONT

1.

Research has shown that ballads were produced by all of society
working as a team. They didn't just happen. There was no guesswork.
The people, then, knew what they wanted and how to get it.
We see the results in works as diverse as "Windsor Forest" and "The Wife of Usher's Well."

Working as a team, they didn't just happen. There was no guesswork.
The horns of elfland swing past, and in a few seconds
We see the results in works as diverse as "Windsor Forest" and "The Wife of Usher's Well,"
or, on a more modern note, in the finale of the Sibelius violin concerto.

The horns of elfland swing past, and in a few seconds
The world, as we know it, sinks into dementia, proving narrative passé,
or in the finale of the Sibelius violin concerto.
Not to worry, many hands are making work light again.

The world, as we know it, sinks into dementia, proving narrative passé.
In any case the ruling was long overdue.
Not to worry, many hands are making work light again,
so we stay indoors. The quest was only another adventure.

2.

In any case, the ruling was long overdue.
The people are beside themselves with rapture
so we stay indoors. The quest was only another adventure
and the solution problematic, at any rate far off in the future.

The people are beside themselves with rapture
yet no one thinks to question the source of so much collective euphoria,
and the solution: problematic, at any rate far off in the future.
The saxophone wails, the martini glass is drained.

Yet no one thinks to question the source of so much collective euphoria.
In troubled times one looked to the shaman or priest for comfort and counsel.
The saxophone wails, the martini glass is drained,
And night like black swansdown settles on the city.

In troubled times one looked to the shaman or priest for comfort and counsel
Now, only the willing are fated to receive death as a reward,
and night like black swansdown settles on the city.
If we tried to leave, would being naked help us?

3.

Now, only the willing are fated to receive death as a reward.
Children twist hula-hoops, imagining a door to the outside.
If we tried to leave, would being naked help us?
And what of older, lighter concerns? What of the river?

Children twist hula-hoops, imagining a door to the outside,
when all we think of is how much we can carry with us.
And what of older, lighter concerns? What of the river?
All the behemoths have filed through the maze of time.

When all we think of is how much we can carry with us
Small wonder that those at home sit, nervous, by the unlit grate.
All the behemoths have filed through the maze of time.
It remains for us to come to terms with *our* commonality.

Small wonder that those at home sit nervous by the unlit grate.
It was their choice, after all, that spurred us to feats of the imagination.
It remains for us to come to terms with our commonality
And in so doing deprive time of further hostages.

4.

It was their choice, after all, that spurred us to feats of the imagination.
Now, silently as one mounts a stair we emerge into the open
and in so doing deprive time of further hostages,
to end the standoff that history long ago began.

Now, silently as one mounts a stair we emerge into the open
but it is shrouded, veiled: We must have made some ghastly error.
To end the standoff that history long ago began
Must we thrust ever onward, into perversity?

But it is shrouded, veiled: We must have made some ghastly error.
You mop your forehead with a rose, recommending its thorns.
Must we thrust ever onward, into perversity?
Only night knows for sure; the secret is safe with her.

You mop your forehead with a rose, recommending its thorns.
Research has shown that ballads were produced by all of society;
Only night knows for sure. The secret is safe with her:
The people, then, knew what they wanted and how to get it.

~

BARBARA HENNING
CENTRAL BOOKING

1.

Everyday decisions of the modern city dweller
are becoming almost completely a matter of habit
Predictably, the human female ceases to be seasonal
while many children are chronically undernourished

Becoming almost completely a matter of habit
the pyramid texts warn happiness depends on self discipline
While many children are chronically undernourished
I would rather be a work of art than own one

The pyramid texts warn happiness depends on self discipline
She seats herself comfortably in an armchair
I would rather be a work of art than own one
With one machine turned off, an even quieter buzzing

She seats herself comfortably in an armchair
waiting for the flow of the universe to come uncaged
With one machine turned off, an even quieter buzzing
Little promises are always broken

Waiting for the flow of the universe to come uncaged
slave traders are less likely to slaughter their captives
Little promises are always broken
Don't tell a soul about it

2.

Slave traders are less likely to slaughter their captives
administering one punishment to cure the effects of another
Don't tell a soul about it
The definition of duration implies pain

Administering one punishment to cure the effects of another
Last week he was dying. Today he's in a holding cell
The definition of duration implies pain
and no one ever answers the telephone at central booking

Last week he was dying. Today he's in a holding cell
The books are condemned and sent to prison in a boat
and no one ever answers the telephone at central booking
The habit of hunting still in our blood

The books are condemned and sent to prison in a boat
Ants keep crawling over our legs like Lisa's sea lyrics
The habit of hunting still in their blood
identity flowing along with the waves

Ants keep crawling over our legs like Lisa's sea lyrics
Freud made cocaine a cure for morphine addiction
identity flowing along with the waves
Kenneth Rexroth read an entire shelf of Britannica

Freud made cocaine a cure for morphine addiction
I used to scorn nature poems, but now
and then he read an entire shelf of Britannica
We're sleeping and his hands smell like an old ashtray

I used to scorn nature poems, but now
four hundred are waiting in a cell and the computer's down
We're sleeping and his hands smell like an old ashtray
The rich managed to survive. The poor died by the thousands

3.

Four hundred are waiting in a cell and the computer—
Do we need to feel as if we are getting somewhere?
The rich managed to survive. The poor died by the thousands
Yet a disaster always has some creative outcome

Do we need to feel as if we are getting somewhere?
My reading list extends beyond this life's possibility
Yet a disaster always has some creative outcome
Sleep comes over me with the blanket

My reading list extends beyond this life's possibility
A modern day authority is a floating credit report
Sleep comes over me with the blanket
They gather data on your character and then sell it

A modern day authority is a floating credit report
I shut a window in one room and then in the next
they gather data on your character and then sell it
Even so the heat of summer is falling off the globe

I shut a window in one room and then in the next
the everyday decisions of the modern city dweller
Even so the heat of summer is falling off the globe
and predictably the human female ceases to be seasonal

~

NOTES

Ashbery, John. "Hotel Lautréamont." *Hotel Lautréamont,* Alfred A. Knopf, Sept. 1992, 14-16.

Henning, Barbara. "Central Booking." *Me & My Dog,* Meeting Eyes Bindery, 1999, 13-14, 17-19.

#8: Quilting and Migrating

Background / Examples

In 2007 or 2008, I finished a journal and put together a series of poems that I later called "Twirling: The Spirit Flies Off Like A Falcon." The poem is in *Cities and Memories* (Chax Press). In the early process, I selected several words in each poem in the series and then quilted them into the next poem and so forth all the way to the end and back to the beginning. Sometimes the newly collaged words or phrases would just appear and give a kind of chant like effect to the next poem. When writing, I was very conscious of the effects of manipulating syntax so that at times there might be a slippery surprise.

I also incorporated research. With "Twirling," for example, we were at war with Iraq/Afghanistan at the time and I wanted the awareness of that situation to be in the poem. (I had very strong feelings and ideas about the war, especially since I had a friend who was in Afghanistan working on women's rights.) I selected certain words in each poem and searched on the internet or in *The Times Archives* for the words and either "Iraq" or "Afghanistan." Then I spliced some of the material I found (usually a few words or phrases here and there) into the poem. So there would be Tucson (or wherever I happened to be at the time—Detroit, Upper Michigan, New York City, wherever) and also Kabul or Baghdad.

I also used a similar process with a few other serial poems published in *A Swift Passage*: "Twelve Green Rooms" focused on the Gulf oil disaster; "A Swift Passage" on migration; and in "A Slow Curve," I collaged words and phrases from a story by Bobbie Louise Hawkins.

Below are five from "Twelve Green Rooms." At the end I describe the process of writing this serial poem.

from TWELVE GREEN ROOMS

Third Street, Tucson

The light is white today and the oranges are glistening with rain water. Orange trees were brought here by the Spaniards, along with the Jesuit missions. Today the birds are quieter than usual. Maybe when they sing a lot, it's because they are thirsty. The Santa Cruz used to flow year round, but then ranchers gold miners farmers   population   suburban   water drain   sprawl   On Third Street, a young man comes out of a seven bedroom house to smoke on the porch. I pass under a big sparse tree with low branches, so old and just standing there, one of the tallest trees in the neighborhood. It appears deciduous, but in fact it's a low pine, an Allepo, an ancient tree from the Mediterranean. The estimated appraisal value is well over $20,000. Brought to Tucson as seedlings by a gas station as a gimmick 70 years ago   too much   too little   water flows from the Colorado River to the Gulf of California and Tucson gardens   overflow downpour   perennial springs   irrigation tree-lined   rivulet   monsoon   riverbed   barren   run dry

Stein says that the work of man is not in harmony with the landscape, it opposes it and that is the basis of cubism. Peddling along, I look down at my blue socks, one higher than the other. No city money for street repair this year, but instead an incredible pattern of intersecting cracks and potholes.

Bayport, Long Island

A shock of black hair, little cleft chin, round face, little feet like a fish. Pelican. Pelican. Pelican. Two weeks later he is more than one-third larger. One day he'll be over six feet. With a ten foot wing span and a layer of webbed fibers. Throat pouches full of water   fish oceanic   ripple   spill   sentient   brim over   full over   The terns are fragile little birds, one dive into the oily water and they don't resurface. I take the baby into the kitchen, and then in the red glow of the night light, we sway that baby sway. Pelicaniformas, ancient symbol of   spill out   spill over   Later I come down the stairs for a glass of water. In the dark, the tv is on with no sound and Greg is stretched out in the chair, his big line-backer body and the infant curled up in his armpit, both sound asleep. Half a mile south, the Atlantic laps against the shore.

Barrett Avenue

Linnée sits cross-legged on the sofa nursing the baby. Little Luke starts zipping and unzipping my vest. I put his two little stuffed rabbits inside my vest and zip them in. I'm pregnant I say. I'm pink. His eyes light up and then unzip—two babies! He looks at Né nursing Logan, and then back at me. I unzip his pjs and put the babies in there. Luke is pregnant. Where is Luke? I play it on the piano. Full of glee, he's shaking, laughing and running in circles. Come outside and help me plant these flowers. It's windy. The wind is lifting his curls. He picks the hyacinth up by the stem, breaking off the roots and then he walks across the yard, holding the purple flower. Yesterday, nearly 60 pelican chicks washed onto an island in coastal Louisiana, fragile, wading into oily puddles or smeared by oil from their parents' feathers   floating too much   too little   down to the ocean   A crown of plastic flowers for British Petroleum   In the park, an old woman holds a string and a bat kite flying high up in the sky. Her daughter says— she keeps everything. It was mine when I was a child. Oil is used to make plastic, preservatives, food packaging, hair curlers, telephones, televisions, balloons, ammonia, insect repellent, heart valves, trash bags, body bags, but not paper kites and cotton string. Luke runs out into the center of the field, watching it waver back and forth   eons oh   sand   oh   pressure   oh my sword   oh the tempest squall   hurricane   oceanic   subaquatic   At dusk, Luke takes me by my hand and we walk slowly down the street under the big maple trees.

Deepwater Horizon

Unable to fly, float, escape or find food—irritation, vomiting, diarrhea, oil aspiration, ulceration, skin death, confusion, vertigo tremors, seizures, cardiac arrest, hemolytic anemia, liver and kidney damage, sudden death, chemical pneumonitis, choking, coughing, gagging, swelling, bronchospasms, bleeding, fever. For long haired animals and birds it is worse. The chemical dispersants break the oil into tiny droplets, causing irritation, inflammation, headaches, genetic damage and mutations, difficulty breathing, vomiting, kidney and liver damage. *Baby turtles leave their sandy nests and head straight for the sea knowing everything a turtle needs to know*   wavering back and forth   spread out   spill over   brim over   The largest fish on earth are four miles from the leaking wellhead. From Belize to Hondouras to Alabama. *They filter plankton and tiny fish from the water through sieve-like mechanisms in their mouths*. Each animal particular. Like a fingerprint. When the whale shark dies it disappears, sinking to the bottom of the sea   plastic   lifting   too much   too little wavering back and forth   When one animal is extinct another proliferates. Biodiversity. The bristel worm is churning up the bacteria

245

on the sea floor. The fishermen will die or relocate. And beach houses in Texas keep tar sandals as regular guest items, the oil just a nuisance, after all BP has been good to them, pouring money into their economy, and so they vote, yes, yes, yes.

Between the Sound and the Atlantic

The criminals have been found and law and order and the stars and actors are passing in front of the screen as their mortality is documented. I'm in the rocker with a newspaper on my lap remembering this and that and then I remember my grandmother sitting in her chair weeping about her dead friends as we were chasing each other around the house, passing her by, six, nine, eleven, and twelve. Then she'd sit up, start yodeling—yo-dli-oh-laa-haa-dee—and she'd take a newspaper and reach out and whack us as we passed her by. Ecstatic. Static. Wet. Rivulet. Inlet. Droplet. We keep going until the last word and then someone else finishes the sentence and starts another. Maybe tomorrow. I pick up the newspaper and start reading about the oil spill, a photo of a dead baby pelican on the front page. Maybe tomorrow. Lolo can't walk yet but he stands next to the sofa, sways, claps and hums to music. That's the way children's language takes shape, I think, as a shadow that slowly gains detail and then the sun goes behind a cloud, and I drift off for a moment, coasting over the deep water horizon and then slipping into a hot oil slick. When the man leans over the bird, carefully wiping off the oil, she turns her head to the side. Then from the shadow another sound emerges   a squawk   gush   surge   2100   get to   well I will   As the ice cap melts and the sea level rises   squawk   well I will perhaps the pelicans will   multiply   20 million years   pelicanus squawk   gush surge   flying   *well I will*   clumsy   graceful ungainly   and their ancestors will   majestically fly   too much too little   over our flooded shores and cities

After excerpting vignettes from my journal, editing them until I liked the way time and space were woven, then cracking apart the narratives, splicing in words and phrases from research about the oil spill, water pollution, shortages and the effects on animals—after all this, I excerpted words in the shape of a W from each piece and then wove them into the next one. I am now calling this process sequential quilting. Written in 2009-2010, the final quilting took place in summer 2010 in Marquette Michigan, next to Lake Superior, one of the largest freshwater lakes in the world. The water on earth and in our animal human bodies plants lands air is the same water that was here when the dinosaurs were lumbering   water   sound earth   ether   moving   reassembling   to destroy   re story call forth   again   om nama shivaya

NOTES

Henning, Barbara. "Twelve Green Rooms," *A Swift Passage,* Quale Press, 2013, pp. 3-14. Also published in *Poets Gulf Coast, 2010,* https://poetsgulf-coast.wordpress.com/2010/08/22/three-poems-by-barbara-henning/.

Henning, Barbara. "Twirling the Spirit Flies Off Like a Falcon." *Cities & Memory,* Chax Press, 2010, pp. 75-91.

#9: Detective Motifs

Prompt

Go to the library (or find a way to search online in newspaper archives); research obituaries and articles for everyone you know who has died. If you are older and the list is too long, narrow your search to a particular group. Collect your data in your journal and write about memories related to each person. Then make a list of some of the categories for detective fiction (or make up your own categories). Then clip apart your notes and data looking for promising narratives, images, and words. Sort, arrange and form poems. Perhaps work against getting too morbid.

Background / Examples:

When my father died in 1996, I was in Detroit for a few weeks. After the funeral, I decided to research obituaries for friends, family and colleagues. In the main Detroit Public Library on Woodward Avenue, I went through old newspapers and took notes. Meanwhile in my journal I explored memories and thoughts about death. At the time, I was in my late 40s.

Back home in New York City, I was teaching a course on detective fiction. So when I came home, I merged the two interests. I made a list of motifs. I don't have the draft for these poems anymore so I'm just guessing that the list might have been something like this: (1) A crime: there must be a corpse, (2) A detective-seeker, (3) Investigation, (4) A baffling puzzling situation, (5) Clues and motives, (6) Analysis, (7) Inevitable solution and (8) Resolution.

Then I took the journal with all my notes on the obituaries and whatever else I had been thinking about that month, and I went through it and typed up whatever I thought was interesting, poetic, moving, whatever struck me. I wasn't working with the internet like we do now, so I clipped away with scissors, cutting the text into pieces. Then I sorted them into piles, one for each motif.

Again, I wasn't a purist. If it seemed puzzling, it went into the puzzle file. If it seemed like a motive or clue, it went into that file. It could have been a bee buzzing around a flower, and I might have put it into "Investigation." I don't know what I did exactly, but I know that I was inventive with the category decisions.

Previously in other poems, I had done this same type of inquiry with journaling, cutting and sorting into various categories; one time I worked with Lacanian categories, studying and writing about Diane Arbus photographs; the poem was entitled, "Watching Things Work" and was later published in *Lacanian Ink*.

Below are three poems from the series of seven poems. "Detective Sentences," later published in a collection, entitled, *Detective Sentences* (Spuyten Duyvil); "Closure & Closure" was published by *The Paris Review* in Fall 1997 and reprinted as the "Daily Poem" on January 23, 2020.

Barbara Henning
Detective Sentences

> A sentence is an interval in which there is a finally forward and back. A sentence is an interval during which if there is a difficulty they will do away with it. A sentence is a part of the way when they wish to be secure.   Gertrude Stein

Closure & Closure

The newborn fell asleep beside her mother who died in the early morning from
      a blood clot in her brain.
Quiet and lovely, Beth's death was a loss for millions of little girls.

Their bodies were found five miles apart in the kitchens of their homes.
The boy's mother died on a kidney machine. He died at nineteen from a virus.

He drank too much one night and then died from an overdose.
He was shot in the back. The other was stabbed and slashed repeatedly.

He passed through the door of the hotel with a little pistol in his pocket.
Both were bachelors. Both lived alone. Both were discovered at 8 a.m.

The deadly fire they started in the rafters spread to his crib.
My feathers ruffle. There's no record of his death, but he died.

Things get better, get worse and then your body is cold and stiff on a
        table in the mortician's room.
Your feet, once tucked into your mother's body, warm and slippery, are now
        hidden inside a box.

THE MISTAKEN GINA ARBOR

With terrible guilt and financial loss, they moved to Florida.
I woke up thinking about the possibility of divine meanness.

Mose Allison reminds me of Allen bopping around Detroit.
He drinks a bottle of chalky syrup for the catscan.

When those around you understand your jokes, you are home.
Under a pseudonym, there remains the possibility of absolute honesty.

The stranger spoke to me about my handwriting.
The guy at the next table talks into a cordless phone and burps.

He would be doing her a favor if he broke up with her.
This is someone who can take care of herself.

After she married a Presbyterian, her father disinherited her.
At age ninety he moved back in and let her nurse him to his death.

She spent the rest of her life refusing to write poems.
Mathilda Unknown is at the top of my list of ancestors.

MOTHERESE

I put my left hand on his forehead, my right on his folded hands and I said goodbye.
He never visited you because he was afraid of the neighborhoods where you lived.

A flurry of white supremacist propaganda and graffiti, a Cadillac post-office box.
In order to drink a glass of water, your heart must be strong enough to pump it.

Everything parched takes a drink.
If she had never died, everything would have been so different.

Words linked together stretch out to form a series of sentences.
Something distracts.

A letter from the landlord informing the tenant he is a health hazard—
The police return my television set wrapped up in newspaper and plastic.

A whole new situation's unfolding, cards up.
I wonder if they ever find the murderer.

It's all a matter of numbers explains the insurance investigator.
You can live a long time. Now I want to go to sleep.

NOTES

Henning, Barbara. "Detective Sentences." *Detective Sentences,* Spuyten Duyvil, 2001, pp. 49-55.

Henning, Barbara. "Watching Things Work. *Love Makes Thinking Dark*. United Artists, 1995. 74-80.

#10: Oulipo Constraints

Prompt

Write a paragraph story or prose poem about some something that happened to you when you were a teenager or a young adult. Capture one moment, and perhaps an earlier memory. Then transform the poem using a few of the constraints below.

Background / Examples

OULIPO is short for *Ouvroir de Litterature Potentielle*. A group of post-surrealist writers (lovers of literary madness) initially formed the group in 1961. In *Oulipo: A Primer for Potential Literature*, Noel Arnaud writes, "We call potential literature the search for new forms and structures which may be used by writers in any way they see fit." Some of the early members included Georges Perec, Jacques Roubaud, Italo Calvino, Michèle Métail and the American writer, Harry Mathews. One of the ideas is to apply mathematical constraints to language or to "put machines to poetic use." Most were purists, rarely wavering from the rules. I find using constraints like these, however, as also useful in the beginning of a writing project. Even when following the rules, you are not rule *bound* because most of the experiments can continue endlessly; you close whenever you close, tending toward multiplicity rather than singularity.

In the early 90s, **Harry Mathews** compiled a list of OULIPO constraints and circulated it among poets at the Poetry Project. When Lynn Crawford gave me a copy of the list, I took an earlier poem from my first book, *Smoking in the Twilight Bar*, "Satin Ribbons" and transformed it into seven different poems, titling the final series, "Fabric Reins." I never used those particular constraints again, but after working on this project, I suddenly had many new ideas for experimenting with language. I still have the Mathews handout; it is crumpled up and faded, but I managed to keep some of it. See below for some of his constraints.

In my poem for the N+7 and LSD prompts, I used a Webster dictionary as well as an old comic dictionary. In one of my poems, my mind became a

252

"causal" dictionary and I rewrote the poem searching for the root causes/in-fluences of the words in the poems. In another I broke it down into parts of speech with some kind of dictionary (I don't now recall). In the last stanza, I transformed my poem, using the syntax of Hamlet's last speech.

I read "Fabric Reins" a couple of times at the Nuyorican Poets café in the early 90s for Bob Holman's poetry slams, dressing in black lace, reading from a big ornate aristocratic looking velvet folder with gold trim (made by the artist Sally Young). It was my performance poetry year. The poem is below.

SMOKING IN THE TWILIGHT BAR

BARBARA HENNING

Photo by Harriette Hartigan

BARBARA HENNING
FABRIC REINS

A strobe spins light on the girl's black velvet skirt and high heels. She stands in the middle of a ballroom, listens to Lorraine talk about the man who used to tie her up with satin ribbons. And she's amazed at the design the wrinkles form around her eyes, like snowflakes. They remind her of her mother's eyes when she was dying on the sofa. She picked up a high heel, threw it, put a crack in the plaster. The girl stood across the room, looking at the lines on the walls, at her mother's wrinkles, and listening to her moan. Father would not wake up. Satin ribbons, satin ribbons and wrinkles.

*

With back erect, she weaves her open ear closer to the full-bodied dancer who sings of the hero who once bound her with cords of satin. So much more than just a recognition, the duplication of lapping and looping white pressed around the lights like snow-covered hills. As if with the turning of the globe, the leaf on the ground, the axis is lost: the landscape of a leg, heels nailed to the bed, the wild child looking through the keyhole. The other in the mirror. In the mirror, putting on lipstick—

*

And garments of vengeance while the sun stands still and the moon keeps a bird's-eye view of the upper room where men talk. My waters are bound up in their thick clouds even though I have lost my children and am desolate with the unprofitable talk. The only thing worse than being talked about is being born into trouble—he comes along and ties me on the fringe with a band of blue. Some girls die young, couch as couch can be, easier to pick up, harder to drop, like a low shoe or an eye for an eye: what every young man should know, neither written nor spoken—if at first you don't you will always know how they cry and throw dust into the air. If he wants his dreams to come true, he must wake up and fill me with wind. some people wake up and find themselves female. Others wake up and find themselves late. or a pretty package just for Adam and his ribbon of blue—

*

a statement of happening   a well-proportioned sentence   stillness   breathing   quiet at the same time a preposition qualifying another related group of words   a rhetorical conclusion   added emotional phrases and images   placed in or occupying a lower position   pause and rest   compare to elsewhere   a pronounced memory   of some other submissive image   the object conclud-

ed shut up   one other Capitalized past action   inhale   more
action   exhale again the repetitive result: a position prefaced
STOP   Another time inaction   stupor   breathe the image   the
breath   the sound   A DIVIDING HALT   the Capital's habitu-
ally negative action finished   a comma fault   a thing   a thing

*

A strobe spins light on the girl's black velvet skirt and high heels. A
stroke spins a light emitting diode on Gisarme's black velvet skiv-
vy and high Hegelians. She stands in the middle of a ballroom, in
the middle distance of baloney, near the balm of Gilead, listening
to Lorraine talk about the man who used to tie her up with satin
ribbons, listening to the loss ratio talk about the management
who used to tie her up with riboflavin. And she's amazed at the
design the wrinkles form around Lorraine's eyes, like snowflakes.
And she's amazed at the desirability of the writs forming around
the loss ratio, like snow mold. They remind her of her mother's eyes when she was dying on the sofa. They remind her of
her mother-in-law's eyeful when she was dying on the soft drink.
Mother picked up a high heel, threw it. Motherhouse picked up a
high Hegelian, threw him, put a crack in the plaster, a crackpot in
the plasticity. The girl stood across the room, looking at the lines
of the walls, at her mother's wrinkles, and listening to her moan.
Gisarme stood across the roost, looking at the linear equation on
the wall creeper, at her mother-in-law's writ, and listening to her
moan.   Father would not wake up. Fathom would not wake up.
Father Time would not wake up. Satin ribbons, satin riboflavin,
satin ribgrass and highspeed light—

*

Plunging through the young woman's sinister garment and her
contemptible soul, that upright object regarded as female gives an
ear in the midst of a large room for dances to a cross who offers
secret information about the primate with his highly developed

brain and faculty for abstract thought, the particular primate who once tied knots in her horizontal arms with glossy fabric. The young female is bewildered by the patterned ridges taking shape around the organs of sight lodged tightly in her bony orbit, like feathery crystals. This plural of indefinite thirds brings to mind the spherical organs of her female parent as she too longed desperately to pass into an inferior state on the upholstered couch. The head of the establishment learned in a casual manner of a grave sole hurled violently with an abrupt erratic shift into a pasty preparation applied to the body, as a curative, a counter irritant. The woman of any age remains across the partitioned inside of the living quarters, directing her eyes at the elongated mark drawn at the boundary of the slimy substance formed by bacteria as the skin puckers due to age, and an unexpected sound occurs, a lamentation. the man who had begotten this child will not rouse. The inventor will not keep watch or vigil. Glossy and dull long narrow strips, creases in the skin, fabric reins for controlling an animal.

*

This distraction is of metal, rock, oil, space, labor, time, unknown wars, of brick, of paint and stone. My distraction is body, hands, that which is seen, in this case, a membrane, the vibrations and nuances of melody and rhythm—in one and out the other. This stillness born of chaos, the connection that presupposes two others and a woven fabric, cut into strips, polished and sold by the yard. An animal's skin drawn tightly over the toe and hurdled into an enclosure built by someone else's grandfather. A declaration of awe, after eating, after talking, after thinking: born of my mother's mother, departed for the margin in black, not white, not yellow, not red, but everything, in a factory or a sweat shop or torn from the antler of a deer, locked in battle, woven by women in fields and factories, as opposed to our parents' slippery cohabitation. If we place her in full form on the couch, asleep, she will wake up and die. An opening is something flat like mother's love, static bound by father's remorse. And so the sound of my lungs, the first words uttered and directed toward the gender of my friend. Listen: I think green, no beige, the warm linoleum beneath my ant-infested bed, the pattern of the fabric laid out perfect and geometric on my knees, tied up tight just for you and your pleasure—

*

Dark Pleasure—

Strobe light in the ballroom, oh distract me!
Listen,
Once you were bound with satin. Still,
I who stay by the side in black velvet
am amazed with the likeness
of my mother's lines to yours—
If we could but place her on the couch again
Her eyes, your eyes, her high heel
thrown across the room—
A crack in the wall. Lorraine, I feel dead
with these ribbons: Father would not wake up
or listen to me and my mother weeping,
now silence—

Please speak, like patterned snowflakes
tell me of her shape again, reclining
and of this man with his tight cords—
All for my pleasure

~

from HARRY MATHEWS' HANDOUT

The N+ 7 Method.

In the method called N + 7, N stands for "noun." And +7 means that in a given text each noun is replaced by the seventh noun following it in a dictionary of one's choice . E.g. ,

> To be or not to be — that is the quickness .

(The choice of a dictionary is—at least apparently—the user's only chance of exercising his or her freedom, and it should not be taken lightly. The basic rule to remember is that the larger the dictionary. the smaller the changes and vice versa: e.g., head/header and head/heap.)

The Eclipse

An eclipse combines the results of the N+7 with the source text from which they are derived.

I loaded my pockets with stones. I loaded my poets with stopgaps.

LSD

This acronym stands for litterature semo-definitionelle, or semo-definitional literature. The words of a chosen passage are replaced by their dictionary definitions with a view to producing a text not only longer than the initial one but radically different in meaning and/or style. The process of substitution can be exploited several times although, after the third, length may become a problem.

Homosyntaxism.

In its original form homosyotaxism requires the replacement of all words in a given text (usually selected because of its curiosity or the interest of its author) by other words belonging to the same grammatical category—nouns by nouns, verbs by verbs, and so forth. This is most easily done by making as an intermediary step a syntactical translation or scheme of the original text.

    I   like   cheese.
    pr   v   n

From this one can complete the process more readily oblivious of one's point of departure:

    pr   v   n
    They industrialized handicrafts.

. . . it is not necessary to replicate the original text word by word—adverbs, for instance, can be replaced by adverbial phrases and vice versa. Nor need one change every word: common words such as "and" more usefully survive the process than be turned into "but's and "or's" (although of course they can be.)

An example:

    In this case the restaurant should be no problem. Almost any place not currently in violation of the health code will do.

    Afterward the car was a relief. The various comforts generally forgotten in clement weather were consoling.

The Chimaera

This procedure requires two texts of approximately equal length. From one of them, the nouns, verbs, and adjectives are removed and their places accordingly marked. A list is then made of the nouns, verbs and adjectives of the second text in the order in which they appear, and in that order are introduced into the first text to replace the original words. The punctuation of the first text is maintained.

The Lipogram

The Lipogram has a long history: it was apparently first used in the second half of the sixth century B.C. by Pindar's master Lasos of Hermione. The procedure requires foregoing one or more letters when writing. If Shakespeare had been lipograrnatically inclined. he might have written: ·

(without a)To be or not to be. this is the question
(without t) Being or nonbeing — such is our quandary
(without e) Survival or oblivion — that is our quandary

~

For other Oulipo inspired prose poems, see Mark Wallace (268) and Harryette Mullen (79.) Also, see Harry Mathews (133), Lynn Crawford (292) and Georges Perec's "Tale" (151).

Notes

Arnaud, Noel. "Forward." *Oulipo: A Primer for Potential Literature,* edited by Warren F. Motte, Jr., University of Nebraska Press ,1986, p. xiii.

Esar, Evan. *Esar's Comic Dictionary*. Harvest House, 1943.

Henning, Barbara. "Fabric Reins." *Love Makes Thinking Dark*, United Artists, 1995, pp. 62-67.

Mathews, Harry. Handout.

Shakespeare, William. "The Tragedy of Hamlet Prince of Denmark." *The Complete Signet Classic Shakespeare*, edited by Sylvan Barnet, Harcourt Brace, 1972.

INDEX OF POEMS, STORIES AND AUTHORS

Part One: Prose Poetry / Poetic Prose

Part Two: Flash Fiction

Part Three: Chronology of Mind

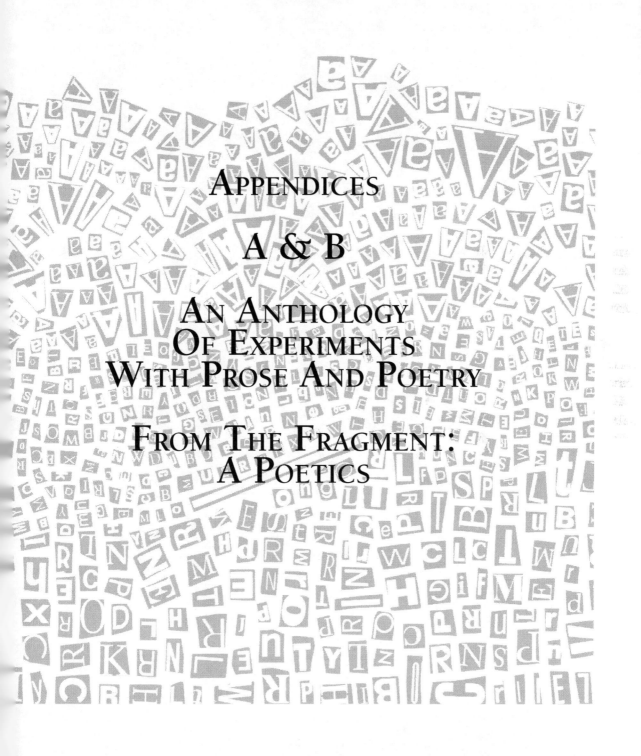

APPENDICES

A & B

AN ANTHOLOGY
OF EXPERIMENTS
WITH PROSE AND POETRY

FROM THE FRAGMENT:
A POETICS

Experiments
An Anthology Of Prose Poems And Poetic Prose

In 2003, I invited a group of poets I admired to each give me a prose poem and an assignment or a process note. I first used this anthology in the Prose Poem class I taught at Long Island University in Brooklyn. The anthology changed shape each time I taught the course. This is a selection from that ongoing project. Some of the process notes were mini-interviews I did with the poets. Some of the poets consider a prose poem a poem with a prosaic voice.

Contents

Diane Di Prima
Wisteria Light

In the early days of eternity when none of us was naked as yet, and a good thing too, I opted to plaster the back stairs. Not that the stairs wanted to be plastered, but I was certain that was the only way the billiard table would fit. Workmen dropped hammers here & there. You were vacuuming, by god, though the plaster wasn't dry, as if you were going to get an A for neatness. There were two slots in this greeting card, a kind of microchip it was, with Franz Kline wiring, not that we thought then that black & white would be a problem even for the moon. Our returning to the same haven as uncertain as coming out each time in a different one. No one distinguished between the blessed & the unblessed, no immortals had immigrated here for some time. I wanted to order wisteria, something to mitigate the light in those canyons. When you wisely pointed out it wouldn't grow there, I thought to murder you with the pail with which you were mopping the windows. I clearly saw brick walls, the red mellowing to yellow, or brown shingle shadowed with the ancient vines. I wanted none of those we had invited, whoever they were. Or the flat light they loved. I saw that clearly. Return to the present was an unhappy business, saturated as it was with murdered swallows. *I Vesperi Siciliani* slid into one slot, and I was afraid *Pagliacci* would find the other. And there we would be, like the king who drives his chariot around & around in that tiny courtyard, circles of paving stones without even a pear tree. Stuck as a crow on a telephone pole, once you've seen it, the pole is never again empty, there's always a crow, black in your mind's eye in front of the white sky before sunrise.

~

Process Note/Assignment: This poem happened immediately on waking from a dream in which much of the imagery occurred, but the dream slid painlessly together with what I saw out my window on waking, my study, my desk, etc., the pole where the crow or raven often sat (wasn't sitting then), etc. so that dream and writing and waking environment weren't separated out at all. Not only was one as "real" as the other, but they were really one thing. I suppose that could be an exercise, if people have dreams they remember, and can write as soon as they wake up.

Brenda Coultas
from *The Bowery Project*

Glass BeachTide was in and so looked at tree line of the landfill, could see bottles entwined in the roots, glass shards, and garbage compressed to a great density so as to become brown matter. I could see whole bottles that would be free in time and pulled one out, it had a brown liquid in it. Became entranced, curious if this was the original content. Or was it just rot and seawater? A newspaper from the 1940s was lying on some wood, intact except for the edges; in fact so fresh, one could easily turn the pages. I wondered if someone had wedged it out from the roots or had the waves worked it free. Some person who cared about such things as history had placed it there. In fact, there were other scavengers who worked the beach silently setting aside vintage pop bottles and curiosities in a safe place for others like us.

Picked up 2 toy guns, ink well, sm brw, sm brw, 2 wh cold creams. Went home. (July 27, 01, Glass Beach , Brooklyn)

We spoke to a man scratching the sand with a stick for marbles. He knew the history of this place, said it a was horse rendering plant and indeed on the map it said Dead Horse Bay, and it had been a city dump that became a town composed of the dump's employees, then the city closed it down stating it was too toxic to live in. Now it was an unmarked stretch of public beach that the residents returned to regularly and bitterly.

The old glass had a lot of lead and it gleamed. I tried not to be greedy and to take only what I could carry. Meanwhile I left thousands. The broken glass tinkled in the surf and if I ever were to believe in mermaids, this is where they'd be. (July 24,01)

Thought I'd never look like "money." (Aug. 1,01)
Looked in regular spot, nothing. (April 27,01)
Went to Coney Island with some poets. We had a good time although the garbage was unremarkable. (May 5,01)

70s fake Victorian settee with toaster oven and orange juicer in original box. (Aug. 30, 01, 2st & 2nd Ave)

Four panels of fake bookcases, 2 tabletops, glass chandelier, slightly broken, and man, with a cart painted blue and decorated with glamorous dolls, sizing it up. We stopped to discuss the objects. We guessed at the origin of them, maybe from the vaudeville days of a famous Bowery theater and shook our heads in shame that we couldn't take any of it with us although it was cool stuff. (Labor day weekend, 1st & Bowery).

Shopping cart painted red, metal 70s office chair. Man put small table in trash can and walked away. (Sept 4-01, Houston & Elizabeth)

From *A Handmade Museum*, Coffee House Press, 2003.

Process Note: The Bowery Project is centered on documenting and reacting to the layers of debris including human kind that layer the streets of the Bowery in NYC. Specify the brief section between Cooper Union and Houston, an area that contains the remnants of SRO hotels and the remains of the 1890s Bowery that are slated to be demolished by The Bowery Development Plan in the next decade. I live a block from this section and travel through it daily. It will no longer exist by 2010, the artist coop (Kate Millett lives there) that used to be McGurk's Suicide Hall (named so because prostitutes flung themselves out the windows in a symbolic protest of their working conditions), the Sunshine Hotel, and various soup kitchens will be extinct. My intent is not to romanticize the suffering or demonize the Bowery residents but rather to comment on poverty, class, suffering, and my own dilemma and identification as a teacher and poet one paycheck away from the street.

Bob Holman
Usher

This is the true story of an Usher who gets called to the stage when the star gets sick. It all happens so fast that she has to do the part while still dressed in her usher's uniform. But unbelievably, her performance is so great, so believable, that everyone in the audience swears they saw her wearing the star's red nightgown. In fact, so many people mention this that other people get suspicious, and finally the entire audience is ordered to undergo lie detector tests.

The audience members report to individual rooms for their polygraphs, while the friends and relatives who accompanied them wait in a huge antechamber. Here, after an initial tense silence, pleasant conversations are struck up. Through the idlest of chatter, certain similarities of habit of the audience members are noted, strange coincidences and patterns.

By the time the polygraphs are over, many discoveries have been made. When the audience members leave their tiny cubicles, those waiting for them clam up immediately. The audience members are sweaty, shaken, furtive; it is clear that many of them flunked the tests. Gradually, a giant conspiracy is uncovered, a conspiracy led by the Usher, who has developed a whole new theory of the theatre.

~

From *PANIC*DJ: Performance Text (Poems, Raps, Songs)*, University Arts Resources, 1988.

Process Note: I am always interested in how you get the sound (action) out of (off) the page. The Futurist performance pieces that have a part for the audience also woke me up, as Willie the Shake says, that we are but the players. What do we see when we see something that is something else (actor)? and especially the class shift to get the usher on the stage (she is, after all, the god who shows you your place in the world). So be it! A poem in disguise as prose, some theory for you "Thought is made in the mouth" (Tzara) types.

RICHARD HELL
THAT TO THE SIDES OF THE DARK SHINE THE THEORIES

Yesterday, late in the evening, I started feeling thick and heavy as if I were being pulled down, as if something deep underground had started to exert a new kind of gravity that was sucking my body and senses towards it, while my floating mind stayed above. I could hardly keep my eyelids raised and I had to lie down. Once I did that, my body hollowed and lightened, like a drawing of itself. My mind seemed to float loose while leaking into my body like molecules: sex, sax, six, socks, sucks... It was like my body liquified, then evaporated, the whole prehistoric breathing, and my mind was a rudderless little boat that drifted in it. I seeped and haltingly flowed according to the permeability and slant. In the puddles at the bottom of the boat was a tumbled messy litter of everything imaginable that had happened or could happen to me. How could it be so small? My senses seemed to have returned, but were caught in the contents of the boat, as if perception were engendered by those objects.[1] It seemed that if I looked at one item—a tan-colored lifesize hobbyshop model of a robin, for instance— everything else in the strew became possible, so that when my attention left the glued-together plastic bird, the items around it had become something other than what they'd been before. Oh, it was too beautiful, this surrender. It is the secret standard of worthiness. All who do it are good! My mind[2] opened and the boat, being one, the only, wasn't a boat.[3]

---

[1]Later I heard "that to the sides of the dark shine the theories."*

[2]If the brain-neurons are buzzing, are individual, can choose, aren't they all of life and history? Each person is God and the brain's neurons are all the people of the history of the world. We are the neurons in God's brain. (Is God asleep? Will God awake? And then what happens to us? God's wakefulness the laws, God's sleep the activity...)

[3]Somewhere in the ocean I started getting an erection. Marilyn Monroe had a penis. The boat sprang a leak. I "woke up"** with come all over me.

---

*If you want to be an artist, go to sleep.

**Falling, going to, then coming, up...

~

From *Hot and Cold*, powerHouse Books, 2001.

Process Note/Assignment: Since you ask, one of my favorite poems of my own is the prose poem, "That to the Sides of the Dark Shine the Theories." Incidentally the title of it is actually words I woke up remembering from a dream. As far as an assignment suggested by the poem. . . .What comes to mind is to solicit pages that find a form that's as close to possible to a specific mental moment, an instance of consciousness, chosen by the writer. In other words, take one instant of experience (of any kind, from the most seemingly placid to the most intense) and try to represent it as scientifically as possible. Nabokov used to talk about striving for the passion of science and the precision of poetry. That's kind of the idea. I mean we know that the brain functions largely as a filter: emphasizing what it determines is significant in the data at any given moment and keeping the rest in the background in varying degrees. But always we're aware of much more of a given moment than we usually pay attention to. The assignment is to try to make a piece of writing that corresponds to what's actually happening in the instance of one's consciousness chosen.

Lewis Warsh
Suggestion

I suggested to you that it wasn't necessary to feel unhappy about something you couldn't do anything about. That it wasn't necessary to feel anxious about something that hadn't happened. Just because it might happen, I suggested, didn't mean you had to assume that it was going to happen. I suggested that thinking that something might happen was one way of protecting yourself against the possibility that it would happen. The thought, I said, was a way of preparing you for the possibility. I suggested that it was pointless to make yourself unhappy by thinking about things that hadn't happened. I thought (but didn't tell you) that some people have a propensity for making themselves unhappy by purposely thinking about things that cause them anxiety. That it wasn't necessary, for them or for you, to spend your time thinking about things that might create a state of anxiety or unhappiness, that it wasn't necessary, for instance, to invent scenarios in which people acted or said things that made you unhappy. I suggested that thinking about things in this way was one way of preventing them from happening, but that the thoughts themselves (with no basis in reality) were in themselves a source of unhappiness. I suggested that even though everything has a basis in reality it was possible not to dwell on things that hadn't yet happened, that thoughts themselves were a form of reality, that thought-forms loomed like shadows in the distant past & distorted our way of thinking in the present, that the way we thought about things in the present had no connection with what was actually happening. I suggested that it might be possible to live more fully in the present if you could avoid being victimized by things that had happened in the past. I suggested that it was pointless to make yourself unhappy by having these thoughts. I suggested that you needed a new perspective on reality.

~

From *Inseparable: Poems 1995-2005*, Granary Books, 2008.

Process Note/Assignment: Write a prose poem in which you give advice to someone you know. Think of a specific person—a lover, a friend, a relative, and address that person as "you." You can tell the person what their problems are and what they should do to correct them or feel better. You can address the person psychologically—the more intimate you are with this person the more you'll have to say. The purpose of the work is to help the other person in a concrete way but you can also give radical advice. You can also tell the person what they shouldn't be doing. Experiment, in this work, with repetition—you can say the same thing, if you like, in different ways.

MAUREEN OWEN

POEM TO PISS EVERYONE OFF

I had the feeling early this summer of discovering
Gertrude Stein. I borrowed a copy of her selected
writings from Dick and retired here to read them.
I had this dazzling image of running through a wide empty
field towards her as she rose from a white rattan chair
during her garden tea. As I gradually drew within less
distance of her I felt some of my initial exuberance give
way & just as I came abreast of her I was stricken with
such overwhelming boredom that I instantly kicked her cane
out from under her and sped on by.

~

From *Hearts in Space*, Kulchur Press, 1980.

Process Note/Assignment: Choose and research a particular writer whose work is lauded and who is proclaimed by most critics and reviewers to be an outstanding figure in contemporary literature. Read their work and imagine that you are initially intrigued, but gradually come to disagree and taking this opposite viewpoint write a prose poem that incorporates and describes your dissenting view.

HARRYETTE MULLEN

DAISY PEARL

More than a woman's name. Her traditional shape. Rapidly spread and rubbed with a wedge. Straight drunk with a crooked lick. A brief suck on time. Diminutive. Promptly popular still on the border. As one version of stamina went. A great show of suffering in order to arouse. There were sweet ones. Frozen ones and fruity ones. Her little resemblance to the original. Shake her one key part. Control her ice. Shake her poor stem. Her rim rubbed. Slice juice and pour control out with dusty salt. Or to taste if desired.

SUZUKI METHOD

El Nino brought a typhoon of tom-toms from Tokyo, where a thrilling instrument makes an OK toy. Tiny violins are shrill. Their shrieks are musical mice. The color of a mechanical clock is lost in translation. Whatever you're telling me sounds like the straight teeth of rodents. My dreams throw the book at the varmint. We both shudder as the dictionary thuds. You've got to admit, our Esperanto's hopeless. Your virgin is unfaithful. My savory hero boards the ship of Marco Polo, loaded with soy from Ohio.

~

From *Sleeping in the Dictionary*, University of California Press, 2002.

Process Note: Some of the language in "Daisy Pearl" came from a recipe for margaritas that I found in a magazine. It's not exactly a Dadaist cut-up, because I didn't literally cut and paste the recipe text. I looked up the name "Margarita" and incorporated that information into a poem that recycles words and phrases from the recipe. The recipe writer had included a brief history of the margarita, including its origin on the Mexican border. "Suzuki Method" is a record of a visit to the Watt's Towers in Los Angeles with a Japanese friend. My friend's name appears in the poem as an anagram, which was suggested by the fact that Tokyo and Kyoto are anagrams. The title comes from a method of music education pioneered by violinist Shinichi Suzuki. He called it the "mother tongue" method of teaching, because children learn music in the same way they learn to speak their native language. Simon Rodia, who created the Watt's Towers, called them "the ships of Marco Polo." While the units of "Suzuki Method" are grammatical if somewhat zany declarative sentences, "Daisy Pearl" is mostly a construction of abrupt, staccato fragments. The multicultural landscape of southern California is part of the visual and linguistic background of both poems.

MARK WALLACE
PROSE POEM

What seems noise to some seems music to others. What limits do you place on darkness? The sun cuts across my body on a day when light is hard to find. So much glorious aimless wandering. Who knows who will sit beside me, saying they've been far away. The love I lose that comes back again. Cars and plastic and signs for stores, the earnest exchange of dollars! Don't remember to find me. We make mistakes before they're mistakes—is it a wonder the body's beautiful? Isn't it shocking the sky never crashes?

~

Process Note/Assignment: This prose poem is from my poetry collection, "Party n My Body." Each poem in the collection is ten sentences in length (some of the sentences may be fragments) and works with the following formal elements:

1) Each line must, on the level of narrative, have nothing to do with the previous sentence. By frustrating overt narrative connections, a complicated set of associational connections appears instead.

2) Each ten line poem must include at least one question, although it can include more.

3) One sentence in each poem must end with an exclamation point that's used improperly–that is, an exclamation point that doesn't really seem like it belongs at the end of that sentence.

Invent your own formal rules for a prose poem, and use those rules to write a series of poems, 8 or 10 at least. While the rules of the form should remain rigid, try to vary the way they are applied from poem to poem. Think of the rules as the basis for a game that should be played differently every time.

Try, as at least one of the rules that you use, to work with punctuation that is handled improperly. The goal is to think of punctuation as an element of the composition of a poem that one might use creatively, rather than as a grammatical restraint.

ALYSTYRE JULIAN
SIX FROM SEVEN DAYS

I met you when we were birds, we were lovers, you sang from your branch, then we were cats, I licked you to sleep, and then we were owls, yes birds again, birds of prey, these were nights of visions, and then we were leopards, yes cats again, and we stalked separately and feasted, but we prowled near each other, and then we were birds again, of the soaring variety, and we were often apart, mantles over our own catch, but we flew past each other in the sky circuit, and then we were saber-toothed tigers and we bared our sharpnesses, but we lay together, yes we did that in secluded parts of the jungle, yes, when we were sleepy and sullen tigers we did that; if I was nicked from a kill you salivated over my wound and I would find the best spot for our grand sprawl, and then we were lost to each other when I stayed a tiger and you became a bird again and I craved your wing span and then when you were down, talons in some rodent, I leaped for you, your feathers could have choked me but I bit into you and swallowed, yes I did that and I went on after that, snarling and still looking for you in all our favorite spots—

~

Process Note: I started a little experiment called Seven Days. For literally seven days, I tried everything I could think of, letting my imagination "run free." Each day was a different angle of coming towards the writing—each day I started over again. The first day of the project was simply "ONE" and it was a scripted dialogue between abstract voices. The second day I used the memory of a photograph and called it "108 degrees." "Three" became sub-headings: "Three Divided By Three," "Three-Fourths," etc., each with text to follow. The prose poem "Six" must have come on the sixth day.

I'd felt up to that point that the experiment was exploratory as an exercise, but that I didn't really see anything that I would take further, or that could stand on its own. After staying with the loose daily structure of "Seven Days," "Six" came out of nowhere as its own pocket of prose. I had to edit very little of it from the original version. Somehow the experiment had let me mine surface texts, small frames, until "Six" revealed itself as something all of a piece, both more cohesive and fluid than anything else from the days previous—something that was, to my understanding, a prose poem, complete in itself.

I knew abstractly what the relationship of the animals was about—based very loosely on someone in particular—but even that particular someone was more a compilation of feelings and relations circling my sub-conscious.

The best part is that I have found it fun to read aloud.

Tom Savage
Classical German Song

May we all get to where we want to be. There is no housing shortage in Heaven. Angels arrive and leave all the time. The rent is free. The view keeps you awake, whatever the effect of your fellow or sister angels' conversations might be. You have a choice of God, gods, or no gods at all. Few preachers make it to these heights so you never get telemarketing messages trying to convert you or to sell you anything.

You've left all your "don't call" numbers behind through lack of need. At first, the fact that all your thoughts can be heard, without translation into speech, by anyone who chooses to hear them might seem disconcerting. Gradually you discover that due to an absence of loneliness in heaven, few intrude in this way. Each merely waits for her or his timely or untimely re-entry into birth. That is almost always the way it is. There is return to Earth as somebody else, sooner or later. That is the only limitation to your stay here.

Process Note/Assignment: I wrote this poem last summer while I was listening to Mahler's Fourth Symphony a lot. At the end of that work, there is a long soprano solo which takes place among angels in Heaven. When I gave my then-students in the senior center the assignment to write a prose poem, it was an easy thing to do. Most of them never really understood the function of line breaks in modern and postmodern poetry so it was a relief to be free of arguments about that for a while. Still, one of the most enthusiastic of these older people began writing a lot of these and calling these "essays." Anyway, I was trying to produce a prose equivalent of a classical German song, thus the title. As for a possible assignment, the only one which comes to mind is to ask your students to write a prose poem about the most "unpoetic" subject or thing they can think of. Of course, Heaven is not that unpoetic. It's a treacly cliché in most contexts and presents its own difficulties. Still . . .

BILL KUSHNER
BUILDING

So they wound up building a 2-story. In the one story the man he kept washing his hands & wishing away & that's not good. He was one of these people was always in the background on his back on the ground & I think I loved him. Tell me how you feel about it & I'll tell you how I feel about it & tell me if I'm wrong. I think some loves you can't do a thing about. You just love & you love your little red heart out, & that's well that. In the 2nd story lived a little box. Little box just sat there in the middle of the room, so neat & so fine, what a perfect tenant. Colorless to begin with, box gradually turned a white, whiter & whiter, until I swear it glowed. Just beautifully blinding, as if another sun, why it was always daylight, why even at midnight, & this too was love, for how could it not be? Love yes, but a pure my love, an almost divine love, it was hard not to feel not like bowing to that hot little box, it was love that intense. Little by little the man of he on the ground he began to crawl, then to up, then to walk, & walk into the fore-ground, & then into the sky. He rose into & up into blue sky & sighed a goodbye, & so long he was gone. I suppose I could have cried, but no, no tears, love, no good-byes. Little by little, white box began to change, it was truly strange, little box turned the strangest of a color, there was no word for it, that color, not pink, not red, nothing other. One day black, the next brown, it was eerie. You never knew what, until one day puff, lovely box was gone. Gone, taking all our love with it, goodbye oh little, bye bye. So now our story it is over. Both stories empty, vacant, over, & the building yes all torn down. Some say, however, they still see it, some say it still exists, see? there in the mist. Love? some say that still exists. Me, I found another place to live & so that's where I live.

~

From *3rd Bed*, no. 10, Spring/Summer 2004.

Process Note: I gave myself this assignment: write a city poem.

COLE SWENSEN
BEASTIARY
for V.P.

1

Eight crows fly up form the field though it's odd that you can't count them once
they're in the air as if the moving number unraveled on rising—that motion and
altitude both. This is especially true in books where the crow often stands for a
tear (that is, something torn) whereas here it is simply a black mark on a blue
sky or a grey sky or against the sun.

2

Close observation of the black beetle reveals an inverted architecture in which
subterranean vaults flay themselves against noon. While inside, a different night
takes over. Awakens in a small room with the impression that a small piece of
paper is being folded over and over in your lung. It's still dark out and the moon
is down and the dogs pace nervously back and forth, hearing the air, caught in
the grid of its living there.

3

The grey swan is a solitary thing. Spun steel surrounded by all that air and there
is something cold in the world today and you shudder. They make no sound and
the water moves soundlessly along in the canal. If something were to move, the
earth would turn on its axis, tilting slightly according to the season and it would
either snow. It turns alone, an elongated planet orbiting its own heart, which is
about the size and shape of a walnut.

4

The crows fly up among the sounds of smaller birds. Invisible millions orbiting
two or three notes and vacillating, a little wavering that shudders the air like
the sheets of heat that rise from a fire you don't actually see. What you see are
the crows—fifteen in the field stubbled with the broken ends of wheat, eating
something that must be there in the dirt.

5

Birds without name or number. It means it's going to rain. There where the sky
has gone away and it's not a continual sound but rather in neat pieces as if the
throat were composed of dozens of rooms. Some birds can imitate the sound of

pouring water, of a closing door. Others can call you by name, but it's not clear if they are aware that it's your name, which is to say, aware that it is you, the person who left, the person who shut the door.

6

There is always something incongruous about seeing an insect on a paved road. For instance, this bee, determined to walk to the other side yet unsure of the direction so traveling in a rough circle as if he were circling something unapproachable and probably attracted by the heat. By the gravity of the color black and by the enormity of a road. It is as wide as it is long and circular in shape and in it he sees a face that is his own, though it seems so much smaller when rooted to the ground.

7

The saint had such large hands. They struck the casual viewer as deformed. They were deformed and covered easily twice his chest, each one, and when he held them out, but a saint cannot move but if. This is the root of the word. Belief is never so assured as when the glance falls—you're only passing through the town—and if a hand, like a sail could cut such a neat triangle from empty space. I write letters in which every word is a single word and I see his lips in my mind begin: no part of the body can live alone, repeat: no part, no.

8

I think it is a wren. A sequence of points across a blue field. Points by definition have no shape. They mark. There is a constellation nailed in place just behind their suspended forms. It never gets dark here anymore. And the compass floats and the angle bends and this is just a small service they perform while all along they have their own lives, beautiful lives and delicate, hollow bones.

9

The grey carp hover suspended just below the surface of the water. Why do we stare at anything alive? We are passersby. There are five of them. And we stare as though they are not quite possible, verging on the visible but fading back. The sky is cloudy today. There are grey clouds in a grey sky reflected in the grey water. There is no reflection on its surface, none. Sometimes for moments at a time and they too are breathing.   ~

From *Noon*, Green Integer, 2005.

Process Note: Cole and I spoke over the phone on August 2, 2011. The following is culled from our discussion.

The book that this comes from, *Noon*, is a book about a specific place, a site just north of Paris called the Abbaye de Royaumont. I was part of a multi-arts residency there for eight weeks one summer, and I wrote most of the book while walking in the countryside around there. The bestiary section in particular was written in response to a friend's manuscript, which was also a bestiary, and so it's dedicated to her—Veronique Pittolo.

The whole book is based on nines—there are nine poems, with nine sections each. And the title comes from that—it's just one sound off of nine. Nine has always seemed to me a powerful number, particularly in relation to our use of the base ten—like an asymptote, it approaches and approaches but never quite reaches ten, and thus remains one off. In searching for a word that would be similarly one off, the one that really rang, that seemed to echo the book, was *noon*. When it was translated into French, the translator first translated the title as *midi*, which is *noon* in French, but he then decided to keep with the principle rather than the word, and ended up with *nef*. The French for nine is n*euf*, and he went through all the words that are one sound off of *neuf*, we both liked *nef,* which means both *nave*, as in a church, and a ship. I mention this only because I think it brings up an interesting point about translation—how it often goes below the words, behind them. Sometimes you don't translate the meaning of a word but instead translate the action of the language.

To go back to the poem "Bestiary"—it focuses on the animals I saw around Royaumont on my walks; the writing process itself incorporated an exchange of observation and sound—the entire book was very much led by sound. I would start with an observation, say of the black beetle on the road in section two, and then just see where the momentum of writing would lead me. I would mentally head for off-rhymes—I think when we write, we have hovering in our minds not only the words we put down, but also their entire associative fields. We don't notice them consciously, but hundreds and hundreds of words related by sense and by sound are stirred up, and so I listen very lightly for ones with sounds I like. In that section, to my ear, it's the words noon, room, lung, and down that internally hold the piece together, sealed by the air/there rhyme at the end.

When the momentum of an initial observation wound down, I would look up again, make another observation, and ride its momentum for awhile. It seemed a way perhaps to interweave the concrete world, the things I was observing, in with language as a concrete object in itself.

ANNE WALDMAN
FROM *MARRIAGE*

Marriage marriage is like you say everything everything in fall fall on the bed bed at dawn dawn because you work work all night. Night is an apartment. Meant to be marriage. Marriage is an apartment & meant people people come in in because when when you marry marry chances are there will be edibles edibles to eat at tables tables in the house.

House will be the apartment which is night night. There there will be a bed bed & an extra bed bed a clean sheet sheet sheet or two two for guests guests one extra towel. Extra towel. How will you be welcomed? There will be drinks drinks galore galore brought by armies of guests guests casks casks of liquors liquors and brandies brandies elixirs sweet & bitter bitter bottle of Merlot Merlot Bustelo coffee. Will you have some when I offer. When you are married married there will be handsome gifts for the kitchen kitchen sometimes two of every thing. Everything is brand brand new new. Espresso coffee cups, a Finnish plate, a clock, a doormat, pieces of Art.

And books of astonishing Medical Science with pictures. Even richer lexicons. When you are married married there will be more sheets sheets & towels towels arriving arriving & often often a pet pet or two two. You definitely need a telephone when you are married. Two two lines lines. You need need separate separate electronic mail electronic-mail accounts accounts. When you are married married you will have sets sets of things things, of more sheets and towels matching, you will have duplicates of things, you will have just one tablecloth. When you are married married you will be responsible when neighbors neighbors greet you. You will smile smile in unison unison or you might say he is fine, she is fine, o she is just down with a cold, o he is consoling a weary traveler just now, arrived from across the Plains. She my husband is due home soon, he my wife is busy at the moment, my husband he is very very busy busy at the moment moment this very moment. Meant good-bye, good-bye. When you are married married sex sex will happen happen without delay delay. You will have a mailbox mailbox and a doorbell doorbell. Bell bell ring ring it rings rings again a double time. You do not have to answer. That's sure for when you are married people people understand understand you do not not have to answer

answer a doorbell doorbell because sex sex may hap-pen happen without delay delay. You will hear everything twice, through your ears and the ears of the other. Her or him as a case case maybe be. He & he & her & her as a case case may be may be. When you are married married you can play play with names names and re-name yourself if you like. You can add a name, have a double name with a hyphen if you like. You can open joint accounts when you are married.

Marriage is no guarantee against depression. A shun is no guarantee against anything. Marriage is no guarantee against resolution. Revolution is a tricky word word. Here, you hear here? Marriage is sweeter sweeter than you think. Think.

- stereo

~

From *Vow to Poetry*. Coffee House Press, 2001.

Process Note: I wanted to see how far the sentence would go in the arrangement of the writing of marriage, which is itself a term, a turn, of various lengths and measures. How could a sentence—possibly a same-sex sentence—sustain itself through thick and thin, turn of a page or climax of desire as a point at which it lathers up to the weaker "poem." I saw couples in the arrangement. This was a gender poem . . touching on genre as well as gender. He & He & She & She & She dressing like He to love He, and undressing to love Her, infinite possibilities of coupling desire. A lucrative contract. Then a separation, a divorce, a common law arrangement. It gets confusing, dizzying like an opera. How to keep track of all the conjuncts and their performances in a grammar of sentences?

NIjinsky might dance and complain, Blake would become a saintly husbanding apparition. Participatory in its nature, do you read into me? Think up your own examples and follow the lengths the sentence goes to. Queer customs from other continents, histories of chattel and patriarchy. In the haibum you might insist upon a "capping" haiku, a summation to hold that thought. . . . Back and forth, forth or back. I wanted sentences that joke around, make fusses and historical "points" at times, and snub the sentencelessness of poetry.

Simon Pettet
Two Prose Poems

Yearning even in Paradise. Greedy bastards. Probably made
someone in the school pay for it, Villiers Street. Fog
on the Embankment. You were so flawless. Someone always gets
the wrong idea. And so when you discovered him about what
age were you? Oh I suppose it must have been about twelve years
before I married him. We were living on Station Road.

* * * * * * * * * * * * * *

The books on the sidewalk are dutifully arranged.

The officer's a moonlighter since he works at the other precinct.

Dance performers from around the globe are advertised on a torn

poster. I can't see them since my dog is blind. I make a wish. I wish

for another one. The tethered akita is granted a reprieve. All of this all

the time. Every conceivable moment. All the worlds you ever wanted to know.

~

From *Hearth*, Talisman, 2008.

Process Note: These two pieces were written independently and, although I wouldn't
lose sleep over it, I think they're both prose poems. What do *you* think? Does it have
something to do with the cumulative (one thing building on another thing)? So when
you start with a long(er) prose(y) line (or even a fragment/phrase), and that line dictates
the next line (tho' not at all, or not necessarily, a "logical" progression)... "One perception must immediately and directly lead to a further perception" (Charles Olson) - "Direct" doesn't have to be "obvious". "Poetry" - or the varieties of prose, for that matter
- doesn't have to be pre-ordained.

Is James Joyce writing poetry in his famous book *Ulysses?* or only in his "book of po-ems", *Chamber Music?* or how about Jack Kerouac (his "Duluoz" novels and his poetry book, *Mexico City Blues*?) Can you think of any other "famous prose writers" who also published books of poems? - Is there an *essential* difference between the "novels" and the "poetry"? What do you think that is?

CHARLES ALEXANDER
SOME SENTENCES SEARCH FOR SOME PERIODS 2

Something that mothers and does not know where to go in the night, or is it morning now? Will you tell me it is morning now so that I might think of the sunlight before the sun is visible, before its letters proclaim the day in heat and light and one sharp motion that might blind or displace the insects from their sleeping places? If I might write just a moment of the day I might begin with "As you wish" or "Ripeness is all" whereas we all know the end is "The rest is silence" as in the movie about Carl Jung and Sigmund Freud, as in the words of Hamlet, as if words were in words and sunlight twisted around the letters until lost at the end of day in a graying haze. One upon the string, the G string the C string the sing string. *To mother to foal* she said and mother left a year ago but mother of my children remains and we hold each other in scheduled time on a Sunday morning and in unscheduled time whenever we may please, does it please you if you please? Pleasure and a lover, and what else does one need? Don't forget to breathe on a Friday for this is the day of release, hold hold hold and then let go. One can't build a snowman here unless the climb leads to forests in February, if lucky in the open field between the ever green branches, but snowmen are a part of my past, once with a red corduroy jacket that my father wore, too, or perhaps this is a memory-mixture, i.e. the way truth isn't what happened but an invented memory of what happened, for is and isn't are not divergent, just different sides of a coin, whereas different coins might reveal entirely different vistas. From where I sit at this moment shelves are going out from me and there, upon them, one by one, a blue book, an orange book, a black book, a purple book, a silver book, rows and rows of parti-colored things made of paper and ink and thread, these are such dreams as stuff is made on. But in the corner, an orange coffee cup, and a transportation not a transmogrification to a town among mountains with coffee and sunlight and words words words. No matter, no matter, no water, no wafer, no was, no is. Who am I to call the kettle black, to call you to me for a bright wet kiss on the pillow, in the pillow one sinks and rises, falls and emerges, breathes and stops. A backstop stands behind the catcher, the catcher sits behind home plate, home plate is buried in the dirt at the corner of the basepath, the basepath forms a triangle around the pitcher, the pitcher gets things going with a windup and a pitch to a batter, the batter may be anyone at any given time trying to understand what is given to her, trying to return what the world throws at her, trying to find a way to the fence, to an opening in a fence that might allow more than simply a rearrangement of the parts. Parts are assigned, actor A will play character Q, amateur volunteer B will portray character T, truth will be evident from the emotional conduct of arms and heads. Heads and deads. *I am aweary, aweary, I would that I were dead.* Deads and beads. Those beads that were his eyes pearl up in my heart of all wonders, I wonder in my bead of all hearts, wander in eyes that curl up and ball up and fall into the time before I was born. I have not come here with empty hands, the lines throughout them will tell you stories of what I have come here with. I have not come here alone, for wherever I go she and he and she and she and she and she come with me it is not possible to imagine being alone, no, that game with bases and fences is a team sport, as is the making of snowpeople the playing of strings the rising of the sun in the morning for as long as that may last. To come through conflicts and inventions and waxy worlds and earthquake palaces and hopeful buildings and near acts and random acts and waters pushing slanting certain and uncertain and still to float, even to power that floating with strokes of arms and legs with pulses of torsos and un-flinching willingness to play the game, even to finish the game despite the rather growing sense that there is no finish there are no cells that complete the pattern there may not even be colors one can trust. Some sentences for some periods look and for some periods find naught but ripeness, all the rest is breathing. *Pli selon pli*, the music and the dance, the composer and the choreographer, the chromosome and the coloration, the painter and the poet, the step step step and turn. Bowls and bowls, holes and holes, mothers and others loose in the night (in the light).

~

From *At The Edge Of The Sea: Pushing Water II,* Singing Horse, 2018.

Process Note/Assignment: There really was not a plan to these poems. Rather, it was a matter of beginning somewhere, and linking the second sentence to the first, the second thought to the first, but not generally through logical connections, but instead con-necting a word, or an image, and sometimes, if there was a break in such connections, that was fine. The idea was just to keep it going until it seemed either some "end" was reached, or perhaps the energy of the piece had done all it might do. In this one, there's a circling back, from "mothers" to "mother" at the end. But where it might go within is really quite open.

I was aware of trying to keep a more or less flat tone, i.e. when the linkages are of words/ideas and not some other kind of development, one doesn't quite get rises and falls in tone or emotional output, rather a sort of steadiness, though that doesn't mean no emotional intent at all. There is a combination of memory in this work, and imaginative thinking. There is of course some allusion, to a film, to Shakespeare, to Tennyson, to Kathleen Fraser, and more, but that's just roving in one's mind, my mind. "Mind movie," perhaps, and mine is fairly literary. Some of the material here is quite personal, but it is like life as the personal flows in and around everything else, i.e. the reading, the memories, working life, etc., and they all make sentences together, but sentences that perhaps, taken all together, do not have an ending, a "period" in that sense. But they do have a "period" in the other sense, i.e. a period of time, the period of time that they take. And that does seem to be a manner of energy in that Olsonian projective sense.

If one were to use this as a model, I would say, think of a memory, one that has images, some color, some depth. Let that stand as a first sentence. Make a second sentence that links, not to the memory, but to just a word in the first sentence, repeating that word in a different context. The second sentence can be another actual memory. Keep going in the same way for ten or more sentences, i.e. making connections that seem to occur more by chance than by intention. Somewhere along the way, include not only something from the previous sentence, but from an earlier sentence, and keep doing that, until by the end, you have a sentence that includes, in some way, the beginning.

LYNN CRAWFORD
FANCY*

> For Gina Ferrari

Normally I interview heavily made up but today my face is naked. Coats, creams, foundations wear me out, not just because it is spring. I do wear lipstick do NOT powder my cheeks, neck or nose. Do NOT use the tinted moisturizer I bought at the discount beauty branch. Talking with the beauty-clerks, I learn why their expressions are so grave. Smiling cracks the heavily applied face paint; chips crumble into cleavage, chokers, uniform buttons.

Mom says, Fancy, you have a way of nailing points, perceptions, observations smack on the button. You think and talk bare naked. She delivers this with her brand of humor: initial grave presentation. Dad frowns, I flush, we start to suffer an ugly silence then—her face springs to a smile. Mom is a successful joker, consistent with her maternal family branch. I do not carry that gene, every time I try to pull a prank something happens to my nose.

I get an itch, a pain, an unpleasant sensation in my nose. Then it turns red, a glaring globular button. Dad discovers a homeopathic repair; he rubs it with a flower petal, then a flower stem, finally a small tree branch. He tries the last method first using a bark covered tree part, but is most effective when he used one stripped naked. That works best; I remember that he discovered this cure on a warm day, late spring. Plenty of foliage and hope in the air; mom busy planting, cooking, canning, an impossible day on which to feel grave.

I can't remember, even in dark weather, our family atmosphere being grave. This could be fact, or my re-remembering, who knows. In truth, sometimes, very late at night, or early in the morning, other types of pictures spring into my head. Is it a good joke when mom makes a stew and stirs in, along with peas, beef, carrots, a half dozen buttons? Is it funny when our neighbor chews a spoonful and breaks a tooth where once was a firm, white piece in her smile now is a space gaping, empty, naked. Is it a good joke to steal my prom dress from its carefully wrapped paper, so when I look for it an hour before my date should come I find it outside, dangling from a tree branch?

Yes, mom's pranks are funny; maybe not the tooth destruction, but in general; I consider that tooth incident an exception, a breach. Like I said, my childhood memories are amusing, which is perhaps why I am drawn to stories and people you might call grave. A life spent around mom's practical, naked humor. Once she saw dad smile at a clerk in the discount beauty store and glued a skunk sprayed leaf beneath his nose. Wearing latex gloves, she holds the pre-glued, foul smelling, object behind her back, asks dad to come over and help her with dress buttons. When he gets near she shoots her hand to his face, he springs back. She'd planned well: gloves off, in the garbage bag, tossed outside, with lightening speed; hands rinsed with tomato juice, a skunk spray remedy popular in our house during summer and spring. Shamed, Dad goes behind our shed and whacks his legs and back with a tree branch. But that picture may be something I dreamed rather than an actual event; it is hard to get your past right on the button. Did I see him again whacking himself by that murdered clerk's grave? A boyfriend shot her through the back of her head; the bullet emerged through her nose. According to the police, she was wearing panties but otherwise was naked.

I'm glad it is me interviewing for her position at the discount beauty branch; I replay her funeral, people sobbing as she is dropped into her grave. I review those police photos, nose unrecognizably disfigured, legs and torso naked, little blue buttons up the front of her panties. Some shots are close up, others longer range through the panes of her window and just budding trees, it had been a chilly spring.

~

From *Fortification Resort*, Brooklyn Rail/Black Square, 2005.

Process: Fancy is a sestina (morphed). The six words are: naked, spring, nose, branch, grave, button. I wrote it in a writing workshop in Key West taught by Harry Mathews. The class chose the words. As I started to write I kept thinking of the work of an artist, Gina Ferrari. So I wrote it with her drawings and sculptures in mind and it turns out to be an homage to that work.

From Marion Kleinschmidt, a student in one of my writers.com classes:

This story gives me goose bumps. Similar to Mathews' "Cigarettes" there is a tension between two emotional qualities: the hilarity of everyday humour and pranks vs. the sinister reality of violence. The six trigger words (naked, spring, nose, grave, branch, button) are permutated through these two qualities and various anecdotes, culminating in the words "nose" and "naked" (so commonplace) as code for the beauty clerk's mutilated body. The idea of "grave" aspects in our world finally topples into an actual "grave". And to me, this feels not at all like a literary gimmick. It embodies the truth that language just like human behaviour seems to signal one thing on the surface, but often hides something else beneath. (Does the mother with her pranks REALLY wish to make people laugh?) In a way, here the sestina technique helps to turn the trigger words into connectors between surface plot and sub-plot.

MARTINE BELLEN
CUSTOMERS WHO HAVE BOUGHT "SLEEPING BEAUTY"
HAVE ALSO BOUGHT THIS

ME. Pron. The objective case of I.

1. *A state in New England.*

2. *ME is a concept in the cosmology of Sumerian mythology.*

3. *Net energy available in certain foods.*

4. *A think group that resides in my head. A large, furry animal. A ME. The me.*

5. *A bullet's point of entry.*

Upon awakening from a story, before walking through the portal to the hallway into a land where language is required, I confirm I'm ME (a state in New England) (a think group). Some days I don't arrive at the threshold of my body and a deep, cavernous loss resides where ME would have been. The cave paintings in Lascaux. Horses, bulls, and stags—motifs that repeat when I can't see where I'm headed, when I'm in a forest. Some days I ingest donuts and sour dough, some days I sleep deep in mud like a fish that wants to stop drifting, day into night into day.

I stand before the portal/window/screen door (or other port of entry). Beside ME (a large, furry animal) appears another ME (of Sumerian mythology). Look, I have spread! Mother feels my finger and knows that it has grown.

A little girl with 100-year-old crone legs wakes from her blackout. She hands a poison apple to a drop-dead beauty. One must wonder

What she's hiding under her dress. In her heart. The apple spiked with E.

"Mirror, mirror inside ME

Spinning out fate

Who do WE hate?"

The beauty bites. SLEEPS (*sleep meaning a cheap way of travel, a calming narcotic, a monk with mu mind—verb, passive and active*).

*

She rushes through an hour like a hallway. The alarm rings as she attempts to outrun the wolf, the wind. Music imprisoned by its bars (the breath of bars and their throbbing beer-soaked walls). Flesh and time swap outfits—either way, a jailor enforces a life sentence. Either way we wither.

*

I eye her through a mirror. She eyes me as I sleep through life—

      lying/dreaming that I'm a fairy princess,

           A God-fearing goblin A talking bird.

     <u>I am none of these</u>.

       not this knee, not this shyness, not this shiny halo....

I take the shortcut through the forest. I ax down trees. I chop off hair. I revise

the story. I win. I live; still, I am eternally forever after.

*

Smoothing out despair

Isn't as easy as steaming wrinkles from silk to be worn by Cinderella.

She took the remedy out of an old story

By painting herself into a dream

Of self. Mostly air disturbs

The sea // mostly light (noon light), parabolic light,

Finding the tree beneath its color. Poison knowledge.

On the threshold of a land where language is required. I dream

I'm hiking among Weimaraners that scamper through pet doors

Into a past and recite Howl. We clap paws and run sharp claws

Across a pearlescent perfect moon. Morning fog unwraps pond

To reveal a soggy sandwich. The wax paper is oily, transparent—

Through it I see diverse divinities running

The Greatest Show on Earth, now playing

On a distant planet called Barnum & Bailey—

Its deities: misfits, freaks, manifestations of me.

In order to talk to her I have to enter her world

And remember precisely who she is/I am.

Once there, I arrive at Mother's

Who is cavernous, a dark space painted with primitive stags, bulls, horses.

~

From *This Amazing Cage of Light: New and Selected Poems*, Spuyten Duyvil, 2015

Process Note: When writing "Customers Who Have Bought 'Sleeping Beauty' Have Also Bought This" (which is a play, of course, on <u>amazon.com</u>'s sales tool), I was thinking about culturally-determined connotations of written and oral language and the friction between fluid denotations and dictionary definitions or social signifiers and how when one chooses words for poems, one is unlocking a lexical cage. I wondered if we let words out of their cages, which traces of their behavior would remain. I set this mechanism of inquiry inside the party dress of fairy tale motifs because in that familiar garment, there are possibilities of uncanny transformation and simplistic duality (good and bad, beautiful and ugly). Also, I was thinking about the Japanese and Chinese languages and how, I've been told, in even more pronounced ways than in English, context creates meaning. For instance, in Japanese, *kai* can mean the ocean, the earth, shellfish, food, or to gather food, to name a few possibilities. I, then, wove threads of symbol and dream into the mix.

Julie Ezelle Patton
Email To Barbara Henning

From: julie patton <julieattonp@yahoo.com>
Subject: Re: hola
Date: December 14, 2016 at 1:15:35 AM EST
To: Barbara Henning <barbhenn@mac.com>
Reply-To: julie patton <julieattonp@yahoo.com>

Dear Barbara,

I am hoping to come this weekend. I haven't been in touch due to health reasons. Plus lost cell phone. I apologize for the inconvenience of being incommunicado and planned, hook or crook, to inform you of what's going on. Unfortunately for me, the fact that I am able to type thru blurred vision means my brain might be adjusting to dim sight. I don't want that. And beef I tarried along to find an allopathic doctor wished to first consult with my old feel-good standby: Chinese medicine. Works for me to get at the root of the problem, purge on my own. Before going down such an uncomfortable rabbit hole with cold instruments. Brrr... I'll take my chances on me. Not only financial; this system makes one pay for its use in more than cash. Sigh, the memory of doctors visiting us at home. How I miss the warmth of being tended to without moving an inch. House calls. Imagine that!

Speaking of which, I am a new auntie again today. Girl. Over 7 lbs. I am troubled that I can't bring myself to jump up and down with joy. Sad. Children bring hope. The thought of tumbling down the umbilical shoot in these times make me shudder. Clouds gather. May Light disperse the h20 (2 for t-t-t-2ears0?) and replace it with baby blue.
Take a powder,
Rump!

Love, I accidentally touch, tapped your cardboard name spine looking for Pinky. The text meowed, said, "baby, come back & see me sometime."
"I will," I thought, breathing edge
of books on a shelf

the weather of convenience
central furnace
clouds
over head
moisture
heat,
excessive tongues... flagging
damp

just sitting there,
wrist out
lean forward &
bleed . . .

O, o, oh!

vain words (I
       v
       a
       n
       kgb...east
in general
3
in Rump's inane
asylum. Putrid
smell of war with
money to
burn

               ~

Process Note: Julie in an interview with Drew Gardner in 2001—

You can make an art of daily living so that everything is "art." There is no separation between art and life, sacred and mundane—it all depends on the awareness, attention we bring to the things we are doing—from cooking, to lovemaking, dressing, writing, walking, talking—finding the patterns that connect. It is all performance. An art to everything done well. I don't believe in the idea of artist as creative specialist (here there are artists, at the edge of the known/unexplored world). On the other hand, there is something to this category in the sense that people who "play," like children, and the elderly taken off the conveyor built of useful productivity, and the mentally ill are shut up, isolated, on the brink of society. Diss function, isolation terns them into artists more than the fat of creativity itself. The artist, like the shaman lives on the edge of society, near forest, city dump (soon to be so ho'd into prostition wariness) negotiating in betweens.

I like to be in service of the materials, forget my "self" and become the page or the sound trying to have its say. My mother's father Roy Ezelle was forever making things remake him, his environment, mind, etc. He didn't call it art; just "making-do." He hand-stitched suits, knitted beautiful brown dolls, made collage paintings—used everything on hand. I'm the same, found objects, situations, opportunities, words, sentences and sounds form the basis of my work—and the reason for it. Cause—the world is amazing! What to do with all of this stuff? I am the one transformed in the process. The important thing is to try something. Look! I like walking down a street and being surprised by something. Forget people as the only or most significant domain of talking, everything is yak, yak, yak! Orange can with the swimming peanuts and writing (Japanese) I can't make out sid "Julie, pick me up!" I live in a Dick and Jane reality where everything is "see," "come here," "look," and exclamation points. Words of marvel.

I chafe against type, have a compulsion to free language from con fetters, make it breathe, walk, move—I am, of course, very walky-talky. On the re-staged page wondering as I wander *em* body of Language as multi-dimensional phenomena. Nevertheless, "writing" re mains the common ground most of my projects arch from. That's why I can float away from them, writing is as much in the body as out, it only gives the *appearance of being* outside it. Maybe we should replace the word writing with scoring. Still, for me, no matter the technique or form, this scoring (writing) is apriori—even if it's just the gesture, felt impulse per swaying me. You would never know this given my tendency to balk at fixing words to the page as forever condition—thass why per formance, I get to change the hook...run interference between page and stage for multiple interpretations, breath of readings, divining.

Folks call this improvisation but I'd choose another word—one I remember my grandfather using whenever I asked him what he was doing, simply *making*-do. I like the accent on the word "making" and the verb-activity of "do" (in line with the roots of poesis.

Julie in Conversation with Barbara Henning on September 8, 2018.

When I was younger, as long as I had a desk and a view with some trees—perhaps it had to do with leaves, least to leaves. Perhaps when I'm writing I'm like a tree trunk rooted. Most of those letters come while I'm standing up . . . you know how it is here always in motion going down the hallway, going up the stairs, down the stairs, always this sense of motion and so my thought patterns and my creative output no matter what medium or material I'm working with tends to have this flow of moving through thoughts or impressions or ideas, many many fluttery leaves and they all kind of spill out in a giant leaf pile that someone else can jump into and discern meaning or glean whatever is coming at them or through them through the multi colored flora of everyday life.

What's in a blank sheet of paper is an openness. It did come from something living . . . That's when I sit down and write and touch paper but these letter poems you are talking about they are coming out of the machine not hand writing . . . that's my dream body of a poet. . . I give myself permission not to be me, the character . . . A lot of what I do that entails the part of me that involves language is a performance, is an act, it's not really me, it's me in conversation with all these others I know . . . So I get to correspondence on the machine because there is a there-ness, a person I'm connected to, someone I'm in correspondence with.

*Gardner, Drew. "Interview with Julie Patton." *Interviews. Reviews. Essays,* edited by Gary Sullivan, Spring/Summer 2001, home.jps.net/~nada/patton.htm

KIM LYONS
TINTA

There is no better day than a Sunday in late August in the northern hemisphere to look for it. The overly stretched, scorched exhaustion of things lays open a kind of skin at the very instant a rectangular shadow is crawling across the yellowed grass. A gap is revealed. A cleft or splinter inside the blazing light like a cooled finger, beckoning. While looking around, I find a quieted locust, belly up with a surprising flash of blackened silver in the wing. When I lift my head, I see an enormous, powerful tree trunk within which braided arteries lean precipitously under a dome of shimmering leaves. A fantastic creature that at a distance across a field seems as though a foiled, immobilized God in an epic. Something that had witnessed and travailed and radiates its burden to the extent that I turn away, instantly haunted. When I return home, no ink remains in a small, oddly configured glass bottle for "tinta." I look for its essence as a recoverable pool in which one may be immersed. The remains of a glacier lake that you might slide into until only your head—the organ most in need of submersion—glides above like a splattered gull with two dark eyes that twitch over the horizon. I peer at the assemblage of objects the raucous world has deposited here. I read "25 Besos" then "Astral" and below those the words "Beata Solitudo" handwritten on a stained tile. A man talks to a wolf inside a nimbus. A small campfire fire flickers at his foot. Just to make certain, I raise the violet teardrop of octagonal glass to my right eye and look into the collaged, oblique windows that expand the space horizontally and bring the far-away perimeter close. Disoriented by the perspective, yet confirmed, I sense that its traces are near, unfixed, subliminal. And, I am writing this to tell you the news.

~

Process Note: This prose poem comes into being as it articulates the search for itself. Or, a something inside itself. Or, perhaps, the "thing" remains undisclosed to the poem which contains the enigma as a possibility. The imposed constraint was that the writing would not name its ineffable object.

TYRONE WILLIAMS
THE UGLY STICK

Wailing away until her arms went rubbery, phlegm already starting to cake as
future snot-no-more, her blond weave withering into a post-Jeri curl, she fell on
blubbering ashy knees before a white-sheeted beanpole, squeaky with Jordans,
they put a cap sideways on his ass...

From *The Elderly* 4 (Summer 2014).

INMATE

Driven by imaginal gut bacteria a taxicab driver goes rogue from the standstill traffic of rush hour, pulling off onto the shoulder of the freeway. He exits the vehicle
as ordered, free tenor with a prayer rug, spreads it out upon the gravel, falls to his
knees, and amid the fumes of gasoline, tar and oil, the cacophony of blaring horns,
squealing brakes, and rumbling mufflers, begins his ministrations to the brains.

Process Note/Assignment: When I am preparing to write, I go back through my journals
(you must keep a journal--paper or electronic--of conversations, ideas, overheard phrases,
etc.) and begin stringing together things that might resonate with one another. For "The
Ugly Stick" I wanted to collapse a certain part of 20th c. black history into objects, fashions
and trends, all of which index our desire for relevance. If you want to try this, perhaps
you could select six or seven phrases or objects that concern trends and fashions. Avoid
conjunctions and focus only on descriptive words.

"Inmate" derives from an actual experience: I was driving into D.C. and was stuck in traffic. I noticed a cab driver on the shoulder of the freeway, kneeling on a prayer mat. This
observation, along with my readings from the Koran and medical reports examining the
"second" brain (intestinal bacteria) influenced the writing of this poem. It was, as it were,
a collage of observation and readings.

BERNADETTE MAYER
TO ADMIRAL SCOTT ABOUT SPACE
courting a form for mr. space

Fractious glaciers, there is
In it no mention of the rest
Some of the stuff seemed his
Oh God, the house was a mess

Next antimatter drove spaces
To shuttle a black white ink
Into homogenization of races
And the old hold of the sink

Once in connection with poem
Mention was made of emending
The chaos as if it were home
Which too is merely unending

Nothing too neat—or deadness
Ever, is there? Or is there?
On Jupiter red was a redness
As Picasso pitied a red pear

Generoisty makes even a date
Look silly & I wouldn't like
Ler/him to have to stew/wait
As I sewed dumplings of pike

Or put soles back on my feet
That had fallen off from any
Reason—frostbite and sweet
Unconscious love of the many

Discovery is an artful ninny
As people know form the home
Maybe these verses are tinny
But they do look like a poem

Discovery is an artful ninny
As people know form the home
Maybe these verses are tinny
But they do look like a poem

To Mr.Dead Scott about space
Alive I mention to Mr. Alone
The cannibal who would erase
All that's been with & known

Amen! a deal has been struck
Let's all get back to our bed
Let's all be back to our bed
Let's all go back to our bed
And perfectly entirely fuck,
And idealistically utopianly
And headlong utopianly fuck,
And atavistically, utopianly
& how can we fuck? utopianly
Let's all go back to our bed
And fuck and fuck utopianly,
And fuck, and utopianly fuck
Until we are done in & dead,
Until we're done in and dead

Amen! a deal has been struck
Let's all go back to our bed
And fuck, and utopianly fuck
Until we're done in and dead
O.K. would you mind moving o
Okay and would you mind that
O.K. and would you mind moving
Over a little bit so I could
Have some room and would you
Please abdicate the form and
Kiss me right there where it
Kiss me exactly there where,
Kiss me just there where I'm
Pointing and please do it in
Exactly the way you did it I
Just the way you once did he

306

Do it precisely as it was if
Do it exactly as you did it,
Do it just as you once did I
O.K. and would you mind moving
But they do look like a poem
Just as I noticed you'd done
Something like that before I
Something similar which was,
Something I remember & it is
Something I recall which was
Quite perfect & not like any
Quite perfect unlike anyone
I'd ever had the fortune to,
But they do look like a poem
Fractious glaciers, there is
Quite perfect & unlike notes
Quite perfect & not like her
Something I recall which was
Amazing, not like anything I
Ever think I had felt before
In the rigorous form of love
In the rigorous trek of love
Over the continent's wastes,
Over my dead body continent,
In love all this walking and
All this work & I say love o
All this working, I say love
Seems like a tight belt that
As people know from the home
Cold feet of the only living
Love who is a tight belt I'm
Love's a tight belt I'm to o
Love's a tight belt I wear &
Love's a tight belt I put on
Every morning before I get a
Every morning when I get out
When every morning I forget,
Where every morning I forget
The form while you still are
The form while you know me &
The form in which I and you,

As people know from the poem
Like a litany of exacting be
Like a litany of purest love
From the living to the dead,
From the living to wild dead
From the wild living to dead
Wild living to wild dead was
Wild living to the wild dead
Just in bed mention the dead
Space goes on forever I went
Space doesn't go on forever I
Am just coming by to see you
For a visit onto your street
For a little visit your home
For a little visit my friend
For a visit I seem to love a
For a visit I do love you, I

For a visit I really love oh
As people know from the home
For a visit I still love you
Till the spacious bitter end
with thought to everything I
With a thought to everything
That I can go over & correct
You're my fortune & my form,
You're my fortune in a form,
You're my blessing and form,
What's this rigid form you I
Is this rigid form you and I
Do you and I make this rigid
Do you make this rigid or I?
We shuttle & return to earth
We don't pay homage to anyone

~

From *Scarlet Tanager*, New Directions, 2005.

Process Note/Assignment: Phone conversation, July 11, 2001.

Bernadette: I was writing as I always do on the typewriter. I started writing with lines of the same number of characters and then I thought it would be interesting to just continue to do this. That was my aim.

Barbara: Why did you start writing about Admiral Scott?

Bernadette: Because I read all the time about Admiral Scott. The Admiral from World War Two. Yeah the guy who went to Antarctica.

Barbara: How long did it take you to write this poem?

Bernadette: I don't really know, a couple of weeks I guess.

Barbara: Each line must have taken a while to get the same amount of characters.

Bernadette: I had to write all these different versions to make them be the same length. And I know nobody cares about this anymore because they just write on the computer. It's an idea I got from Catallus who was writing in hendecasyllables, which are eleven syllable lines, and when I was translating Catallus, I suddenly found myself writing hendecasyllable lines without even knowing it or counting the syllables, so I thought here's a talent I could develop. But do you know what is interesting about this poem. When I read it out loud to an audience, it's very hypnotic.

Barbara: Oh, yeah, it is totally hypnotic.

Bernadette: Amazing.

Barbara: Maybe because of the way you use repetition and then you turn on to another topic. Maybe the repetition came from sitting and working with a line over and over until you got it right.

Bernadette: Yeah, I think so. And not having meaning matter, just the number of characters.

Barbara: But there is meaning anyhow.

Bernadette: Oh yeah, definitely. When I read it in public, I hold it up and I say, "Well, it sounds like prose, but it looks like a poem." And then I hold it up. My students used to ask me all the time, "What is the difference between prose and poetry?" And I used to say, "Well if something looks like a poem, you can say it is poetry."

Bernadette: An assignment from this poem would be counting the number of characters or syllables in your poem. It's an interesting poetic exercise. You could tell your students to consult Moliere's *LeBourgeois Gentilhomme*. Turning prose into poetry is something Buckminister Fuller did well in his book of poems; poetry into prose is just a matter of design. Read *La Vita Nuova* for a mixture of the two. Another good assignment would be to write a *Vita Nuova*, imitating Dante.

from "The People Database"
Kristen Prevellet

During the Gulf War, US troops set up their battalions in the middle of the desert. My cousin told me that to keep from going mad she dug a mile-long circular track in the sand. The tanks and tents that made up her battalion were encircled by her track, and on the outside was nothing but the wind, the dunes, and the miles and miles of sky. She ran around the track for two hours every day. Her hair is red like the sun pounding down on the track and there she ran, with the desert and the war all around her. Tanks on the inside of the circular track and sand on the outside. My cousin told me this. In this war tanks buried enemy civilians alive in the sand, and misguided bombs attacked houses in the night. In the desert she could not hear bombs falling into the night, and saw no enemies buried alive in the sand. She did not venture beyond the circular track, and witnessed nothing outside of the roaming circle made by her battalion. She was protected from the enemy, but not from the weapons used to kill the enemy. She was instructed to take little white pills because chemical warfare was being used by the enemy, and chemical warfare was being used by the Army to counter the chemical warfare being used by the enemy. My cousin threw the white pills in the white sand behind her as she ran the circular track. My cousin told me that she now wonders at herself in the desert running around the tanks to keep from going mad, tossing behind her the little white pills that were supposed to protect her from the chemical warfare of the enemy and the chemical warfare of the Army. It was rumored that the little white pills had never been tested on humans, and that even if they did counteract the chemical warfare of the enemy and the Army, there were other side effects, known and unknown, to taking the little white pills. My cousin debated the logic of taking pills with unknown side effects to protect herself against the chemical warfare of the enemy and the Army. Her red hair in the red sun blaring down on the war, and there was my cousin running madly around it.

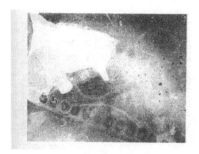

Planes just drop form the sky and disappear into the middle of the ocean. There are pockets of swiftly moving vortices that have suction capabilities so powerful that plane flying into their path would stall and drop. This is the result of global warming. Or highly charged fiberoptic cables that are woven into the ocean floor. Temperature fluctuations are so extreme over the Atlantic that patterns of warm and cold waters are all mixed together. Birds in New York drop out of the sky. One after the other, shooting stars. Flying over the parks and houses and then suspended airborne, dead in mid flight. A strand of encephalitis never before seen in North America has arrived on the East Coast. Now that the world has gotten smaller, airplanes move from one country to another picking up passengers and exchanging packages. Parasites fly. We have set them free. Canals constructed for shipping in the early part of the century allowed lampreys, normally restricted to the ocean, to float into the Great Lakes. By 1960 trout populations had plummeted and once prosperous fishing towns became economically depressed. Planes fall from the sky just as lampreys cup their round incisor mouths around the body of the trout. Parasites are nothing to fear. As humans we are all half parasite. No one is purely human. We are filled with the blood and infections of the entire human race. With time we will evolve to accept our hybridity. birds fall from the sky and land in playgrounds where children witnessing the descent, will forever after believe that it is natural and right for birds to remain for a moment suspended airborne and then fall down dead. Those who refuse to accept this will fall from the sky in planes and sink to the bottom of the ocean where their flesh will become wrapped in fiberoptic cables and send signal to outer space. When the aliens finally arrive it will be clear to us all. We are aliens, and we have been here all along.

~

From *Scratch Sides: Poetry, Documentation, and Image-Text Projects*, Skanky Possum Press, 2003.

Process Note/Assignment: "The People Database" was a public art project conceived by Annemie Maes, a sculptor and installation artist who lives in Brussels. I first saw these photographs at Matrix Art Project and contacted Annemie about the possibility of doing a collaboration. Collected from passport-photo shops, the photographs included in "The People Database" represent real people who had just had their photographs taken. The artist made no alterations of any kind to these photographs—the back flaps were scanned, and each revealed its own unique reaction to the Polaroid chemicals. The website is now closed but you can go to other sites of lost passport photo websites or perhaps foundpoems.net and pick a photograph or two, and write your own reaction to them. Use the photographs to write your own story, or articulate your thoughts, desires, philosophies, and dreams. Annemie writes about her passport photos: "I see these photographs as mirrors. A thousand mirrors, and their thousand reflections give us a critical portrait of the contemporary society."

Appendix B

From The Fragment

A Poetics

(A Dialogue In Quotes Between 63 Writers)

Edited & Collected By
Barbara Henning
1996-97

Antonin Artaud – John Ashbery – Houston A. Baker – Roland Barthes – Jacques Bens – Charles Bernstein – Ted Berrigan – William Blake – Robin Blaser – Bertolt Brecht – Nicole Brossard – William Burroughs – Hèléne Cixous – Catherine Clément – Clark Coolidge – Hart Crane – Robert Creeley – Robert Duncan – Ernest Fenollosa – Rob Fitterman – Michel Foucault – Allen Ginsberg– Pierre Guyutat – Lyn Hejinian – Fanny Howe – Susan Howe – LeRoi Jones (Amiri Baraka) – Franz Kafka – Richard Kostelanetz – Richard Lanham – Ann Lauterbach – Francois LeLionnais – Bernadette Mayer – Vladimir Mayakovsky – Douglas Messerli – Warren F. Motte, Jr. – Harryette Mullen – Alice Notley – Frank O'Hara – Charles Olson – Ron Padgett – Pound Ezra – Raymond Queneau – David Rattray – Kenneth Rexroth – Laura Riding – Alain Robbe-Grillet – Rena Rosenwasser – Jerome Rothenberg – Ed Sanders – Leslie Scalapino – R.W. Sellars – Ron Silliman – Gertrude Stein – Wallace Stevens – Ronald Sukenick – Lorenzo Thomas – Chris Tysh – Anne Waldman – Alan Watts – William Carlos Williams – Virginia Woolf

Table Of Contents

Intro—

Several years ago, I began to collect these passages from various essays by poets, philosophers and critics, ideas of importance to many experimental writers. The intent was to promote dialogue, not to write a manifesto.

Some of the areas covered: (1) To approach language as material; (2) To live a poetic life, collaborating with other poets and artists; (3) To break rules and make up new forms and constraints; (4) To write the truth, as you know it; (5) To acknowledge and consider the slippery nature of truth, language and thought; and (6) instead of trying to reproduce reality, to change it.

There are approximately 125 passages, including my own text; the passages range from one short sentence to 150 words. I hope that this fragmented collection of manifestos, interviews, essays and statements on poetics will introduce you to some of the history and slanted thinking about experimental poetics and poetry, at least by those writers who have influenced my writing and thinking.

With humor and confusion,
as poetry baffles,
so may this
Barbara Henning
1996, 2020

Material & Expression

Language as a real thing is not imitation either of sounds or colors or emotions it is an intellectual recreation and there is no possible doubt about it and it is going to go on being that as long as humanity is anything. Gertrude Stein ("Poetry and Grammar" 238)

***

I do not transcribe. I construct. This has been even the old ambition of Flaubert: to make something out of nothing, something that would stand alone, without having to lean on anything external to the work. Alain Robbe-Grillet (162).

***

One isn't putting things *into* poems, then at least not as my own experience of writing informs me. There is never a "subject" *about* which one constructs an activity called "poetry." Nor can one, as Williams says, "copy nature," take from that which is elsewise informed some felicitous appearance, whether a rhyme or a so-called sentiment.. . . what emerges in the writing I most value is a content which cannot be anticipated, which "tells you what you don't know," which you subvert, twist, or misrepresent only on peril of death. Robert *Creeley* (272-73)

***

It is no accident that Pound and Williams both were involved variously in a movement which got called "objectivism.". . . What seems to me a more valid formal action for present usage is "objectism," a word to be taken to stand for a kind of relation of man to experience which a poet might state as a necessity of a line or a work to be as wood is, to be as clean as wood is as it issues from the hand of nature, to be as shaped as wood can be when a man has his hand to it. Objectivism is the getting rid of the lyrical interference of the individual as ego, of the "subject" and his soul, that peculiar presumption by which Western man has interposed himself between what he is as a creature of nature . . . and those other creations of nature which we may, with no derogation, call objects. For man is himself an object. Charles Olson ("Projective Verse," 24)

***

Literature is concerned with plot and character. Its intention is to be "well-written" and "comprehensible." It's a very commonplace activity. Then there is the progression towards writing . . . In any case, by "writing," I mean simple textual writing.. . . It is that desire to do something new which compels one to move from literature to writing and from writing to *matière écrite* . . . brutal matter . . . no wasted words or wasted time. I also colored in the paper on which I wrote my poems . . . For me, the manuscript itself is a piece of visual art.. . . There is an *oral* aspect to it, as well as a visual and a musical architectural aspect . . . This is no longer "writing," it's the process of working with a material that is common to all art.

An artist who reaches this point-like Beethoven in music of Cézanne in painting—no longer knows, in the final count, how he does what he does. I am convinced of this. I call this a state of wisdom. Pierre Guyotat (19)

***

If you start with rules, you've really got a tough road. What I think is that you start with materials. You start with matter, not with rules. The rules appear, the limitations appear, and those are *your* limitations and the limitations of the material. Clark Coolidge (159-60)

***

Once again I want to insist that I offer no rules to make anyone a poet, by following which he can write poetry. Such rules simply don't exist. A poet is a person who creates these very rules.. . . . (13)

I make this reservation: establishing rules is not in itself the aim of poetry, otherwise the poet turns into a scholar exercising his powers in formulating rules for non-existent or useless things and propositions.. . . (14)

Materials. Words. Fill your storehouse constantly, fill the granaries of your skull with all kinds of words, necessary, expressive, rare, invented, renovated and manufactured (19).. . .

A poet regards every meeting, every signpost, every event in whatever circumstances simply as material to be shaped into words. (24)
Vladimir Mayakovsky

***

I think a simple one phrase definition of poetry is: the invention of life or reality through language. To invent reality through words, this is what poetry does. And it isn't such a high falutin' thing . . . It must make people want to dance, or to make love, or to sing. It must fill them with the impulses to do something real in life; it must stimulate their imagination and their mind. It must entertain them and give them something to think about and provide them with solid information. I believe that good poets and good poems do this. David Rattray (5)

***

Think of a poem as a place in which you can put a lot of strange beautiful things, in strange beautiful settings.. . . when the feeling arises in me that I have enough material to make three or four poems, I will sit down perhaps and make one. And I'll use that material plus what comes to me from starting to put the material in the places that it should go, in the places that it indicates it should go. Ted Berrigan ("The Business of. . . " 54, 56)

***

When I was about eight years old, my mother gave me a diary with a key. When I was eleven and she died, my diary became a place to talk to her, a place to grieve, wonder and plan my get away. Later as a young adult, I began to collect quotations and ideas in my journal. Then I began experimenting with various approaches to journal writing by using different books, pens and typewriters, and also by pasting in objects and subverting a linear approach to writing by using columns and entries on entries.

My mother taught me how to make quilts from circles of fabric that were cut out of old clothes and sheets. We would cut and sew around the edges, pulling the thread to create little pockets. The pockets were then flattened, sorted by color and design, and sewn together to make the a cover for the quilt. Because her resources were limited and she had four children, she was an expert at collecting and organizing scraps of this and that to make doll clothes, our clothes, drapes and other household items.

Perhaps that why I enjoy sorting scraps of language from my notebooks into different categories depending on the questions and designs I am thinking through. Information, images and partial encounters are part of my everyday urban life. Some of the fragments I find are beautiful. Some are disturbing. Filth and decay can be swept up and recycled. Nails and screws can be sorted. A terribly difficult book can be enjoyed and traces kept with notes. I pull out the beautiful-terrible-banal from my journals, my reading and listening and I write poetry—discovering, layering, experimenting. BH

***

Don't imagine that the art of poetry is any simpler than the art of music, or that you can please the expert before you have spent at least as much effort on the art of verse as the average piano teacher spends on the art of music. Ezra Pound ("Retrospect" 38)

***

The poet is never inspired, because he is the master of that which appears to others as inspiration. He does not wait for inspiration to fall out of the heavens on him like roasted ortolans. He knows how to hunt, and lives by the incontestable proverb, 'God helps them that help themselves.' He is never inspired because he is unceasingly inspired, because the powers of poetry are always at his disposition, subjected to his will, submissive to his own activity. Raymond Queneau (43)

***

Inspiration which consists in blind obedience to every impulse is in reality a sort of slavery. Raymond Queneau (41)

***

Today, many use marijuana or LSD in order to come into a reality larger than tehir own personality or case history or their one family or one city or one nation or one species. But I do it on language. *Words* send me. Robert Duncan ("Man's Fulfillment . . .," p. 121.)

***

A professor once corrected me on my ideas about poetry: "Lyric poetry should express desire directly. It should please the heart and mind. It is meant to be sung or with elevated words and figures of speech." But desire is that which flees reality, that which can never be satisfied let alone clearly articulated. Perhaps those who are born with a promise might experience their desire as more tangible. Those, however, who live their separation, fissure, splinter and division as a given part of their human condition speak of desire indirectly. Should we attempt to speak directly? Or remain mute and wordless? Or allow desire to pass through our songlike talklike machinelike poems indirectly. At a slant. BH

***

Suddenly I was in Iowa with all these people who were aspiring writers . . . and I met some people that were writing poems, and I thought that was really strange because I had never met anyone who wrote poems before. And they were writing poems, and I almost instantly started writing poems. And I was really fascinated by the fact that you could do all your manipulations on a single page, and that the material was right there in this block, and there were terrific kinds of control over words that you didn't have when you were writing stories, and it all came down to the words, and I guess that's when I found out that I was a poet. So it really turned out that I was more interested in words than I was in stories or a kind of narrative flow. I wasn't interested in creating a reality. I was interested in doing something with words and truth. Alice Notley (Interview 89)

***

THERE is too much of human material now everywhere: the world is covered with "the man-made." None of our problems can be solved by making more of it, more of the material, including books. Shiny-covered, same-looking books everywhere. To go into a bookstore & be made sick by all the books there, is almost the same as to be made sick by all the dead cars in New Jersey, seen from the train window, early in the morning. All achievement, writerly & poetic achievement included, must become more invisible. The notion of "soul," of the Invisible, must be taken up again. Alice Notley ("Introduction", v)

***

There is an inner and subtle quality that creates the fundamental difference between expert and artist. This quality is to achieve the technique and forget it. A truly spiritual artist is one who forgets himself and in that self-forgetfulness achieves the bliss which is called Ananda. (Rukmini Devi)

***

—No. No. Picasso said [to the character, Vladimir Tatlin] Waste not a minute. Go do what you want to, what you can. Get a lifetime of work into a week. Plan nothing: make. Guy Davenport (23)

CONSPIRE & COMMUNE

Be influenced by as many great artists as you can, but have the decency, either to acknowledge the debt outright, or to try to conceal it.. . . Let the candidate fill his mind with the finest cadence he can discover, preferably in a foreign language, so that the meaning of the words may be less likely to divert his attention from the movement. Ezra Pound ("Retrospect" 38-39)

***

I read all of Pound and saw what to put into poems, I got the direct message from Pound--put everything in your poems, everything that's going on in your life, what it says in the letters you get, in the books you read, what you see in the street . . . What you're reading . . . Ted Berrigan (Homage 109)

***

And it [our poetry] has come out of a conflict—more or less deeply felt—with inherited forms of poetry, literature, language, discourse: not in every instance but where there are recognized repressive structures, forms of categorical thinking that act against that other free play of possibilities just alluded to.. . . The past, come alive, is in motion with us. It is no longer somewhere else but, like the future, here—which is the only way it can be, toward a poetry of changes. Jerome Rothenberg (135)

***

And the best thing to do when you begin is to pick some poet whose poems you like, and imitate some. And then find other poets & other poems and imitate them. The worst thing you can do is to tell anyone who you are imitating. Because then everyone will think that all the good parts in your poems come out of being a good imitation. When, in fact, the exact opposite will be true. The good parts will come out of where you misunderstand entirely what the poet you are imitating is doing, & so write something that is completely dumb, but that turns out to be very good. Misunderstanding is one of the truly creative procedures in writing. Ted Berrigan ("The Business of . . . " 43)

***

RC: I'd advise students to read. Study with someone who intrigues you, or provokes you, even confuses you. SH: People have to find their own voices somehow. To me poetry is, I hate to say it, something holy, and I hate to confuse it with a career. The brochure of the creative writing program I'm teaching in now says things like, "We have so and so students published in *The New Yorker*, *The Antioch Review*"—this whole thing of contests and magazine publications connected to poetry makes me sick. RC: it's particularly offensive with poetry because poetry is a communal art. Poetry is company, however sentimentally that puts it. I feel it has a kinship with music. I always admired or envied the way musicians would hang out together. In the literary arts, the only group that hangs out together are poets. SH: The one good thing about a writing program is the community. Robert Creeley & Susan Howe (21-22)

***

In the spring of early summer of 1912, "H.D.," Richard Aldington and myself decided that we were agreed upon the three principles following:

    1. Direct treatment of the "thing" whether subjective or objective.

    2. To use absolutely no word that does not contribute to the presentation.

    3. As regarding rhythm: to compose in the sequence of the musical phrase, not in sequence of a metronome. Ezra Pound ("A Retrospect" 36)

***

When I returned from deportation [in 1960], we began to meet more and more often, for no other reason than to wallow together in that which interested us so passionately. Imperceptibly, as we gradually became conscious of belonging to a sort of knighthood of the heteroclite, the affinity we felt in the beginning was transformed into profound friendship. François Le Lionnais (74)

***

I will describe experiments I performed with Brion Gysin and Ian Sommerville twelve years before *Breakthrough* was published and, in fact, before it was written. These experiments started not on tape recorders but on paper. In 1959, Brion Gysin said, "Writing is fifty years behind painting," and applied the montage technique to words on a page.

These cut-up experiments appear in *Minutes to Go*, in 1959. Subsequently, we cut up the Bible, Shakespeare, Rimbaud, our own writing, anything in sight. William Burroughs (63-64).

***

Then I learned about *Evergreen Review* and suddenly started reading all these modernist poets such as Leroi Jones and Frank O'Hara, and I subscribed to the magazines advertised in *Evergreen Review* like Leroi Jones' *Yugen* and Wallace Barman's *Semina*. And when I looked at magazines like *Yugen*, I saw they were just little things stapled together, and so I went down to a local printer and asked, How to you do this? And he said, Oh, it's nothing—it's real easy. So I decided to start my own magazine. I invited Dick Gallup, who was still across the street and was writing poetry, to be co-editor and Joe Brainard, who was the best artist in school, to be the art editor.. . . Yes, I met Ted in the spring of 1959, I was working in the bookstore, and Ted walked in with three friends of his. Ron Padgett (102)

***

In 1974 Kit Robinson published a one-shot magazine, *Streets and Roads*, in San Francisco, bringing together for the first time writing by himself, Watten (who had also settled in the city and was now entirely in charge of *This*), Provincetown poet Alan Bernheimer, Bob Perelman of Boston and two Los Angeles residents, Steven Benson and Carla Harryman. Within three years, all would be living in San Francisco. Watten would begin a reading series at the Grand Piano. Perelman, who began *Hills* before he came west, would host talks on poetics by writers at his Folsom Street loft. This concentration was further deepened with the arrival of Lyn Hejinian, Tom Mandel and others. Ron Silliman ("Language, Realism and Poetry" xvii)

***

When we, the six founders of Kelsey St. Press, began as publishers we were aware of the authorial presence of the female voice in literature. The actuality of Woolf, Stein, and H.D. resonated in readings that we read to ourselves and to each other. We were going back to sources, conscious of how these writers had been neglected in our own college studies. The textual sound of Adrienne Rich reading *Diving Into The Wreck* had just occurred. We were women, five of us poets, who had been meeting in a group to read and provide critical commentary on each other's work. It was nineteen-seventy-three. . . . An anthology of Bay Area Beat Poets had just been released. It neglected to mention women writers. We bitterly resented this deletion in a history that canonized the Beat poetic voice. Co-founding a press to publish new writing by women was a means of questioning the centrality of the male figure in writing. Rena Rosenwasser (92)

***

And so I had a long talk with Ron Padgett, who at that time was eighteen years old, and I told him everything I understood and then I didn't remember any more about it until a good number of years later, and then I asked Ron one time if he remembered that talk, and he said he remembered it very well, it had changed his life. So I asked him what I said, but he didn't remember either. Ted Berrigan
("The Business of . . . " 47)

***

The avant-garde movement of the Lower East Side in the early 1960s—when it turned, for some people at least, into the "East Village"—was a remarkable period. Grim though the walkups might have been, the atmosphere of creative and artistic energy was exhilarating. There was ludic buoyancy—perhaps from hunger, or too much herbal tea. Maybe it was because there was so much jazz in the air, maybe because the poets knew the musicians who knew the painters who knew the dancers. (537)

. . . The most remarkable thing about the Lower East Side scene was that, while race remained a powerful engine of social upheaval, the artists seemed able to work together almost in spite of it. (575) . . . Because they were all outsiders in an immigrant community, the avant-garde artists became a community. Because those who were African American came there to become artists, not to avoid being black, there was a kind of integrated society that did not seem to exist elsewhere. (576)

. . . As Harlem had been the locus of the Renaissance of the 1920s, it was—in part—to the Lower East Side that *Time magazine* turned in 1970 to assess the new directions in the arts pioneered by African American artists. Lorenzo Thomas (578)

***

Ken: When the young language folks were in the workshop, what was the dynamic like?
Bernadette: It was great. It was over that period of years that we made the experiment
list. Then, after a while, the workshop became a true collaboration. The very last year
that I was doing it I wasn't even doing it anymore. We had a rotating leadership, so that
every week somebody in the workshop would do something else. People came up with
different experiments and it would go on for 4 or 5 hours. We talked a lot about theory,
Jacques Lacan, semiotics, and stuff like that. Though theory didn't have much to do with
the way I had evolved as a writer, I was very interested in all those things. They were
much more interesting then than they are at the moment, you know. Bernadette Mayer
& Ken Jordan (8)

***

Ezra Pound admonished, "Make it new!" Gertrude Stein had said, "Anybody that creates
a new thing has to make it ugly." I took these as urgent commands to get on with my own
work, however raw and crude it might be, as well as to help create a forum for younger
writers, which would simultaneously honor the "elders." The only criterion for judgment
would be whether the work truly "breathes," (in Emily Dickinson's sense of the term).
(2) . . . We decided to call our new venture a poetry "project" because we saw it as an ongoing event requiring hard work and perseverance. We also had in mind the sense of an
outward *projecting*, "to direct one's voice to be heard clearly at a distance." Public readings
were at the heart of the plan." (Anne Waldman. ("Introduction" 4)

*****

BREAK & REMAKE

In April of 1997 I was sitting beside a dear friend. His body was full of fluids and his penis had slipped back inside. In his wretched/agitated state, I sang, calming him as we had calmed our babies. His sex became meaningless. And yet as I talk about him, I mark him, I gender him. The first thing we announce when a baby is born is, it's a girl, it's a boy, it's a question. And this helps us imagine a life to come, a life to pass, in our community and in our language. As gender marks out a social order, along come expectations and demands and sometimes a rigid armor. We often forget the whisper before the words. The poetic word undoes, confounds, so I perpetually eraser and re-arrange. A powerful poetry, I think, breaks and remakes, speaking differently, the language of the mad, the genius, the imaginary, the ordinary—rhythm, music, hunger, timbre, loss, gesture, color, form, laughter, agony. All art disrupts the symbolic order (and conventional notions about gender, the real, normal and natural) unless it is made to keep the king in power. Even then, it might secretly be a little disruptive. I like poetry that disturbs rather than supports the status quo, the conventions and my own expectations about gender, genre, sentence and sense. To revise examine analyze and introduce other voices and discourses into everyday language and everyday thought. To listen to noise. To call into question culture, history, the future. To call into question what I think. what I write. what I say. Easily. what I leave out. What eye. BH

* * *

Ideally an experimental writer reinvents language anew for every work or every phase of his artistic life. . . .[Quoting Pound:] Willingness to experiment is not enough, but unwillingness to experiment is mere death. ("Avant-Garde" 245-6) Richard Kostelanetz.

* * *

Experimentation. The devising of experiments is one of the important methods of interrogating nature and getting significant data. The essence of an experiment is the *control* of the factors and conditions of an occurrence. By means of control, the experimenter is able to eliminate factors and notice the effects, or combine them, or vary them one by one, or introduce new factors. Within certain limits, he can do with nature as he wishes and make it answer his questions. Thus experimentation is a method of controlled analysis, synthesis and variation which enables men to get nature to do definite things repeatedly. (R. W. Sellars The Essentials of Logic 185)

***

It is not the poet, but the poem: the most that the poet can do is to be a wise, experimenting parent.

Experiment, however, may be interpreted in two ways. In the first sense it is a delicate and constantly alert state of expectancy directed towards the discovery of something of which some slight clue has been given; and the system in it means only the constant shifting and adjustment of the experimenter as the unknown thing becomes more and more known: system is the readiness to change system. The important thing in the whole process is the initial clue, or, in old-fashioned language, the inspiration. The real scientist should have an equal power of genius with the poet, with the difference that the scientist is inspired to discover things which already are (his results are facts), while the poet is inspired to discover things which are made by his discovery of them (his results are not statements about things already known to exist, or knowledge, but truths, things which existed before only as potential truth). Experiment in the second sense is the use of a system for its own sake and brings about, whether in science or poetry, no results but those possible to the system.. . .

Poets, then, who need the support of a system (labourers pretending to be inventors, since in poetry, unlike science, there is no place for labourers) are obliged to adopt not only the workshop method of science, but the whole philosophical point of view of science, which is directly opposite to the point of view of poetry. For in science there is no personality granted to the things discovered, which are looked upon as soulless parts of a soulless aggregate, with no independent rights or life of their own. Such poets, therefore, produce poems that are only well-ordered statements about chosen subjects, not new, independent living organisms; facts, not truths, pieces of literature, not distinct poetic personalities. Poetry of this sort (and there has been little poetry of any other sort, as there have been few real poets) is thus the science of poem-training instead of the art of poem-appreciation. The real poet is a poet by reason of his creative vision of the poem, as the real parent is a parent by reason of his creative vision of the child: authorship is not a matter of the right use of the will but of an enlightened withdrawal of the will to make room for the will. Laura (Jackson) Riding and Robert Graves (Survey 125-127)

***

For the experimenter it is more important to have beauty in one's experiments than to have them fit mathematics.

The most real, the truth, the beauty of the poem is a configuration, but also a happening in language, that leads back into or on towards the beauty of the universe itself. I am but part of the whole of what I am, and wherever I seek to understand I fail what I know. Robert Duncan ("Towards" 79)

***

Where certain individuals see an example of original, conscious, and lucid poetic innovation, others will see only empty acrobatics, pretension, and literary madness. Warren F. Motte, Jr. (3)

***

I'd get American magazines like *Esquire*, open the pages, get a phrase from it, and then start writing on my own. When I ran out, I'd go back to the magazine. It was pure experimentation. John Ashbery (1976 NYT interview).

***

In his earliest verse Williams constantly uses the irregular caesura, the multiple caesura, and the runover line; lines that end in "the," "of," "and," "with," "but," fascinate him. What he is after is a strophe that breaks the syntax and creates an anti-logic, an anti-rational wit which finds a new rationality and a new logic—Gertrude Stein, André Breton, Korzybski, Norbert Weiner, Whorf—the effort to free the thought processes of modern man living in a polyvalent, polymorphous, multiphasic universe opened up by his technology, from the Euclidian patterns of Aristotelian logic based on the idealization of Greek grammar and syntax. This becomes a battle cry of poets, logicians, philologists, psychiatrists, and all sorts of people as the twentieth century grows old. Kenneth Rexroth (82)

***

The classical playwright who writes his tragedy observing a certain number of familiar rules is freer than the poet who writes that which comes into his head and who is the slave of other rules of which he is ignorant. Raymond Queneau (41)

***

Every literary work begins with an inspiration (at least that's what its author suggests) which must accommodate itself as well as possible to a series of constraints and procedures that fit inside each other like Chinese boxes. Constraints of vocabulary and grammar, constraints of the novel (division into chapters, etc.) or of classical tragedy (rule of the three unities), constraints of general versification, constraints of fixed forms (as in the case of the rondeau or the sonnet), etc.

Must one adhere to the old tricks of the trade and obstinately refuse to imagine new possibilities? The partisans of the status quo don't hesitate to answer in the affirmative . . . Should humanity lie back and be satisfied to watch new thoughts make ancient verses? We don't believe that it should. François Le Lionnais (26-27).

***

When Arnold Schoenberg told his pupil John Cage that he had no talent for harmony, the young man disregarded harmony in his musical experiments; when Gertrude Stein was told her writing was often ungrammatical, she made her principle experiment the possibilities of ungrammatical English. Richard Kostelanetz ("Avant-Garde 245)

***

As a method of learning how to write, the obfuscated poem must still cover to hide a real energy in training.. . . . The best obfuscation bewilders old meanings while reflecting or imitating or creating a structure of a beauty that we know.. . . The idea that real change— and its consequent repellent revolution where your best friend's suddenly the prison warden in the rigid stumbling of professional belief—is not at the heart of experiment in which lies the chance for liberation, is the kind of scam where you might find the book you are reading grabbed from your hands. Bernadette Mayer (166)

***

You say that I want someone to Elucidate my Ideas. But you ought to know that What is Grand is necessarily obscure to Weak men. That which can be made Explicit to the Idiot is not worth my care. The wisest of the ancients considered what is not too Explicit as the fittest for Instruction, because it rouzes the faculties to act. I name Moses, Solomon, Esop, Homer, Plato. William Blake. (Letter To the Revd. Dr. Trusler, August 23, 1799)

***

When a poem is attacked for obscurity it is either because the reader has gone to the poem in order to be put into a poetic mood (not to have reality uncovered for him as it can be uncovered alone in poems)—or because the poet has been concerned neither with providing a poem nor with stirring up a poetic mood in his readers, only with enjoying the display of his own faculties.. . . The reply to the charge of obscurity, from the poet who writes poems for the reasons of poetry, can only be: my poems represent so much poetic learning, and you can learn from them as much as I have learned—if you admit the reasons of poetry. (485)

. . . Poems will not serve as reading-matter when you want detective fiction, or a play, or anything but poems. (489) Laura (Riding) Jackson ("Original 1938 Preface")

***

That is the paradox, because to be accessible usually means buying into an established set of formal guidelines and traditions. The very nature of establishing those forms defines the certainty that the moment of their relevance has already past. In other words, any form that's already defined comes from another age. As the inventor or creator, as an artist echoing the present, as someone bringing his/her lineage and sensibility out into new territory, the poet finds him or herself in the arena of inaccessibility as heard through the ears of the reader.. . . And, of course, it's not just the difficulty or discontinuity that makes the poet inaccessible—an accessible poet is not necessarily simple, but safe—i.e. safely using forms of the past without questioning them. Rob Fitterman (7)

***

ONE PERCEPTION MUST IMMEDIATELY AND DIRECTLY LEAD TO A FURTHER PERCEPTION. . . . get on with it, keep moving, keep in speed, the nerves, their speed, the perceptions, theirs, the acts, the split second acts, the whole business, keep it moving as fast as you can, citizen. Charles Olson ("Projective Verse," 17)

***

By 1955 I wrote poetry adapted from prose seeds, journals, scratching, arranged by phrasing or breath groups into little shortline patterns according to ideas of measure of

American speech I'd picked up from W.C Williams' imagist preoccupations . . . [In *Howl*] the whole section typed out madly in one afternoon . . . I depended on the word "who" to keep the beat . . . Ideally each line of *Howl* is a single breath unit.. . . My breath is long— that's the Measure, one physical-mental inspriation of thought contained in the elastic of a breath.. . . So these poems are a series of experiments with the formal organization of the long line.. . . Whitman's form . . . A lot of these forms developed out of an extreme rhapsodic wail I once heard in a madhouse. Allen Ginsberg ("Notes for Howl and other Poems", 318-320).

***

Sonnets always seemed interesting just because of the way they let you think within the poem. Sonnets permit you to think in a way that other poems might not. You couldn't think the same way given another really strict form. You don't think in a sestina the way you think in a sonnet.

I like the idea of fooling around with the question of beginnings and middles and end-ings, those concepts one always hates in writing, especially in fiction and the sonnet has them. The traditional form of the sonnet is to set up the scene, and then develop it in the middle, and come to a conclusion in the end couplet. And that's really stupid.

The traditional form of the sonnet is to set up the scene, and then develop it in th emid-dle, and come to a conclusion in the end couplet. And that's really stupid.

That's not the way we think; but it is structurally fascinating to do it. To not do it while also doing it. I'm not sure of how that's done, but if you're always aware that you're doing that, and you're not doing it at the same time . . . Bernadette Mayer ("The Colors" 9)

***

But my point here is that the minuet, the game of tennis, the heroic couplet, the concept of form as the imposing of rules and establishing of regularities, the theories of civili-zation, race and progress, the performances in sciences and arts to rationalize the uni-verse, to secure balance and class—all these are a tribal magic against a real threat of an upset and things not keeping their place.. . . A change in mode, in what was permitted, once threatened demonic disorder. Now, unconventional usages threaten loss of reason or insurrection. It is an architecture built up of symmetries for the mind feels even visual departures from the norm will bring vertigo and collapse. There must be regular sequences and a repetition of stanzas because thought must not wander, possibility must contain the reassurance of an end to possibilities. Robert Duncan ("Ideas of the Meaning of Form" 102)

***

I think that one reason there is so much ugly antipathy to writers who are breaking form in anyway is because people know that language taps an unpredictable power source in all of us. It's not the same in the visual arts where there are many abstract or form-breaking artists who enjoy wide popularity, are embraced by a critical establishment, and sell their work for a tremendous amount of money. You will see their work in museums and books about the work on large glass coffee tables. Try the same thing with language, and you may find your writing lost. This is because words are used as buoys, and if they start to break up . . . then everything goes because words connect us with life. Susan Howe (65)

*****

Truth & Lies

It is one of the greatest glories of this universe that the common and inconspicuous life of ordinary men contains a thousand daily opportunities of spiritual splendor. Ernest Wood, 41.

***

I think we ought to read only the kind of books that wound and stab us. If the book we are reading doesn't wake us up with a blow on the head, what are we reading it for? . . . But we need books that affect us like a disaster, that grieve us deeply, like the death of someone we loved more than ourselves, like being banished into forests far from everyone, like a suicide. A book must be the axe for the frozen sea inside us. That is my belief. Franz Kafka (17)

***

Why are such books so rare? Because those who write the books that hurt us also suffer, also undergo a sort of suicide, also get lost in forests—and this is frightening. Hèléne Cixous (18)

***

And if there is still one hellish, truly accursed thing in our time, it is our artistic dallying with forms, instead of being like victims burnt at the stake, signalling through the flames. Antoine Artaud (13)

***

Like jazz, poetry must address a deep and total reality of being, and it must, somehow, perform a redemptive function. Lorenzo Thomas ("Communicating" 297).

***

We are led to Believe in a Lie
When we see not Thro' the Eye
      William Blake ("Auguries of Innocence," 153)

**

It is my hope to go through the combined materials of the poem, using our "real" world somewhat as a spring-board, and to give the poem as a whole an orbit or predetermined direction of its own free from my own personality as from any chance evaluation on the reader's part. (This is, of course, an impossibility, but it is a characteristic worth mentioning.) Such a poem is at least a stab at the truth. Hart Crane (163).

***

I got all hung up on Cézanne around 1949 in my last years at Columbia, studying with Meyer Schapiro. I don't know how it led into it—I think it was about the same time that I was having these Blake visions. So, the thing I understood from Blake was that it was possible to transmit a message through time which could reach the enlightened, that poetry had a definite effect, it wasn't just pretty, or just beautiful, as I had understood pretty beauty before—it was something basic to human existence, or it reached something, it reached the bottom of human existence. But anyway the impression I got was that it was like a kind of time machine through which he could transmit, Blake could transmit, his basic consciousness and communicate it to somebody else after he was dead, in other words, build a time machine. Allen Ginsberg (Paris Review, 24-25)

**

Nowadays, anyone who wishes to combat lies and ignorance and to write the truth must overcome at least five difficulties. He must have the *courage* to write the truth when truth is everywhere opposed; the *keenness* to recognize it although it is everywhere concealed; the *skill* to manipulate it as a weapon; the judgment to select those in whose hands it will be effective; and the *cunning* to spread the truth among such persons. These are formidable problems for writers living under Fascism, but they exist also for those writers who have fled or been exiled; they exist even for writers working in countries where civil liberty prevails. (133) . ..What is necessary for all writers in this age of perplexity and lightning change is a knowledge of the materialistic dialectic of economy and history. This knowledge can be acquired from books and from practical instruction, if the necessary diligence is applied. Many truths can be discovered in simpler fashion, or at least portions of truths, or facts that lead to the discovery of truths. Bertolt Brecht (136)

***

The only poetic tradition is the Voice out of the burning bush. The rest is trash, & will be consumed. Allen Ginsberg. ("When the Mode of the Music Changes the Walls of the City Shake". 327)

***

Of course, I circle "the truth" with all kinds of signs, quotation marks, and brackets, to protect it from any form of fixation or conceptualization, since it is one of those words that constantly crosses our universe in a dazzling wake, but is also pursued by suspicion. I will talk about truth again, without which (without the word *truth,* without the mystery *truth)* there would be no writing. It is what writing wants.. . . Paradise is down below. According to my people, writing isn't given. Giving oneself to writing means being in a position to do this work of digging, of unburying, and this entails a long period of apprenticeship . . . Our lives are buildings made up of lies. We have to lie to live. But to write we must try to unlie. Something renders going in the direction of truth and dying almost synonymous. It is dangerous to go in the direction of truth.. . . Thinking is trying to think the unthinkable: thinking the thinkable is not worth the effort. Painting is trying to paint what you cannot paint and writing is writing what you cannot know before you have written: it is preknowing and not knowing, blindly, with words. Hèléne Cixous (6, 36, 38)

**

It's a mistake, I think, to posit the self as the primary organizing feature of writing. As many others have pointed out, a poem exists in a matrix of social and historical relations that are more significant to the formation of an individual text than any personal qualities of the life or voice of an author. Tom Beckett to Charles Bernstein (408-9)

*****

Try to look for the worst in yourself and confide it where there is no process of erasure, where the worst remains the worst. Try to write the worst and you will see that the worst will turn against you and, treacherously, we try to veil the worst. For we cannot bear the worst. Writing the worst is an exercise that requires us to be stronger than ourselves.. . .

The inclination for avowal, the desire for avowal, the yearning to taste the taste of avowal, is what compels us to write: both the need to avow and its impossibility. Because most of the time the moment we avow we fall into the snare of atonement: confession—and forgetfulness. Confession is the worst thing: it disavows what it avows.. . . Hélène Cixous (42, 45)

*****

Poetry (...) could be a force for the re-establishment of the invisible, for making people's inner lives more important than this constant assertion of substance. For poetry is not about words or how one thinks, or makes things. It is about essence—the secret inside the material. It uses rhythmic speech to tell what it knows, because measure helps the defining of essence, because whatever is done should be done attractively, because rhythm is bound up with living. Poetry aims at truth. But the truth is not intellectual, it is the truth Alice Notley ("Introduction", v-vi)

The Slippery & The Certain

Poetry is concerned with using with abusing, with losing with wanting, with denying with avoiding with adoring with replacing the noun. It is doing that always doing that, doing that and doing nothing but that. Poetry is doing nothing but using losing refusing and pleasing and betraying and caressing nouns. That is what poetry does, that is what poetry has to do no matter what kind of poetry it is. And there are a great many kinds of poetry. (231)

...

And then, something happened and I began to discover the names of things, that is not discover the names but discover the things the things to see the things to look at and in so doing I had of course to name them not to give them new names but to see that I could find out how to know that they were there by their names or by replacing their names. And how was I to do so. They had their names and naturally I called them by the names they had and in doing so have begun looking at them I called them by their names with passion and that made poetry, I did not mean it to make poetry but it did, it made the Tender Buttons, and the Tender Buttons was very good poetry it made a lot more poetry, and I will now more and more tell about that and how it happened. (235)

      Gertrude Stein ("Poetry & Grammar")

***

Things are in a continual state of motion and evolution, and if we come to a point where we say, with certitude, right here, this is the end of the universe, then of course we must deal with everything that goes on after that, whereas ambiguity seems to take further developments into account. (46)

      . . . I think I am trying to reproduce the polyphony that goes on inside me, which I don't think is radically different from that of other people.(50)

      . . . on the whole I feel that poetry is going on all the time inside, an underground stream. One can let down one's bucket and bring the poem back up.. . . I don't believe in automatic writing as the Surrealists were supposed to have practiced it, simply because it is not a reflection of the whole mind, which is partly logical and reasonable, and that part should have is say, too. (51)

      . . . I think I am more interested in the movement among ideas than in the ideas themselves, the way one goes from one point to another rather than the destination or the origin. (55) John Ashbery ("The Art of Poetry XXXIII")

***

The method of zen is to baffle, excite, puzzle and exhaust the intellect until it is realized that intellection is only thinking *about.* (19) . . . Thus Zen is sometimes described as 'straight forwardness' or 'going right ahead', for Zen is to move with life without trying to arrest and interrupt its flow; it is an immediate awareness of things as they live and move, as distinct from the mere grasp of ideas and feelings *about* things which are the dead symbols of a living reality. (52) . . . How can truth be known if it can never be defined? Zen would answer: by not trying to grasp or define it. (58) . . . The Zen masters distinguished between two kinds of phrases (*chu*)—the dead and the living—the dead being those which were amenable to logical analysis and solution, and the living, being those which could never be confused to any fixed system of interpretation . . . the realization that life can never be grasped, never possessed or made to stand still (75). Alan Watts (Spirit of Zen)

***

Madwomen, as we saw earlier, invert the order of the world: their ravings reveal the truth because they are deeply subversive. Lacan now embarked upon a systematic inversion of the world. The first paradoxical result was this: the psychoanalyst became the spokesman of silence . . . the reverse of the normal contract. Catherine Clément (110)

***

Writing poetry for me is often more a matter of texture than form.. . . . I continue to use what Stephen Yenser identified as "multivalent fragments," which produce a layered effect of multiple and sometimes contradictory semantic meanings and cultural allusions. I am also interested in the textural effects enabled by what Roman Jakobson called "subliminal verbal patterning" in literary and folk poetry.. . . . My writing process is improvisatory, and certainly I have been influenced by instrumental and vocal improvisations of blues and jazz musicians. Some of the lines I write aspire to certain moments in jazz when scat becomes a kind of inspired speaking in tongues, or glossolalia, moments when utterance aspires to pure music.. . . . Muse & Drudge, like the jazz soloist who plays "mysterious" music, locates itself in a space where it is possible to pay dues, respects, and "props" to tradition while still claiming the freedom to wander to the other side of far. Harryette Mullen

***

Someone asked at the last session what the tape voices have to do with poetics. Answer: Everything. Writers work with words and voices just as painters work with colors. An important point here is the misconception that a writer creates in a vacuum using only his very own words. Was he blind deaf and illiterate from birth? A writer does not own words any more than a painter owns colors. So let's dispense with this "originality" fetish. Is a painter committing plagiarism if he paints a mountain that other painters have painted? Even if he paints a mountain from another painter's painting of a mountain.

Writers work with words and voices and where do these words and voices come from? From many sources: Conversations heard and overheard, movies and radio broadcasts, newspapers, magazines, yes, and *other writers*; . . . voices which he is hearing all the time whether he knows it or not.. . .Look, listen, and transcribe—and forget about being original. William Burroughs (77-79)

***

The mutability of the truth. Ibsen said it. Jefferson said it. We should have a revolution of some sort in America every ten years. The truth has to be redressed, re-examined, reaffirmed in the new mode. There has to be new poetry. But the thing is that the change, the greater material, the altered structure of the inevitable revolution must be *in* the poem, in it. Made of it. It must shine in the structural body of it. William Carlos Williams (In Rothenberg, 14)

***

How can we accept Einstein's theory of relativity, affecting our very conception of the heavens about us of which poems write so much, without incorporating its essential fact—the relativity of measurements—into our own category of activity: the poem. . . . Relativity applies to everything, like love, if it applies to anything in the world.

What, by this approach I am trying to sketch, what we are trying to do is not only to disengage the elements of a measure but to seek (what we believe is there) a new measure or a new way of measuring that will commensurate with the social, economic world in which we are living as contrasted with the past. It is in many ways a different world from the past calling for a different measure. William Carlos Williams ("The Poem as a Field of Action" 283)

343

***

Nonetheless, any poetic line is composed under the compulsion and constraint—the sentence—of syntax.

Just as, in one sentence *you* cannot turn into *she*, *run* cannot turn into *ran*, you can't, in your desire to be free of a certain moment, be somewhere else immediately. This is the judgment of time, history and gender as it is reflected in any written line.

And just as the sentence contains only as much language as it can bear, so can it be viewed as an image of the pressure of temporality. The facing of what is in front of you, by sorting out what is behind, goes into the careful syntactical processing of a sentence. Law and grammar must coexist in that cell. This coexistence requires the exaction of judgement.

Poetic judgment goes to the extreme with this exaction, and the more extreme it is, the more otherly it becomes. It transforms the state of being lost into that of being free, by making judgement on judgement itself. Poetry writes twice and produces another sound from the ordinary. In this sense it is free out of its longing to escape the cell of syntax. Fanny Howe (54)

***

[As opposed to "establishing a sense of verisimilitude"] What Roussel did was to take a completely banal sentence heard everyday, taken from songs, read on walls, and with it he constructed the most absurd things, the most improbably situations, without any possible relationships to reality. (178)

    . . . Roussel's process incorporates word play and *double entendre* which are considered trivial by us, but are basic aspects of Japanese poetics. (180)

    . . . But the knowledge that there is a process throws the reader into a state of being uncertain, and even while knowing that there is no way of rediscovering the process, and even if one enjoys simply reading the text, the fact that there is a secret transforms the experience of reading into one of deciphering, a game, a more complex undertaking, more disturbing, more anxious than when one reads a simple text for the pleasure of it.. . . I'm not convinced that a knowledge of the actual text from which it starts is at all necessary. (181) Michel Foucault

*****

344

The Real & The Universal

To speak well in colonial America was to speak straightforward and in a plain manner, that is to say, within the narrative structure and metaphors of the bible. The successful colonizer was considered a biblical type, a saint (a nation of heroes) and his life was a biblical allegory in the making; perhaps the bible provided a necessary structure to help them justify clearing the land of the people they described as pestilence (the Native Americans). The errand: progress, conquer. Later with the scientific and industrial revolutions, descriptive language became the norm. As I see it, most simplistic descriptions "pretend" to add or subtract nothing, as if a straightforward literal, transparent language is possible, true and accurate. In contemporary America, to be straight-forward and literal is to speak within the narrative structure and metaphors of advanced capital (rather than the bible): the anti-intellectual, journalistic, so-called transparent language of advertising. Speaking and writing in these ways might be interpreted as implicit acceptances of the system. And so some poetic writing questions, disrupts and dislocates conventional notions of "real/ realism" and "normal/natural", refusing to universalize the status quo, and instead of attempting to reproduce reality, attempting to change it. (BH)

***

Realistic poetry, at its best, is likely to meet the following conditions: (1) it will describe normal situations and average characters in ordinary settings (often with emphasis on the lower strata of society); (2) it will renounce the use of far fetched images and metaphors; (3) it will endeavor to reproduce actual speech and tend to approximate prose rhythms. "Realism" (Princeton Encyclopedia, 685)

***

The untruth of a painting or a photograph is that, in spite of its concreteness, it drops the element of natural succession. One superiority of verbal poetry as an art rests in its getting back to the fundamental reality of *time*.. . . . A true noun, an isolated thing, does not exist in nature. Things are only the terminal points, or rather the meeting points, of actions, cross-sections cut through actions, snapshots. Neither can a pure verb, an abstract motion, be possible in nature. The eye sees noun and verb as one: things in motion, motion in things, and so the Chinese conception tends to represent them.. . . . But in nature there is *no* completeness. . . . motion leaks everywhere, like electricity from an exposed wire.

All processes in nature are interrelated; and thus there could be no complete sentence . . . save one which it would take all time to pronounce.

According to this logic . . . thought deals with no bloodless concepts but watches *things* move under its microscope.. . . All truth has to be expressed in sentences because all truth is the *transference of power*. Ernest Fenollosa (16-18)

***

In any given instance, because there is a choice of words, the choice, if a man is in there, will be, obedience of his ear to the syllables. . . . It is from the union of the mind and the ear that the syllable is born . . The other child is the LINE. And together these two, the syllable and the line, they make a poem.. . . And the line comes (I swear it) from the breath, from the breathing of the man who writes, at the moment that he writes . . . Because breath allows all the speech-force of language back in. (53-56)

...

[T.S.] Eliot has stayed inside the non-projective . . . his root is the mind alone . . . in his listenings he has stayed there where the ear and the mind are, has only gone from his fine ear outward rather than, as I say a projective poet will, down through the workings of his own throat to that place where breath comes from, where breath has its beginnings, where drama has to come from, where, the coincidence is, all act springs. Charles Olson (26)

***

The fairy tale of the "realistic" novel whispers its assurance that the world is not mysterious, that it is predictable—if not to the characters then to the author, that it is available to manipulation by the individual, that it is not only under control but that one can profit from this control. Ronald Sukenick. (429)

***

And this unselfconscious transparency has become a stylistic, one might almost say a cultural, ideal for Western Civilization. The best style is the style not noticed; the best manners the most unobtrusive, convincing behavior spontaneous and unselfconscious. Richard Lanham (266)

***

All deep things are Song.. . . The primal element of us; of us, and of all things.. . . Poetry, therefore, we will call *musical Thought*. The Poet is he who *thinks* in that manner. See deep enough, and you see musically; the heart of Nature being everywhere music, if you can only reach it. Robert Duncan quoting Thomas Carlyle ("Towards" 83).

***

The poets in this anthology have all foregrounded language itself as the project of their writing. For these poets language is not something that *explains* or *translates* experience, but is the source of experience. Language is perception, thought, itself; and in that context the poems of these writers do not function as "frames" of experience or brief narrative summaries of ideas and emotions as they do for many current poets. Douglas Messerli (2)

***

One would perhaps admit that it [Oulipo potentiality] opens onto a perfectly authentic modern realism. For reality never shows more than a part of itself, authorizing a thousand interpretations, significations, and solutions, all equally probable. Jacques Bens (72)

***

My statement is this: that poetry to go forward, in my view, has to begin a voyage into the description of *historical reality*. . . . an era of investigative poesy, a form of historical writing—this is as potentially dangerous to the poet as a minefield or those small foot-snuffing blow-up devices the defense dept. used in Vietnam; but it is a danger thrillsomely magnetic to a bard wandering through the electromagnetic aeon. Ed Sanders (366, 370)

***

All writers believe they are realists. . . . Realism is the ideology which each brandishes against his neighbor, the quality which each believes he possesses for himself alone. And it has always been the same: out of a concern for realism each new literary school has sought to destroy the one which preceded it;. . . When a form of writing has lost its initial vitality, its force, its violence, when it has become a vulgar recipe . . . it is indeed a return to the real. Alain Robbe-Grillet (157-158)

***

Words have users, but as well, users have words. And it is the users that establish the world's realities. Realities being those fantasies, that control your immediate span of life. Usually they are not your own fantasies, *i.e.*, they belong to governments, traditions, etc., which, it is must be clear by now, can make for conflict with the singular human life all ways. The fantasy of America might hurt you, but it is what should be meant when one talks of "reality." Not only the things you can touch or see, but the things that make such touching or seeing "normal." Then words, like their users, have a hegemony—socially— which is final, right now. LeRoi Jones (Imamu Amiri Baraka) ("Hunting" 374)

***

By resisting conventional narrative strategies, poetry might call attention to the ways in which those structures have obscured, abraided, and falsified the relationships between cause and effect, subject and object, intention and action, in much of what passes for the telling of our recent common history. Poetry resists false linkages. . . . Resisting false linkages while discovering, recovering, uncovering new ones, poets might help sweep the linguistic path of its polluting and coercive narratives, helping us to re-perceive our world and each other with efficacy, compassion, humor, and mutual regard. Ann Lauter-bach (38)

***

Probably all feelings are cliches which is not to say that they are invalid, or stupid, or even absurd (though like anything else they may be). Feelings are common to us all, never new, stunning only to the person feeling them at the time, and foolish (or boring) to everyone else. Thoughts, however, can be affective whether one shares them at the moment or not, and they can be original.

Feelings have no potential, they can never be anything but what they are. Ideals and thoughts, however, are full of potential. That is to say, love or melancholy only become more or less as they develop as feelings. Yet the idea of love or melancholy ramifies indefinitely and can lead off in an infinity of directions. Lyn Hejinian ("Variations" 507)

***

C.R. Were you challenged by the problem of how to define "found language"? M.F. Well, it is the interest I have in modes of discourse, that is to say, not so much in the linguistic structure which makes such a series of utterances possible, but rather the fact that we live in a world in which things have been said. These spoken words in reality are not, as people tend to think, a wind that passes without leaving a trace, but in fact, diverse as are the traces, they do remain. We live in a world completely marked by, all laced with, discourses, that is to say, utterances which have been spoken, of things said, of affirmations, interrogations, of discourses which have already occurred. To that extent, the historical world in which we live cannot be disassociated from all the elements of discourses which have inhabited this world and continue to live in it as the economic process, the demographic, etcetera, etcetera. Michel Foucault (177)

***

Text means *Tissue*; but whereas hitherto we have always taken this tissue as a product, a ready-made veil, behind which lies, more or less hidden, meaning (truth), we are now emphasizing, in the tissue, the generative idea that the text is made, is worked out in a perpetual interweaving; lost in this tissue—this texture—the subject unmakes himself, like a spider dissolving in the constructive secretions of its web. Were we fond of neologisms, we might define the theory of the text as an *hypology* (*hyphos* is the tissue and the spider's web). Roland Barthes ("Pleasure" 64)

*****

Fixed & Free

To define, pin down. Or instead strive for a subject/object relationship that is open and in-the-process-of-becoming. Begin by ambushing the oedipal structure of Western culture. The sentence. Refigure and confound it. The crucial narrative structure for American realist fiction and poetry rests soundly on repairing and soothing the oedipal triangle (I/you/it - I/Other/other - Subject/Object/object – Father/Mother/boy child) following the law and language of the father; these conventions and triangles often support, ignore and use the other/Other: the poor, the woman, the strange. Rag quilts. In order to dislocate, question and disrupt the power relations embedded within the oedipal triangle, a writer can disrupt the position of the author and character as hero, heroine, great soul, unitary self, natural Americans. Overlap. Disrupt values of unity, significance, identity and defini-tion. Refuse rigid narrative positions and the armor of point of view. Doubletalk. Refuse to speak authoritatively in the voice of the other. Drift away. Exceed the notion of the femi-nine as lack. Holes and details everywhere. Bring the body back into the text. Change the structure, content, and rhythm of the canon and you change lives. Present that which has been repressed, women's sexuality and pleasure. Threaten the order. Écriture féminine as defined by the French feminists is writing that foregrounds that which has usually been repressed and debased. Redraw borders. Let poetic writing strip away the facade of instrumental writing. Shift, transform and stay in the process of becoming, undefinable and particular. (BH)

***

The word "poetry" is a Greek word for making something up. It means to create; it means to make up. And so when you say, is that true, or did you make it up, you're really saying, is that true or is it poetry.. . .Within the Christian world, which is very strongly, of course, Judaic, there was a strong sense that there was something profoundly wrong about mak-ing-up persons. God was the creator and you were stepping into the creator's place. Robert Duncan ("Warp and Woof," 2-3).

***

In the latter part of the twentieth century terms like "The American Dream" and "The American Way of Life" sound like fraudulent propaganda or advertising slogans to us. They did not to Whitman. To him they were terms of a millenarian vision, an apocalypse in which every vestige of fraud or exploitation between human beings had been burned away.

. . . At every point Whitman offers an alternative to the ethics of the rising predatory society.

Whitman's poems are full of men doing things together.

. . . Being is realized in the community of work and love, and love and work, the meaning of the universe. Whitman is the poet of revolutionary hope, and without hope revolution is catastrophe.

. . Whitman's joyous workers swinging their tools in the open air were replaced by a frustrated proletariat in the dark satanic mills, and his independent yeomen by mortgaged farms, tenant farmers, farm laborers . . . So the poetic followers of Whitman became, first radical populists . . then socialists . . . then anarchists . . . then communists . . . Between the wars it seemed as though the Whitman tradition was slowly dying, but it endured underground in hundreds of little magazines, and after the Second War emerged again in poets like Allen Ginsberg and then again swept the world. (Kenneth Rexroth 19-22)

***

That's the trouble—anything I've done has been an accident. Any good has been spoiled by my intentions—the preoccupation with irrelevant and stupid things—Pound said this quietly, rusty voiced like old child, looked directly in my eye while pronouncing "intention." Ezra Pound talking to Allen Ginsberg ("Encounters with Ezra Pound," 8)

***

Charles Bernstein said: "Poetry is the aversion to conformity." This year I would like to add: poetry is the aversion to the assertion of power. Poetry is that which resists dominance. Ann Lauterbach (37)

***

For me it is not enough to simply put a new content in the writing. For example, in some city parks there are squares where people can look at each other and therefore it calls for talking to each other. You can also have a park where the benches are put in such a way that people cannot see each other and therefore it calls for another kind of relationship. It is the same thing if we are talking about form. Formal issues call for different responses on an emotional basis, as well as in a more general way of thinking. Nicole Brossard (2)

***

The best writing is achieved in an egoless state. The writer's defensive, limited ego, his "very own words," these are his least interesting sources. William Burroughs (79)

***

The real "I" in literature should be an avowal. The artist's function is to reveal himself, to confess his guilt. He has to betray himself, to reveal things in his work that he would never reveal in his private life. This can never be done enough. To speak of things that have no connection to his art—mother, grandfather, all this infantile foolishness—has no interest whatsoever neither for the understanding of the work itself, nor for any other person. A work of strength requires an "I" of strength . . .If we wish to really accomplish something in our lives, e have to establish this as a veritable law: to really *live* this understanding. Not to simply accept the world as it is, but to embrace it in all its complex universality and to exclude *nothing*. Pierre Guyotat (21)

***

I have always been averse to talking about, and so I don't write about my life the way the confessional poets do. I don't want to bore people with experiences of mine that are simply versions of what everybody goes through. For me, poetry starts after that point. I write with experience in mind, but I don't write about them, I write out of them. John Ashbery ("The Art of Poetry" 43)

***

Abstraction (in poetry, not in painting) involves personal removal by the poet. For instance, the decision involved in the choice between "the nostalgia *of* the infinite" and "the nostalgia *for* the infinite" defines an attitude towards degree of abstraction.. . . . Personism, a movement which I recently founded and which nobody yet knows about, interests me a great deal, being so totally opposed to this kind of abstract removal that it is verging on a true abstraction for the first time, really, in the history of poetry.. . . . one of its minimal aspects is to address itself to one person (other than the poet himself), thus evoking overtones of love without destroying love's life-giving vulgarity, and sustaining the poet's feeling towards the poem while preventing love from distracting him into feeling about the person. That's part of personism.. . . It puts the poem squarely between the poet and the person.. . . at last between two persons instead of two pages. Frank O'Hara (498-499)

***

So then I immediately regressed into writing poems like Frank O'Hara, because he was a good poet who just said, "I do this in my life and I do that in my life" . . . The idea of the abstract expressionists was, of course, to put how you did your works on the surface, and I decided to do that.. . . (*What did you pick up from O'Hara?*) Personal tone. The way to use a casual tone and then long lines without having to be measured in a slow way. To write fast. I write fast. I'm fast--write as quick as my hands are. Irish line, he used that. I hadn't seen that being used. It's the way I talk.. . . Whatever happened in your life was as interesting as anything else. Ted Berrigan (Homage 110-112)

***

The private life of an individual, his sexual preference and his work are interrelated not because his work translates his sexual life, but because the work includes the whole life as well as the text. Michel Foucault (184)

***

I intended this work to be the repetition of historically real events the writing of which punches a hole in reality. (As if to void them, actively.) Leslie Scalapino (21)

***

Let us record the atoms as they fall upon the mind in the order in which they fall, let us trace the pattern, however disconnected and incoherent in appearance, which each sight or incident scores upon the consciousness. (Virginia Woolf 107)

***

In precisely this way literature (it would be better from now on to say *writing*) by refusing to assign a 'secret', an ultimate meaning, to the text (and to the world as text), liberates what may be called an anti-theological activity, an activity that is truly revolutionary since to refuse to fix meaning is, in the end, to refuse God and his hypostases—reason, science, law. Roland Barthes ("Death of the Author," 147)

***

The Western concept of the cultivation of the voice is foreign to African or Afro-American music. In the West, only the artifact can be beautiful, mere expression cannot be thought to be. LeRoi Jones (Blues People 30)

***

In order to avoid coinciding with the oppressive scripts which, under the pretense of empowerment relaunder the old divisive metaphors of race and subject, in order to elude the panoptic eye of ideology which enlists is as its accomplices, in order to thwart the master positions, one begins by operating a critical negation, a deformation of the very categories: the I, the she, the black, the white, the male. A strategy of resistance. Chris Tysh (75)

***

On the other hand one must not make poetry boring by reasoning the human figure, the poet with mouth & tongue, out of it—leaving only the mannered tracings of a mind which, by constantly denying its own existence as "someone," becomes of interest only to translators of difficult discourse, to critics. *Someone*, at this point, must take in hand the task of being everyone, & no one, as the first poets did. Someone must pay attention to the real spiritual needs of both her neighbors (not her poetic peers) & the future. (Alice Notley, "Introduction", vi)

***

Fixity is a function of power. Those who maintain place, who decide what takes place and dictate what has taken place, are power brokers of the traditional. the "placeless" by contrast, are translators of the nontraditional. Rather than fixed in the order of cunning Grecian urns, their lineage is fluid, nomadic, transitional. Their appropriate sign is a crossing sign at the junction.

The crossing sign is the antithesis of a place marker. It signifies always, change, motion, transience, process. To adept adherents of wandering, a crossing sign is equivalent to a challenge thrown out in brash, sassy tones by a locomotive blowing by: "Do what you can," it demands. "Do what you can—right here—on this placeless—place, this spotless-spot . . ." Houston A. Baker (202)

*****

In a sense, writing begins where words stop. Each time you write, you have to make it new. You have to go beyond the language of the tribe, the old and traditional language. You have to begin where the people before you left off. Revolution in art always begins with the rebel who wants to rescue art from its fatal and presumed place of origin in everyday life. Pierre Guyotat (21)

***

Thought is more important than art. Without thought art could certainly not exist. Art is one of many products of thought. An impressive one, perhaps the most impressive one, but to revere art, and have no understanding of the process that forces it into existence, is finally not even to understand what art is. Leroi Jones (Imamu Amiri Baraka) ("Hunting" 378)

***

When I am thinking about my work, I am often thinking about that thinking—its quality, motives, motifs, and instruments. Then, for me, poetry is the site of the consciousness of consciousness.

  The quality may have its analogues in the scientific method, but it is not so much "experimentalism" as a romance with science's rigor, patience, thoroughness, speculative imagination that informs it. The motives of the thinking spring from intuited necessity and are propelled by something like desire—restlessness, curiosity, anxiety, love. the motifs implode toward a phenomenology of consciousnesss—I write about what I know ('reality'), how I know it, and how I know I know it (articulation). The instrument, for me, of course, is poetic language. Lyn Hejinian (*Mirage* 24)

***

Writing is not arriving; most of the time it's *not arriving*. One must go on foot, with the body. One has to go away, leave the self. How far must one not arrive in order to write, how far must one wander and wear out and have pleasure? One must walk as far as the night. One's own night. Walking through the self toward the dark. Hèléne Cixous (65)

356

***

What do we say about the function of our poetry, the thing we do? That it explores. That it initiates thought or action. That it proposes its own displacement. That it allows vulnerability & conflict. That it remains, like the best science, constantly open to change: to a continual change in our idea of what a poem is or may be. What language is. What experience is. What reality is. That for many of us it has become a fundamental process for the play & interchange of possibilities. Jerome Rothenberg (135)

***

I think the challenge of poetry is the breaking down of the notion of simple truths, the literalness of the word, the notion of fixed commandments of behavior and morality sent down from heaven, the notion of an exclusive culture that can dominate another, the divine right of kings and the not so divine rights of the affluent and comfortable, the notion that God is with us and that these divine revelations we hold to be self evident are equally true for others. The only absolutes for poetry are diversity and change (and the freedom to pursue these); and the only purpose, over the long run, is to raise questions . . . I'm appalled at what people do with answers or what answers do to people. And answers have consequences I don't like. They get fixed in the mind. I don't like to see fixed ends. I like to see the thwarting of ends. Jerome Rothenberg (223-4)

***

The primary ideological message of poetry lies not in its explicit content, political though that may be, but in the *attitude toward reception* it demands of the reader. It is this "attitude toward information," which is carried forward by the recipient. It is this attitude which forms the basis for a response to other information, not necessarily literary, in the text. And, beyond the poem, in the world. Ron Silliman (The New Sentence 31)

***

This is the problem which any poet who departs from closed form is especially confronted by. And it involves a whole series of new recognitions. From the moment he ventures into FIELD COMPOSITION—puts himself in the open—he can go by no track other than the one the poem under hand declares, for itself. Charles Olson ("Projective Verse" 16)

***

I'm interested in a particular kind of narrative—what Jack Spicer and I agreed to call our work the serial poem—this is a narrative which refuses to adopt an imposed story-line, and completes itself only in the sequence of poems, if, in fact, a reader insists upon a definition of completion which is separate from the activity of the poems themselves. The poems tend to act as a sequence of energies which run out when so much of a tale is told. I like to describe this in Ovidian terms, as a *carmen perpetuum*, a continuous song in which the fragmented subject matter is only apparently disconnected. Robin Blaser (237-38)

***

Poetry is the aversion to conformity. Charles Bernstein (37)

***

What a service to poetry it might be to steal story away from the novel & give it back to rhythm & sound give it back to the line. Another service would be to write a long poem, a story poem, with a female narrator/hero. Perhaps this time she wouldn't call herself something like Helen; perhaps instead there might be recovered some sense of what mind was like before Homer, before the world went haywire & women were denied participation in the design & making of it. Perhaps someone might discover that original mind inside herself right now, in these times. Anyone might. Alice Notley ("Homer's *ART*," 402)

*****

NOTES

Allen, Donald and Warren Tallman, eds. *Poetics of the New American Poetry*. Grove Press, 1973.

Artaud, Antonin. *The Theater and its Double*, Grove, 1958, p. 13.

Ashbery, John. "The Art of Poetry XXXIII." Interview by Peter Stitt. *Paris Review*, vol. 90, 1983, pp. 43-55.

Ashbery, John. "How to Be a Difficult Poet." Interview by Richard Kostelanetz. *New York Times Magazine*, 23 May 1976, pp. 19-20.

Baker, Jr., Houston A. *Blues, Ideology and Afro-American Literature*, University of Chicago Press, 1984, p. 202.

Barthes, Roland. *The Pleasure of the Text*, translated by Richard Miller, Hill and Wang, 1975, p. 64

Barthes, Roland. "The Death of the Author." *Image. Music. Text*, edited by Stephen Heath, Fontane, 1977, pp. 147.

Bens, Jacques. "Queneau Oulipian." *Oulipo: A Primer of Potential Literature*, edited by Warren Motte, Jr., University of Nebraska Press, 1986, pp. 65-73.

Bernstein, Charles. "An Interview with Tom Beckett." *Content's Dream: Essays 1975-1984*, Sun & Moon, 1986, pp. 408-9.

Bernstein, Charles. As quoted by Ann Lauterbach. "Links Without Links: The Voice of the Turtle," *The American Poetry Review*, vol. 21, no. 1, Jan/Feb 1992, p. 37.

Berrigan, Ted. "The Business of Poetry (July 9, 1976)." *Talking Poetics from Naropa*, edited by Anne Waldman and Marilyn Webb, Shambhala, 1978, pp. 39-61.

Berrigan, Ted. *Nice to See You: Homage to Ted Berrigan*, edited by Anne Waldman. Coffee House, 1991, pp. 109-112.

Blake, William. "Auguries of Innocence." *The Portable Blake*. edited by Alfred Kazin, Penguin, 1976, p. 153.

Blake, Willliam. Letter "To the Revd. Dr. Trusler" (August 23, 1799). *The Portable Blake*, edited by Alfred Kazin, Penguin, 1976.

Blaser, Robin. "The Fire." *Poetics of the New American Poetry*, edited by Donald Allen, pp. 235-246. Originally published in *Pacific Nation*, no. 2, 1968.

Brecht, Bertolt. "Writing the Truth: Five Difficulties." *Galileo, a play*, Grove Press, 1966, pp.133, 136.

Brossard, Nicole. "A Conversation with Nicole Brossard." Interview by Abigail Child. The
    Newsletter from the Poetry Project, no.143, Dec.1991/Jan. 1992, pp. 1-2.

Burroughs, William. "It Belongs to the Cucumbers on the Subject of Randine's Tape Voices (July
    27, 1976). *Talking Poetics from Naropa*, edited by Anne Waldman and Marilyn Webb,
    Shambhala, 1978, pp. 63-81.

Carlyle, Thomas. "The Hero as Poet." *Heroes and Hero-Worship* (1840). As quoted by Robert
    Duncan, "Towards an Open Universe," *Fictive Certainties*," New Directions,1985, 83.

Cixous, Héléne. *Three Steps on the Ladder of Writing*, translated by Sarah Cornwell and Susan
    Sellers. Columbia University Press, 1993. pp. 6, 36, 38, 42, 45, 65.

Clément, Catherine. *The Lives and Legends of Jacques Lacan*, Columbia University 1983, p. 110.

Coolidge, Clark. "Arrangement." *Talking Poetics from Naropa*. edited by Anne Waldman and
    Marilyn Webb, Shambhala, 1978, pp.143-169.

Crane, Hart. "General Aims and Theories (1925)." *The Complete Poems and Selected Letters* and
    Prose of Hart Crane, Liveright Publishing Corporation,1966, p. 163.

Creeley, Robert. "I'm Given to Write Poems." *Poetics of the New American Poetry*. edited by
    Donald Allen, Grove Press, 1970, pp. 263-273. Originally published in *A Quick Graph:*
    Collected Notes and Essays, Four Seasons Foundation, 1970.

Creeley, Robert and Susan Howe. *Voice Literary Supplement*, no. 124, April 12, 1994, pp. 21-22.

Davenport, Guy. *Tatlin! Six Stories*, Charles Scribner's Sons,1974, p. 23.

Devi, Rukmini. As quoted by Jaynati Patel in *Natya Yoga: A Critical Study*, Ph.d. Thesis in
    Sanskrit, University of Bombay, 1984.

Duncan, Robert. "Ideas of the Meaning of Form." *Fictive Certainties*, New Directions, 1985,
    p.102.

Duncan, Robert. "Man's fulfillment in Order and Strife." *Fictive Certainties*, New Directions,
    1985, p. 121. Previously published in *Caterpiller*, vol. 8, no. 9, October 1969.

Duncan, Robert. "Towards an Open Universe." *Fictive Certainties*, New Directions, 1985, pp. 79,
    83.

Duncan, Robert. "Warp and Woof: Notes from a Talk (June 10, 1976)." *Talking Poetics from*
    Naropa, edited by Anne Waldman and Marilyn Webb, Shambhala, 1978, p 2-3.

Fenollosa, Ernest. "From the Chinese Written Character as a Medium for Poetry." *Poetics of the New American Poetry*, edited by Donald Allen, Grove Press, 1973, pp. 16-18. Previously published in 1936.

Fitterman, Rob. "Access & Context" *The Poetry Project Newsletter, no.* 159, December/January 1995, p. 7.

Foucault, Michel. "Postscript: An Interview with Michel Foucault." *Death and the Labyrinth: The World of Raymond Roussel*, translated and interviewed by Charles Ruas, University of California Press, 1986, pp. 177-181, 184.

Ginsberg, Allen. "Encounters with Ezra Pound." *Composed on the Tongue: Literary Conversations, 1967-1977,* edited by Donald Allen, Grey Fox Press, 1980, p. 8. Previously published In *City Lights Anthology,*1974, pp. 9-21.

Ginsberg, Allen."When the Mode of the music Changes and the Walls of the City Shake" and "Notes for Howl and Other Poems." *Poetics of the New American Poetry*, edited by Donald Allen, Grove Press, 1973. pp. 324-330 and 318-321.

Ginsberg, Allen. *The Paris Review*, interview by Thomas Clark, Spring 1966, pp. 24-25.

Guyutat, Pierre. Interview by Alexandra Tuttle and J. G. Strand. *Paris Exiles*, no. 2, 1985, pp. 19, 21.

Hejinian, Lyn. "From the Person: Statement." *Mirage*, no.3, Spring 1989, p. 24.

Hejinian, Lyn. "Variations: A Return of Words." *In the American Tree*, edited by Ron Silliman, National Poetry Foundation, Inc., 1986, pp. 503-509.

Howe, Fanny. "The Contemporary Logos." *Code of Signals: Recent Writings in Poetics*, edited by Michael Palmer, North Atlantic Press, 1983, p. 54.

Howe, Susan. Interview. *Postmodern Poetry: Talisman Interviews*, edited by Ed Foster, Talisman House, 1994, p. 65.

Jackson, Laura (Riding). "Original 1938 Preface." *The Poems of Laura Riding: A Newly Revised Edition,*" Persea Books, 1938, 2001, pp. 485, 489.

Jackson, Laura (Riding) and Robert Graves. Under Laura Riding. *A Survey of Modernist Poetry*. Heinemann, 1927. pp. 125-127.

Jones, Leroi. (Imamu Amiri Baraka). *Blues People: The Negro Experience in White America and the Music that Developed from It*, Morrow Quill, 1963, p. 30.

Jones, Leroi. "Hunting is Not Those Heads on the Wall" and "Expressive Language." *Poetics of the New American Poetry*, edited by Donald Allen, Grove Press, 1937, pp. 374, 378.

Kafka, Franz. "*To Oskar Pollak* (January 27, 1904)." *Letters to Friends, Family and Editors*, translated by Richard and Clara Winston, Schocken Books, 1977, pp.15-16. As quoted by Hèléne Cixous,*Three Steps on the Ladder of Writing*, translated by Sarah Cornwell and Susan Sellers. Columbia University Press, 1993. p 17.

Kostelanetz, Richard. "Avant-Garde 1973-78." *Claims for Poetry*, edited by Donald Hall, University of Michigan Press, 1982, p. 245.

Lanham, Richard. "The Electronic Word: Literary Study and the Digital Revolution." *New Literary History,* no. 20, Winter 1989, p. 266.

Lauterbach, Ann. "Links Without Links: The Voice of the Turtle." *The American Poetry Review*, Jan/Feb 1992, vol. 21, no. 1, pp. 37-38. From a talk delivered at the Poetry Project in June of 1991.

Le Lionnais, François. "Lipo: First Manifesto." *Oulipo: A Primer of Potential Literature*, edited by Warren Motte, Jr., University of Nebraska Press, 1986, pp. 29-31.

Mayakovsky, Vladimir. *How Are Verses Made?,* translated by G.M. Hyde, Grossman Publishers, 1970, pp. 13-24.

Mayer, Bernadette. "The Colors of Consonance." Interview by Ken Jordan. *The Newsletter of the Poetry Project,* vol. 146, October/November 1992, pp. 5-9.

Mayer, Bernadette. "The Obfuscated Poem." *Code of Signals: Recent Writings in Poetics*, edited by Michael Palmer, North Atlantic Press, 1983, pp.166-167.

Messerli, Douglas, ed. "Introduction." L*anguage Poetries: An Anthology*, edited by Douglas Messerli, New Directions, 1987, p. 2.

Motte, Warren F. Jr., ed. *Oulipo: A Primer of Potential Literature*. University of Nebraska Press, 1986.

Mullen, Harryette. "Kinky Quatrains." *Ecstatic Occasions, Expedient Forms*, edited by David Lehman, University of Michigan Press, 1996, pp. 165-167.

Notley, Alice. Interview. *Postmodern Poetry: Talisman Interviews*, edited by Ed Foster, Talisman House, 1994, *pp.* 88-89.

Notley, Alice. "Introduction" and "Homer's *Art.*" *The Scarlet Cabinet: A Compendium of Books*, by Alice Notley and Douglas Oliver, Scarlett Editions, 1992, pp. v-vi, 402.

O'Hara, Frank. "Personism: A Manifesto." *The Collected Poems of Frank O'Hara*, edited by Donald Allen, University of California, 1995, pp. 498-499.

Olson, Charles. "Projective Verse." *Selected Writings*, New Directions, 1966, pp. 13-26.

Padgett, Ron. Interview. *Postmodern Poetry: Talisman Interviews,* edited by Ed Foster, Talisman House, 1994, p. 102.

Pound, Ezra. "A Retrospect." *Poetics of the New American Poetry*, edited by Donald Allen, Grove Press, 1973, pp. 36-47. Rpt. from *Literary Essays of Ezra Pound*, New Directions, 1918, 1920, 1935.

Queneau, R., "Le voyage en Grece". As quoted in Marcel Bénabou, "Rule and Constraint." *Oulipo A Primer of Potential Literature*, edited by Warren Motte, Jr., University of Nebraska Press, 1986, 40-47.

Rattray, David. "Taking Risks Seriously." Interview by Ken Jordan. *The Newsletter of the Poetry Project*, no. 148, Feb./March 1993, pp. 3-6.

«Realism.» *Princeton Encyclopedia of Poetry and Poetics*, edited by Alex Preminger, Princeton University Press, 1965, p. 685.

Rexroth, Kenneth. *American Poetry in the Twentieth Century*, Seabury, 1973, pp. 19-22, 82.

Robbe-Grillet, Alain. "From Realism to Reality." *For a New Novel: Essays on Fiction*, translated by Richard Howard, Grove Press, 1965, pp. 157-162.

Rosenwasser, Rena. "Chain/Kelsey St. Press." *Chain*, no.1, Spring/Summer 1994, p. 92.

Rothenberg, Jerome. *Pre-faces and Other Writings*, New Directions, 1981, pp. 14, 134-135, 223-4.

Sanders, Ed. "Investigative Poetry: The Context of History Will Be Poetry" (July 8, 1975). *Talking Poetics from Naropa: Annals of the Jack Kerouac School of Disembodied Poetics*, edited by Anne Waldman and Marilyn Webb, vol. 2, Shambhalia, 1979, pp. 365-378.

Scalapino, Leslie. "Note on My Writing." *How Phenomena Appear to Unfold*, Potes & Poets, 1989, p. 21.

Sellars, R.W. *The Essentials of Logic*, Houghton Mifflin, 1917, p. 185.

Silliman, Ron, ed. "Language, Realism, Poetry." *In the American Tree*. National Poetry Foundation, Inc., 1986, p. xxii.

Silliman, Ron. *The New Sentence*, Roof Books, 1977, p. 31.

Stein, Gertrude. "Poetry and Grammar." *Lectures in America*, Beacon Press, 1935, pp. 231, 235, 238.

Sukenick, Ronald. "Twelve Digressions Toward a Study of Composition." *New Literary History,* vol. 6, 1974-75, p. 429.

Thomas, Lorenzo. "Communicating by Horns: Jazz and Redemption in the Poetry of the Beats and the Black Arts Movement." *African American Review*, vol. 26, no. 2, Summer 1992, pp. 297.

Thomas, Lorenzo. "Alea's Children: The Avant-Garde on the Lower East Side, 1960-1970," *African American Review*, vol. 27, no. 4, Winter 1993, pp. 573-578.

Tysh, Chris. "The 'I' Effect: Peeling the Labels of Self-Representation." *Long News: In the Short Century*, no. 5,1994, p. 75.

Anne Waldman. "Introduction." *Out of This World: An Anthology*, Crown Publishers, 1991, pp. 1-6.

Waldman, Anne and Marilyn Webb, eds. *Talking Poetics from Naropa: Annals of the Jack Kerouac School of Disembodied Poetics.* Shambhala, vol. 1, 1978 and vol. 2, 1979.

Watts, Alan. *The Spirit of Zen.* Pantheon Books, 1957. pp. 19, 52, 58, 75.

Williams, William Carlos. "The Poem as a Field of Activity." *Selected Essays of William Carlos Williams*, New Directions, 1969, p. 283.

Wood, Ernest. *Seven Schools of Yoga*, Theosophical Publishing House, 1976. p. 41.

Woolf, Virginia. "Modern Fiction" (1919). Reprinted in *Collected Essays*, London, 1966, p. 107.

BARBARA HENNING is the author of five novels and eight collections of poetry, recently *Digigram* (United Artists 2020), *A Day Like Today* (Negative Capability 2015) and a novel, *Just Like That* (Spuyten Duyvil, 2018). Her current project is a novelized biography of her mother's life and times, "Ferne, a Detroit Story." Henning was the editor and publisher of Long News Magazine and Books, as well as the editor of *Looking Up Harryette Mullen* (Belladonna 2011) and *The Collected Prose of Bobbie Louise Hawkins* (BlazeVox 2012). She has taught for Naropa University, University of Arizona, The Poetry Center in Tucson, The Poetry Project and for the Poet's House in NYC. Born in Detroit, she currently lives in Brooklyn and teaches for Long Island University and writers.com.   www.barbarahenning.com

Made in the USA
Coppell, TX
07 December 2023

25525626R00222